Guidebook to the Historic Sites of the War of 1812

# Guidebook to the Historic Sites of the War of 1812

## Gilbert Collins

*For my mom
who supported me

Gilbut*

DUNDURN PRESS
TORONTO · OXFORD

Printer: Transcontinental Printing Inc.

Canadian Cataloguing in Publication Data

Collins, Gilbert, 1951-
    Guidebook to the historic sites of the War of 1812

ISBN 1-55002-290-3

1. Canada — History — War of 1812 — Battlefields.
2. United States — History — War of 1812 — Battlefields.
3. Historic sites — Canada — Guidebooks. 4. Historic sites — United States — Guidebooks. I. Title.

E364.9.C65 1998          971.03'4          C97-931817-3

1  2  3  4  5  BJ  02  01  00  99  98

THE CANADA COUNCIL | LE CONSEIL DES ARTS
FOR THE ARTS | DU CANADA
SINCE 1957 | DEPUIS 1957

We acknowledge the support of the **Canada Council for the Arts** for our publishing program. We also acknowledge the support of the **Ontario Arts Council** and the **Book Publishing Industry Development Program** of the **Department of Canadian Heritage.**

Printed and bound in Canada.

 Printed on recycled paper.

**website: www.dundurn.com**

| Dundurn Press | Dundurn Press | Dundurn Press |
| --- | --- | --- |
| 8 Market Street | 73 Lime Walk | 250 Sonwil Drive |
| Suite 200 | Headington, Oxford | Buffalo, NY |
| Toronto, Ontario, Canada | England | U.S.A. 14225 |
| M5E 1M6 | OX3 7AD | |

# Contents

# List of Maps

# Preface

T he seed for this book began in 1974, but back then I was completely unaware of this fact. In that year I was a visitor, along with friends, curious to see the battlefield of Crysler's Farm, a historic site that lay an hour's drive from where I had lived all my life. I will never forget what I felt that day. I was thrilled to see the Battle Memorial Building, the Memorial Mound, and the monument on top of it. Adam Scott's mural painting made the battle come alive for me.

Only one particular disappointed me: the knowledge that this famous battlefield was now lost. Along with a number of towns and old cemeteries, most of the site was now under the St. Lawrence River, a victim of progress with the coming of the Seaway. This knowledge, however, sparked a different seed. I became curious to see other sites of the War of 1812. Had any of them survived the ravages of time? I had to know the answer. Little did I know that this curiosity would carry me virtually thousands of miles, and take up large portions of my spare time over a twenty-year period.

During those travels I was struck by the fact that there was no comprehensive guide to direct people to the 1812 sites. The booklet published by the Ontario Ministry of Culture and Recreation was invaluable, but it was not specific to 1812, and was limited to the province only. Sites in other provinces and the United States were left to one's own devices.

My real guide was the author Benson Lossing. This incredible man who lived over a century ago had already travelled to many of these sites by horse and buggy. We can be grateful that he did, for he rescued much obscure material from living witnesses that would otherwise have been lost. With his talented hand he sketched many of the places as they looked between the years 1840 and 1860. As valuable as Lossing's work was, it could not be used alone to find these sites today. The march of time has changed many of the places and in some cases has destroyed them. I had many a disappointment when I encountered a historic site replaced by modern buildings or similar structures.

As time marched by, I waited patiently for someone to create a guidebook to these historic sites, but none was forthcoming. It dawned on me that, with all the travels I had done to these very sites, I should attempt the project. The result has been this humble effort and a labour of love. I have enjoyed these journeys to 1812 sites spanning a number of years that saw a youth turn into a man. I hope the reader, if not fortunate enough to visit some of these historic sites, will gain a little something from the reading of this work.

# Introduction

The historic sites in this book are arranged geographically into twenty-seven areas. The last map is quite different because of its scale, and was necessary to show those sites that were isolated from the main theatres of the war. Each location has symbols associated with it, in order to see at a glance what is offered at each site.

It is tragic that the geography surrounding these sites is changing so rapidly. Some sites that had not altered in over one hundred years have now vanished in less than ten. In more recent times these changes have been rapid indeed compared to even fifty years ago. Trees are cut down, roads are widened, streams diverted, and buildings erected. The largest threat in our century has been urban development, which has destroyed the integrity of some sites and even caused the movement of historical markers from their original locations. In at least one case a monument was moved to a place that had nothing to do with what it commemorated!

# Note on Maps

The maps were designed to give the reader a quick reference to the historic sites in a given area. Some helpful roads are depicted, but the maps are not meant to be detailed instructions to access the site. Provincial, state, and local city maps are essential to finding some of these sites.

# Note on Text

This is not a formal history of the War of 1812. That ground has been adequately covered by such authors as Stanley, Hitsman, Mahon, and others. The bibliography at the end of this work lists the books and articles consulted by this author.

The text that accompanies each site is not "weighted" in any discernible manner. That is to say, because a site has more text than another, it does not follow that there is necessarily more to see; actually, the reverse is sometimes true. Some sites that had little or no interpretation required more text to explain the significance of the site.

# Symbol Key

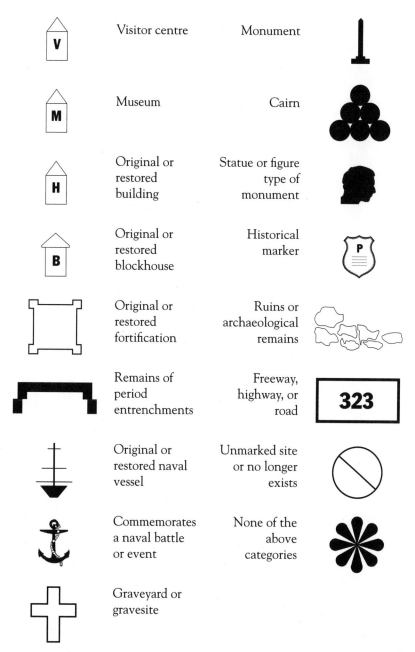

| | | |
|---|---|---|
| **V** | Visitor centre | Monument |
| **M** | Museum | Cairn |
| **H** | Original or restored building | Statue or figure type of monument |
| **B** | Original or restored blockhouse | Historical marker |
| | Original or restored fortification | Ruins or archaeological remains |
| | Remains of period entrenchments | Freeway, highway, or road |
| | Original or restored naval vessel | Unmarked site or no longer exists |
| | Commemorates a naval battle or event | None of the above categories |
| | Graveyard or gravesite | |

# Acknowledgements

I would like to extend particular thanks to my friend Chris Rose, who always seemed to be able to come up with some obscure sources for historical material. Thanks are also due to Mr. Brian Winter, who shared with me his valuable information on the Jabez Lynde house in Whitby. Ms. Hazel Barton and her assistant, from the town of Ancaster Information Services, were very helpful on my visit to their charming town. To my good friends Bob and Linda Fortier, I owe at least the sighting of one historical plaque in New York State that I might have otherwise missed. Thanks are due to the many guides that I met who work at the various historic sites. They were most encouraging and were glad to see that a project such as this was underway. Thanks are in order to the librarians at the many places that I visited. In particular to the lady at the Port Dover library in Ontario, who offered encouragement when this was but a germ of an idea over fifteen years ago. Thanks to the many unnamed individuals who offered simple directions to this "weary traveller." Last, but not least, thanks are due to my darling wife Marla, who offered encouragement and travelled with me to a good many of these sites.

# List of Illustrations

# CHAPTER 1
## DETROIT–WINDSOR

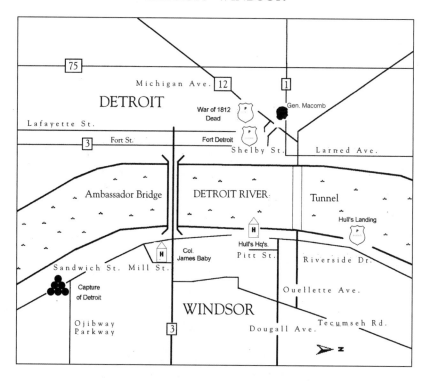

## HULL'S LANDING — WINDSOR, ONTARIO

On July 12, 1812 General William Hull, commanding the American North Western Army, crossed over from Detroit to invade Canada. Landing near here, his army consisted of the 4th United States infantry and three regiments of Ohio Volunteers — in all about two thousand men. The British commander at Amherstburg, Lieutenant Colonel St. George, was out of position to meet the attack. Also heavily outnumbered, he had no choice but to pull his pickets back from Sandwich (present day Windsor), and retreat into Fort Malden. An Ontario Provincial Plaque located on the grounds of the Hiram Walker Company, Riverside Drive, marks the spot where Hull's troops landed.

25

# HULL'S HEADQUARTERS — WINDSOR, ONTARIO

Francois Baby (pronounced "bobby") an early pioneer, built this house just prior to the War of 1812. It was still incomplete when used by American General William Hull as his headquarters on July 12, 1812. When Mr. Baby protested, and recalled their family's friendship before the war, Hull laconically replied "that circumstances have changed now." Hull had to eat his words, however, when he quit the house a few weeks later and abandoned his offensive against Upper Canada. During General Brock's counter-offensive, a battery was placed behind the house to bombard Detroit. The building now houses the Hiram Walker Historical Museum and has displays and artifacts on the War of 1812. The house is located at 254 Pitt Street West in the city of Windsor.

The Francois Baby House as Lossing sketched it in 1860

# COLONEL JAMES BABY — WINDSOR, ONTARIO

James Baby (brother of Francois Baby) served as Colonel of the 1st Regiment of Kent Militia during the war. He was a prominent member of the French-Canadian community, and was elected to the

The Francois Baby House today

executive and legislative assemblies of Upper Canada in 1792. He built this house in 1807, residing in it for nine years before moving to York in 1816. Presently the home is a private residence and not open to the public. An Ontario Provincial Plaque is located in front of the house at 221 Mill Street in the city of Windsor.

## THE CAPTURE OF DETROIT — WINDSOR, ONTARIO

On August 16, 1812 General Isaac Brock embarked his troops here at McKees Point to begin his operations against Detroit. The campaign that began here resulted in the capture of Fort Detroit and the surrender of the entire American North Western Army. The victory was achieved by combined forces of British regulars, Canadian Militia, and Native Indians, and it raised morale at a time when resistance was thought to be hopeless. The twin victories of "Detroit" and "Queenston" saved Upper Canada during the first year of the war. A cairn placed by the Historic Sites and Monuments Board of Canada marks the embarkation area of Brock's troops. The cairn is located at the intersection of Sandwich and Chappus Streets in the city of Windsor.

# FORT DETROIT — DETROIT, MICHIGAN

Fort Lernoult was constructed by the British during the American Revolution. Named for its first commanding officer, it was an important post for the British until 1796, when it was abandoned in accordance with the provisions of Jay's Treaty. The fort's name was never popular, and invariably it was referred to as "Detroit," as if the town and fort were one. In 1812 it was the principal base for General Hull's army in its operations against Canada. On the evening of August 7, 1812, after cancelling his campaign against Canada, Hull's army re-crossed the Detroit River and retired into the fort.

When Fort Michilimackinac surrendered to the British, most of the native forces abandoned the American cause, which led Hull to believe himself greatly outnumbered. This illusion was reinforced by the skirmishes at Maguaga and Brownstown, where native warriors had been engaged, and also indicated that his supply line to Ohio was insecure.

On the early morning of August 16th, General Isaac Brock moved his forces against the fort. Tecumseh used his Indian warriors to great effect, by marching in and out of view, and reinforcing the illusion of great numbers.

When Brock's cannons opened fire on the fort, the bombardment completely unnerved General Hull. In what has been described as "the most disgraceful episode in American history" Hull surrendered not only the fort and his army, but the relief column of troops that was marching to his aid! The surrender of Detroit had far reaching implications and saved western Upper Canada from being occupied in the first year of the war.

After the Battle of Lake Erie the Americans re-occupied the fort on September 29, 1813. Renaming it Fort Shelby, the Americans occupied the fort throughout the war and a garrison was kept there until 1826. Neglected after that time, the fort fell into disrepair and eventually was plowed over. The modern city of Detroit has completely obliterated all traces of the fort. A plaque erected by the State of Michigan is located at Fort and Shelby streets and marks the original site.

# WAR OF 1812 DEAD — DETROIT, MICHIGAN

After the Battle of Lake Erie, the British were forced to evacuate the Detroit frontier, and the American Army took possession of Fort Detroit on September 29, 1813. The American Army however, was to suffer a brutal winter that year, as the post was woefully deficient in shelter and food supplies. At one point over one thousand men were on the sick list, and so many perished that winter that the small town of Detroit could not keep up with the demand for coffins. Many soldiers were buried in a common grave at this site. A Michigan State marker, at the southwest corner of Washington Boulevard and Michigan Avenue, marks the approximate location of the burial site.

# GENERAL MACOMB STATUE — DETROIT, MICHIGAN

Alexander Macomb's first action of the War of 1812 was at the capture of Fort George on May 27, 1813, but since he commanded only the reserve units he saw little action. During General Wilkinson's autumn campaign to capture Montreal, he commanded the advanced guard and thus was not present at the Battle of Crysler's Farm, where the American rear guard was defeated. After that battle the army went into winter quarters, leaving Macomb with little opportunity for action.

In January of 1814 he was promoted to Brigadier General, and took command of the brigade of General Covington, who had been killed at Crysler's Farm. In March he was with the incompetent General Wilkinson on his movement against Lacolle in Lower Canada, but the attack was a complete failure, and Macomb was placed in command of the rear guard on its retreat south. On August 27, 1814 Macomb at last had his own command when he was placed in charge of the defences of Plattsburg, and with a British invasion imminent, he improved the defences which had been started under General Izard.

When the British under Sir George Prevost arrived in September, the American Army was well prepared for defence, but the British attack was uncoordinated, and when their fleet was defeated in Plattsburg Bay, they wisely decided to retreat. Although the land forces had barely been engaged, Plattsburg turned out to be one of the decisive battles of the war. This was because it strengthened the hands of the American diplomatic mission, which was then engaged in peace negotiations at Ghent in Belgium.

Alexander Macomb survived the war and pursued his military career, eventually rising to Commander in Chief of the army. Today General Macomb rests in the Congressional Cemetery in Washington D.C., and a statue to their native son, who was born here in Detroit on April 3, 1782 is located on Michigan Avenue between Washington Boulevard and Shelby Street in the city of Detroit.

## ALEXANDER MACOMB — MOUNT CLEMENS, MICHIGAN

The State of Michigan has erected a plaque to General Alexander Macomb, commander of the infantry forces at the Battle of Plattsburg. The plaque is located at the west edge of the courthouse plaza in the town of Mount Clemens, Macomb County, Michigan. (see prior entry)

# CHAPTER 2
## DETROIT RIVER

In the Town of Amherstburg

1. Park House
2. Gordon House
3. Amherstburg Navy Yard
4. Major John Richardson
5. "Pro Patria" Royal Navy
6. Lt. Col. William Caldwell

# FORT MALDEN — AMHERSTBURG, ONTARIO

After Jay's Treaty in 1796, the British were forced to evacuate their main post at Detroit, and as a direct consequence Fort Malden was constructed between 1797 and 1799. The fort then became the main British base on Lake Erie, where it played a key role in British Colonial Diplomacy. This was especially true in the Indian Department, where contact was kept with the Western Indians, whose aid was essential for a successful defence of the province. The fort's primary purpose though was to protect the vital Amherstburg Navy Yard, which was the headquarters of the Provincial Marine.

During the War of 1812 the garrison participated in many of the battles and skirmishes on the Detroit Frontier. During the summer of 1812, General Isaac Brock and the great Shawnee warrior "Tecumseh" first met at Fort Malden and Brock used the fort as the staging area for his counter-offensive against Detroit.

After the Battle of Lake Erie the fort could no longer be supplied by water, and consequently General Proctor burned the fort on September 23rd, before his retreat to Burlington. On October 5, 1813 Proctor's army was destroyed at the Battle of the Thames, and after this disaster the Americans held the Detroit frontier until the end of the war.

With the signing of the Treaty of Ghent the fort was evacuated by the Americans on July 1, 1815. A smaller fort was then reconstructed over the ruins of the first, but Fort Malden's heyday was over. It was reactivated from time to time as various border crises arose, but it never regained its former importance. In 1921 the fort was deemed of national historic importance, and by 1939 a small park had been established. Today the fort is administered by Parks Canada, and has earthwork remains and four buildings restored to the 1840 period. A museum and interpretive centre are also present. During the summer months, guides in period uniform perform military drills. Fort Malden is located on Laird Avenue in the town of Amherstburg.

# AMHERSTBURG NAVY YARD — AMHERSTBURG, ONTARIO

Naval communication was essential for the defence of Upper Canada, which suffered from a poor road system and thin population. Because of this the Amherstburg Navy Yard and Fort Malden were constructed in 1796 when the British abandoned Fort Detroit. Some of the more famous vessels that were built here were: the brig *General Hunter*, the corvette *Queen Charlotte*, and the *Detroit*, which became Captain Barclay's flagship. After the Battle of Lake Erie the yard was destroyed by the retreating British. Today the site of the Navy Yard is commemorated in "Kings Navy Yard Park" overlooking the Detroit River, and a plaque has been placed by the Historic Sites and Monuments Board of Canada. The only building that remains is the commissariat, which presently houses a small souvenir shop, the proceeds of which go towards Project Detroit. (see next entry)

# "PROJECT DETROIT" — AMHERSTBURG, ONTARIO

Project Detroit is a dedicated group of volunteers whose goal is to build a full-scale replica of the War of 1812 vessel *Detroit*. The *Detroit* was built at the Amherstburg Navy Yard during the summer of 1813, and was classified as a corvette designed to carry sixteen carronades and four long guns.

On April 27, 1813 the Americans raided York, where most of the naval stores intended for Lake Erie were kept, and as a result the *Detroit* never carried her intended armament. When she went into the Battle of Lake Erie as Commodore Barclay's flagship, she was armed with a variety of cannons taken from the ramparts of Fort Malden. At Lake Erie the vessel performed admirably, but was finally captured, along with the rest of the squadron, by the Americans under Commodore Oliver Hazard Perry. The vessel never saw action again, and for many years after her capture she lay rotting at the wharf at Erie, Pennsylvania. Finally, she proved to be a nuisance and was purposely sunk just off of the harbour. Current plans are to have the replica of *Detroit* moored near the site where she was first laid down, which was the old Amherstburg Navy Yard. The historic Gordon House is now the visitor centre for the project. (see Gordon House)

## "PRO PATRIA" — ROYAL NAVY — AMHERSTBURG, ONTARIO

A plaque placed by the Historic Sites and Monuments Board of Canada is dedicated to the seaman of the Royal Navy, the Provincial Marine, and soldiers of the Royal Newfoundland Regiment, who served on the Great Lakes during the war. Members of the Royal Newfoundland Regiment had the distinction of having served as marines on the lake squadrons. The plaque is located in Kings Navy Yard Park in the town of Amherstburg.

## PARK HOUSE — AMHERSTBURG, ONTARIO

The Park House is one of the oldest buildings on the Detroit River and predates the War of 1812. Constructed in 1796, it originally stood on the American side of the river.

The owner, a staunch loyalist, had the house dismantled and re-erected on this site in 1799. The house features pioneer and local artifacts and accents the Park family's mercantile business. The Park House is located at 214 Dalhousie Street in the town of Amherstburg.

## GORDON HOUSE — AMHERSTBURG, ONTARIO

The Gordon House was built in 1798 by local Scottish merchant James Gordon, who provided rope for the King's vessels being constructed at the nearby Navy Yard. James also participated in many of the battles and skirmishes fought on the Detroit frontier. The Gordon House, located at Murray and Dalhousie streets, is now the interpretation centre for "Project Detroit." (see Project Detroit)

## MAJOR JOHN RICHARDSON — AMHERSTBURG — ONTARIO

John Richardson was born in Queenston, Upper Canada in 1796, but when he was six years old, his family moved here to Amherstburg. At the commencement of the War of 1812, through the influence of his father, he joined the 41st Regiment of foot serving as a "gentleman volunteer." Elements of the 41st Regiment were at nearly every engagement fought by the British right division during the first two years of the war, and John Richardson was present at them all. He was captured at the Battle of Moraviantown on October 5, 1813 and was a prisoner of war in Kentucky. He retired from the army on half pay in 1818 and later became a writer. He is best known for his poem "Tecumseh" and the historical novel *Wacousta*. He wrote a classic account of his adventures in serialized form, which eventually became the book *Richardson's War of 1812*, but financial success eluded him, and he died in 1852 in New York City in utter poverty. The Historic Sites and Monuments Board of Canada has placed a plaque dedicated to him near Fort Malden in the town of Amherstburg.

## LIEUTENANT COLONEL WILLIAM CALDWELL — AMHERSTBURG, ONTARIO

Irish-born Lieutenant Colonel William Caldwell served as a captain in Butler's Rangers during the American Revolution, and in August of 1782 he ambushed and defeated a column of mounted Kentuckians at the "Blue Licks Battlefield" in Kentucky. Among those engaged on the American side was the famous frontiersman Daniel Boone, who lost a son in the battle.

During the War of 1812 Caldwell commanded the Western Rangers and participated in the Miami Campaign and was in the Battle of the Longwoods in 1814. Later he was appointed Deputy Superintendent of Indian Affairs and led Indian forces at the battles of Lundy's Lane, and Chippawa, and the Siege of Fort Erie. The Ontario Provincial Plaque dedicated to him is located in front of Christ Church, Ramsay Street in the town of Amherstburg.

## COLONEL MATTHEW ELLIOT — AMHERSTBURG, ONTARIO

Colonel Matthew Elliot was Deputy Superintendent of Indian Affairs at Amherstburg in 1795, but under the shadow of questionable business practices he was eventually relieved of the position. After the "Chesapeake Affair" in 1807, American-British relations were strained once more, and since the loyalty of the Indians was essential — and Elliot had much influence with them — he was reinstated. Although in his seventies, he commanded the 1st Essex Militia and took part in the sieges of Detroit and Fort Meigs, and in the battles of Moraviantown and Black Rock. He held the position of Deputy Superintendent until his death in 1814. An Ontario Provincial Plaque dedicated to him is located on Highway 18 just south of Amherstburg, on what were the grounds of his estates.

# SKIRMISHES AT THE CANARD RIVER

At this spot were fired the first shots of the War of 1812. On July 16, 1812 a British picket under the command of Lieutenant Clemow and consisting of regulars from the 41st Regiment, Canadian Militia and some Indians, was attacked by advanced units of General William Hull's invading army. The American advance guard was under the command of Colonel Lewis Cass and consisted of one company of the U.S. 4th Regiment, one company of Ohio volunteers, four companies of Ohio rifleman and some dragoons: in all about three hundred men. Cass left a covering force at the bridge, and utilizing the knowledge of a local guide marched up the Canard River to a nearby ford and crossed.

The British, outnumbered and completely surprised, fell back to their main position at Amherstburg. In the confusion two British soldiers, privates Hancock and Dean, were left on the north side of the bridge. When the American units advanced, both Hancock and Dean heroically defended the position until both were wounded. Dean kept firing until one of his arms was broken by an American ball. Both privates were captured and Hancock later died that evening.

Both men were later mentioned in a General Order issued August 6th by the Governor General. These two privates were the first to shed their blood in defence of Canada during the War of 1812. The Ontario Provincial Plaque, which is difficult to spot, is adjacent to Highway 18, north of Amherstburg, at the Canard River bridge.

# BATTLE OF BROWNSTOWN — GIBRALTAR, MICHIGAN

In early August, 1812 a relief column to Detroit, consisting of cattle and supplies, arrived at the River Raisin under the command of Captain Brush.

Captain Brush sent a messenger to General Hull, who was at that time on the Canadian side of the river at Sandwich (present-day Windsor, Ontario). The message informed Hull that a party of Indians led by Tecumseh, and possibly escorted by British regulars, had crossed the Detroit River and were at the village of Brownstown. Brush requested that a force be sent from Detroit to clear the way for the convoy, and Hull proceeded to do so. On August 4, 1812, a party of two hundred Ohio Militia, under Major Thomas Van Horne, left Detroit and marched south.

As they were crossing Brownstown Creek, three miles north of the village of Brownstown, the great Shawnee war leader Tecumseh, with only twenty-four warriors, ambushed the Detroit column. The American force retreated in confusion and a running gunfight was kept up until the column reached the Ecorces River, after which the Indians broke off the action.

The American loss was eighteen killed, twelve wounded, and seventy men missing, while the Indians lost only one man, "Chief Logan." Though Brownstown was only a small skirmish, it indicated that Hull's supply line to Ohio was not secure, and reinforced in his mind that he was greatly outnumbered by British and Indian forces. A Michigan State plaque is located at the Parsons Elementary school at 14473 Gibraltar Road in Memorial Park.

## BATTLE OF MAGUAGA — TRENTON, MICHIGAN

After the skirmish at Brownstown, General Hull was determined to re-open his severed supply line to Ohio. On the afternoon of August 8, 1812, a picked force under the command of Lieutenant Colonel James Miller left Detroit and marched south towards the River Raisin. Miller's command consisted of detachments from the 1st and 4th regiments of U.S. regulars, some Michigan and Ohio militia, two cannons, and a detachment of cavalry — in all about six hundred troops.

On the afternoon of August 9th the column approached the Indian village of Maguaga, fourteen miles from Detroit. At an oak grove near the river, the column was ambushed by a detachment of seventy-five British Regulars of the 41st Regiment, sixty Canadian Militia, and seventy Indians under Tecumseh, the whole force commanded by Major Adam Muir. At one point in the engagement the British regulars mistook a body of Indians on their right flank for the enemy and fired on them. This produced much confusion, and when the British centre broke, the survivors fled to the river, hastily embarking in boats and retreating back to Fort Malden.

According to John Richardson, who was present at the engagement, the British lost one man killed and twenty-three wounded, while the Americans lost eighteen killed and sixty-three wounded. Although left in possession of the ground, Miller was ordered by General Hull to fall back to Detroit. Hull was now more convinced than ever that his supply line to Ohio was severed, and after this small skirmish he decided to evacuate his army from Canadian soil.

After Maguaga, Hull's senior officers were in open contempt of him for his lack of nerve. The twin skirmishes of Brownstown and Maguaga laid the seeds for the surrender of Detroit just ten days later. A plaque from the Michigan Historical Commission is located in Elizabeth Park at Slocum and West Jefferson Avenue in the town of Trenton, Michigan.

## LANDING PLACE OF AMERICANS — AMHERSTBURG, ONTARIO

After the Battle of Lake Erie, the American fleet under Commodore Perry began transporting the American Army for the invasion of Upper Canada. By September 25, 1813 nearly five thousand troops were concentrated on Middle Sister Island for the amphibious attack. On the morning of September 27th, the flotilla of sixteen armed vessels and nearly one hundred boats left the island and sailed north.

The selected landing spot was at Hartley's Point, opposite the lower end of Bois Blanc Island, and expecting fierce resistance the troops were vigilant as they landed on the smooth shore. But there was no opposition, as the British under General Proctor had evacuated Fort Malden after burning the public buildings. To the tune of "Yankee Doodle," the American Army occupied Amherstburg. Presently there is no marker to indicate the landing spot of the Americans.

# CHAPTER 3
## MAUMEE VALLEY

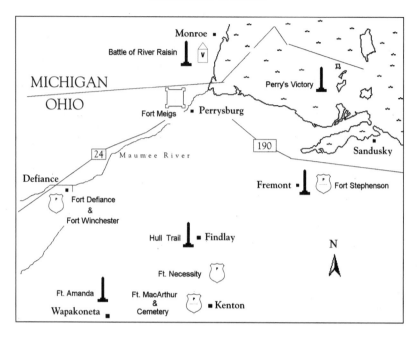

## FORT DEFIANCE — DEFIANCE, OHIO

Fort Defiance was constructed in the summer of 1794 by troops under the command of General "Mad" Anthony Wayne, who defied the British and Indians to take it. It was an earth and log structure, but by the time of the War of 1812 it was a dilapidated ruin. In September of that year, a small detachment of British regulars and Miami Indians, under the command of Major Muir, had been sent to capture Fort Wayne. At this site they had to cross the Maumee River and fall back before the superior numbers of General Winchester's advancing army. When Winchester took possession of the fort, repairs were undertaken, and for the rest of the war it was used as a staging area for troops moving to the Canadian front. After the war it was abandoned, and the site of the fort is now in a small park overlooking the Maumee and Auglaize rivers in the town of Defiance, Ohio. A marker and small cannon are at the site.

Site of Fort Defiance as Lossing sketched it in 1860

The site of Fort Defiance today, overlooking the Maumee and Auglaize rivers

# FORT WINCHESTER — DEFIANCE, OHIO

When General William Henry Harrison arrived at the site of Fort Defiance in October of 1813, he ordered a new fort constructed just eighty yards away. This was the fort that became Fort Winchester, and was a more substantial work than Fort Defiance. The fort was never seriously threatened during the war, and was used mainly as a supply point and staging area. The modern city of Defiance, Ohio has obliterated the site, but it stood about one block south of the present Fort Defiance marker. A state historic plaque is at the location. (see prior entry)

## HULL TRAIL

Just prior to the declaration of war in June of 1812, Brigadier General William Hull assembled an army at Dayton, Ohio. With the British in control of Lake Erie by means of the Provincial Marine, a new road had to be constructed to the Michigan Territory. It was decided that Hull's army would construct the new road on the march as it advanced towards the frontier town of Detroit. At that time Ohio was a virtual wilderness, but the road was finally cleared during the summer of 1812, and at various intervals, blockhouses protected the route. The "Hull Trail" is a series of markers which have been placed by the Ohio Historical Society and highlight various points along the historic route. Sites which are part of the "Hull Trail" have been indicated.

Fort MacArthur — Kenton, Ohio
Hull Trail

Between June 11th and June 19th of 1812, Brigadier General William Hull and his army advanced from Dayton, Ohio to the banks of the Scioto River. Here, under the direction of Colonel

Duncan Macarthur, they constructed Fort Macarthur. It consisted of a palisade, log huts, and a blockhouse and was built to secure the road. After the war it was abandoned and fell into ruin. A stone marker is located at the site, about three miles west of Kenton, Ohio in Hardin County.

Fort MacArthur Cemetery — Kenton, Ohio
Hull Trail

During the winter of 1812–1813, General Tupper and one thousand soldiers encamped on a hill near this spot, and at the foot of the hill is the burial place of sixteen soldiers who died that winter.

Fort Necessity — Hancock County, Ohio
Hull Trail

During Hull's march, a small party under Colonel Duncan Macarthur was sent ahead to scout out the route and clear the road. At this site the party was delayed by heavy rains and mud and was forced to halt. They built a small stockade and blockhouse, calling it "Fort Necessity." After the war the fort performed no function and was abandoned. A stone marker, just north of the county line, is on County Road 2, west of Route 68.

## Eagle Creek Crossing — Findlay, Ohio
## Hull Trail

At this spot Hull's army crossed Eagle Creek on their way to Detroit in June of 1812. A plaque placed by the Daughters of the American Revolution, Fort Findlay Chapter, is located on the east side of Route 68, just south of Findlay, Ohio.

## Blanchard Creek Crossing — Findlay, Ohio
## Hull Trail

At this spot Hull's army crossed Blanchard Creek on their way to Detroit in June of 1812. A plaque placed by the Daughters of the American Revolution, Fort Findlay Chapter, is located at Riverside Park south of the city swimming pool in the city of Findlay.

## Fort Findlay — Findlay, Ohio
## Hull Trail

When General William Hull reached this spot on June 26, 1812 he was unaware that war had been declared. At this point he was about thirty-five miles from the Maumee River, where he would be able to utilize water transportation for part of his baggage. When he reached the Maumee, he sent his private correspondence on board the brig *Adams*, and this was to have disastrous consequences when the British captured the vessel. Now they knew all of Hull's plans and the strength of his army. At this spot Fort Findlay was constructed under the direction of Colonel James Findlay. It was a stockade fifty yards square, and served as a supply depot during the war. The historical marker is on South Main Street, at the Blanchard River Bridge, in downtown Findlay.

## FORT MEIGS — PERRYSBURG, OHIO

Fort Meigs played an important role in the history of the War of 1812. It was constructed in February 1813, at the foot of the Maumee rapids by General William Henry Harrison and it was a large fortification, encompassing an area of ten acres. British General Henry Proctor laid siege to the fort twice during the war, but both sieges were unsuccessful.

The first siege commenced on May 1, 1813, when Proctor brought 520 regulars of the 41st Regiment, 450 militia, and some 1500 Indians to bear against the fort. General Harrison, defending the fort, was aware that a relief column under Brigadier General Green Clay was on its way from Kentucky. On the morning of May 5th, part of the relief column under Colonel Dudley struck the British batteries on the north side of the river, but the British counter-attacked, and with the aid of Tecumseh's Indians dealt a serious blow to the column. Many were captured and killed, including Colonel Dudley.

On the south side of the river the Americans were more successful, for here they managed to capture Proctor's secondary battery, which had produced a crossfire on the fort. After a two-day lull and prisoner exchange Proctor resumed the siege, but the momentum had been lost. His Indian allies began to leave, and his Canadian militia were needed at home to sow the spring crops. On May 9th Proctor lifted the siege and returned to Amherstburg.

When Major General Francis de Rottenburg became the new Commander-in-Chief in Upper Canada, he suggested that Proctor's army abandon the Detroit frontier. Proctor informed him that this action would undermine the whole Indian alliance, and he searched for an alternate plan. Finally, at the insistence of Tecumseh, Proctor reluctantly agreed to a second attack on Fort Meigs. The British were once again before the fort on July 25th, but this time the operational plan was Tecumseh's.

Tecumseh's plan was to stage a "sham battle" outside of the fort, which was meant to trick the garrison into thinking that a relief column was being ambushed. However, the commander of the fort, Colonel Clay, had been present at Dudley's defeat two months before, and was not easily deceived. Restraining his men, he wisely kept them inside the fort. With the plan gone awry, and light guns having no effect on the fort, Proctor and Tecumseh both agreed to lift the siege. Proctor's army left the vicinity the next day, but to keep the Indian alliance active they moved on to smaller Fort Stephenson. On August 2nd, Proctor's army was repulsed in a general attack on the walls, and after they retreated back to Amherstburg.

Fort Meigs has been fully restored and is administered by the Ohio Historical Society. There are interpretive displays and visitors may take an audio cassette tour of the grounds. The fort is located in the town of Perrysburg just outside Toledo, Ohio.

## FORT AMANDA — WAPAKONETA, OHIO

Fort Amanda was built by Colonel John Poague's Kentucky troops under the direction of General William Henry Harrison in the summer and fall of 1812. During the war it was used as a supply depot and rest spot for troops moving to the frontier, but after the Treaty of Ghent it was abandoned. The fort was located on the west bank of the Auglaize River, about nine miles from present-day Wapakoneta, Ohio, in Auglaize County. A fifty-foot high granite obelisk, erected in 1915, marks the location of the fort.

# FORT STEPHENSON — FREMONT, OHIO

Fort Stephenson was constructed in the summer of 1812, and consisted of wooden pickets fourteen feet high surrounded by an eight-foot ditch. Three blockhouses were later added. On August 2, 1813 it was successfully defended by Major George Croghan, 160 regulars of the 17th and 24th U.S. infantries, and one six-pound cannon. The attacking force was under the command of British General Henry Proctor, and was composed of soldiers of the 41st Regiment of foot, several light guns, and Indians led by Tecumseh; in all about one thousand men. Proctor attempted a frontal assault against the fortification, but his troops met a withering fire and were pinned down in a gully. With nightfall Proctor's army re-embarked in boats and returned to Fort Malden.

The site of Fort Stephenson is now occupied by the Birchard Public Library on Croghan Street in the city of Fremont, Ohio. The old cannon, nicknamed "Old Betsy Croghan," is in front of the library, along with a monument, a plaque, and the grave site of Major Croghan.

# PERRY'S VICTORY MONUMENT — LAKE ERIE

This huge monument, completed in June of 1915, towers 352 feet above Lake Erie and is easily spotted from miles away. The monument commemorates Commodore Oliver Hazard Perry's decisive naval victory at the Battle of Lake Erie on September 10, 1813. It was from this spot that Perry's fleet up-anchored and sailed to engage the British about ten miles to the northwest. The battle swept the British navy from the lake and caused them to abandon their post at Amherstburg and all the Detroit Frontier.

Interred below the monument are the remains of three American sailors and three British officers killed during the battle. The monument has an open-air lookout, which is accessible by elevator, and offers good views of the surrounding area.

A visitor centre tells the history of the monument and the battle it commemorates. The monument is located on South Bass Island, Lake Erie, and is accessible by ferry from Port Clinton, Ohio or Catawba Island.

## BATTLE OF THE RIVER RAISIN — MONROE, MICHIGAN

On January 22, 1813, in the dead of winter, Major General Henry Proctor and a force of 597 men, consisting of British regulars, Canadian militia, and Indians, attacked an American detachment at the village of Frenchtown. The attack achieved total surprise and in less than thirty minutes a good portion of the American force of 934 men was in full flight or in the process of surrender. In the general confusion their leader, General James Winchester, was captured.

A portion of the U.S. force, which had not been caught by the initial attack, fought on and repulsed three separate British assaults. After learning of their general's capture, this detached force was surprised to learn that General Winchester himself suggested surrender. On the condition that the American wounded would be protected, they also laid down their arms.

With intelligence that another American army, under General Harrison, was advancing against him, General Proctor decided to retreat back to Amherstburg. Leaving the American wounded behind in the village, many of them were massacred the next day by Indians who had entered the town for the purpose of plunder. The massacre was not forgotten by the American public, and with the rallying cry "Remember the Raisin," the Americans were able to field large militia forces the next spring, particularly in Kentucky. The massacre at the River Raisin was an everlasting stain on the career of General Proctor.

Today the battle site is commemorated at the River Raisin Battlefield Visitor Center, which is at 1403 East Elm Avenue in the city of Monroe, Michigan. The centre features dioramas, exhibits, and a fourteen-minute fibre-optic map presentation on the battle. At various points in the city of Monroe, the Historical Society has placed markers describing the events.

## BATTLE OF THE RIVER RAISIN — MONROE, MICHIGAN

A monument placed by the State of Michigan in 1904 commemorates the Battle of the River Raisin, which was fought on January 22, 1813. The monument is located approximately one-quarter mile west of the Battlefield Visitor Center, at East Elm Avenue and Dixie Highway in the city of Monroe, Michigan.

## BATTLE OF THE RIVER RAISIN — MONROE, MICHIGAN

A monument erected by the State of Michigan honours those American soldiers killed in the Battle of the River Raisin. The monument is located on South Monroe Street in a cemetery that used to hold the remains of 1812 soldiers.

FORT SHELBY — PRAIRIE DU CHIEN, WISCONSIN

In May of 1814, the post at Prairie du Chien was held by a small British artillery detachment under Captain Francis Michael Dease. When William Clark, Governor of the Missouri Territory, sent a mixed force of regulars and militia against the fort, the British abandoned the site. The Americans began construction of a new fort on May 6, 1814, with regular soldiers of the 24th U.S. Infantry.

The fort was named for Governor Isaac Shelby of Kentucky, and a garrison of seventy soldiers of the 7th U.S. Infantry was left under Lieutenant Joseph Perkins. The fort had two blockhouses and was armed with several cannons.

On July 17, 1814, British troops and Indians, under the command of Brevet Major William McKay, laid siege to the fort. McKay had with him only 75 Michigan Fencibles and 136 Indians. Aiding in the American defence was the gunboat *Governor Clark*, which was anchored in the river, but when Sergeant James Keating directed the fire of his single cannon against the gunboat, it was forced to slip its cable and retire down river.

Two days later, with most of their ammunition expended and the fort's only well completely dry, the garrison surrendered. The British renamed the post Fort McKay to impress the local Indians and held the fort for the entire war. After the Treaty of Ghent they abandoned it on May 25, 1815, and burned it on their departure. The site of Fort Shelby is now covered by the Victorian mansion "Villa Louis," and the old carriage house has been converted to a museum, which features artifacts and displays on the fort. The museum is on Villa Louis Road, in the city of Prairie du Chien, Wisconsin.

## BATTLE AT ROCK ISLAND RAPIDS — ROCK ISLAND, ILLINOIS

In early July of 1814, an American expedition was mounted to relieve the garrison at Prairie du Chien. Under the command of Major John Campbell, a force of 120 regulars and rangers was assembled at St. Louis, Missouri. Ascending the Mississippi River they were ambushed at the Rock Island Rapids by Chief Black Hawk and four hundred Sauk and Fox warriors. Campbell's force lost sixteen men killed and twenty-one wounded, but they were rescued by the timely arrival of the gunboat *Governor Clark*, which was itself retreating down river from the siege of Fort Clark.

A larger expedition was then mounted against Prairie du Chien, and this was under the command of Major Zachary Taylor, who had with him 350 men and eight gunboats. The British were warned of the second relief expedition and they commenced assembling another force to meet it. Lieutenant Duncan Graham of the Indian Department, assisted by Sergeant Keating of the Royal Artillery, moved down to the Rock River with a small contingent of thirty men and one field piece. There they rendezvoused with a party of over 1,200 Sauk, Sioux, Winnebago, and Kickapoo Indians. On the morning of September 5, 1814, this large force ambushed Taylor's flotilla, which was anchored in the Rock River.

The accurate fire from Sergeant Keating's field piece, and the ferocity of the Indian attack, convinced Taylor of the futility of the relief mission, and his party retreated down the Mississippi with three men killed and eight wounded. After the failure of the second relief expedition, the British and Indians held the northwest for the remainder of the war. Fort Armstrong was built near the rapids in the spring of 1816, but presently the Battle at the Rock Island Rapids is unmarked. (see prior entry)

## FORT DEARBORN — CHICAGO, ILLINOIS

Fort Dearborn was constructed under the direction of Major John Whistler and officially named after the Secretary of War on July 4, 1804. It was a strongly picketed work and had two blockhouses. At the time of the War of 1812, the garrison consisted of fifty-four regular soldiers under Captain Nathan Heald. In April of 1812, prior to the declaration of war, Winnebago Indians had attacked some of the settlers nearby. Although the garrison was on good terms with the local Indians, these tribes were under constant pressure to join the British. This was especially true after the capture of Fort Michilimackinac, which gave the British open access to the fur trade, and contact with the western Indians. Finally, on April 17th, the local Potawatomis struck farms in the vicinity. Although not assaulted directly, the fort was under virtual siege.

On August 7th Captain Heald received a dispatch from General Hull, based at Detroit, which ordered the evacuation of Fort Dearborn "if practicable." Against the advice of local trader John Kinzie, Heald prepared to leave the fort. On the morning of August

15th, the garrison left the fort accompanied by a small contingent of civilians, but near the sand dunes of Lake Michigan just to the south, the column was attacked by Indians of the Miami and Potawatomi tribes. In what turned out to be a massacre, the column was overwhelmed by over five hundred Indians, and the next day they burned the fort. Forewarned of the attack by some friendly Indians, John Kinzie's life was spared.

The modern metropolis of Chicago has obliterated all traces of old Fort Dearborn. The fort originally stood on the south bank of the Chicago River, near where the Michigan Avenue Bridge is today. The fort is commemorated by bronze plaques located at the southwest corner of Michigan Avenue and Wacker Drive.

## FORT MADISON — FORT MADISON, IOWA

Fort Madison was constructed by Lieutenant Alpha Kingsley of the 1st U.S. Infantry, and was completed on September 26, 1808. It was named after Secretary of State James Madison, and its primary purpose was as a trading post to entice the Indians away from the British. On September 3, 1813, the fort was surrounded by local Sac and Fox Indians.

The garrison was in a serious predicament, since they were low on food and could expect no reinforcements. In desperation, the garrison dug a tunnel from one of the blockhouses to their boats moored in the river, but before making their escape they burned the fort. All that remains of the old fort is a chimney, standing like a monument to its memory. The site of the fort has been partially excavated, and is at the 300 Block of Avenue H off U.S. Highway 61 in the town of Fort Madison.

# FORT CLARK — PEORIA, ILLINOIS

Fort Clark was named after the famous explorer William Clark, and was built in 1813 by the United States Army. The fort's main purpose was as a defence against Indian raids, but it saw no action in the War of 1812, and was garrisoned until 1817. Two years later it was destroyed by Indians and abandoned. The site of the fort is now in the city of Peoria. There are no above-ground remains, and presently no marker is at the site.

# FORT MASSAC — METROPOLIS, ILLINOIS

Fort Massac has a history that stretches back to the Seven Years' War. Built by the French, it was originally named Fort Ascension, and was constructed on a site overlooking the broad Ohio River. It was later changed to Fort Massac in honour of the French Minister of Marine, but after 1763, when the British took formal possession, the fort's name was changed to Fort Massac, which the English found easier to pronounce.

In mid-December of 1811, an earthquake destroyed many of the buildings, and at the time of the War of 1812 the fort was still undergoing repairs. The role of the fort in the general defence plan was questionable, and it was finally abandoned in the spring of 1814. Over the years the local populace dismantled the fort piece by piece, for their own homes and farms, and in time little was left but ruins. Today the fort has been restored to the period 1795, and features a museum that interprets the fort's history. The fort is located east of Metropolis, off of Interstate 24, via State Route 45.

# PIGEON ROOST STATE MEMORIAL — UNDERWOOD, INDIANA

After the fall of Fort Dearborn in August of 1812, Indian raids on local settlers increased. On September 3, 1812, a war party of Shawnee Indians descended on the small community of Pigeon Roost, where they massacred twenty-four men, women, and children. Although a pursuit party of 150 men was organized under Major John M'Coy, the perpetrators of the deed were never apprehended.

Though this turned out to be the last Indian raid in the state during the war, local settlers were kept in a constant state of alert. Today the site is commemorated in Pigeon Roost State Historic Site, which features a forty-four-foot monument and an interpretive marker. The site is south of Underwood, Indiana on U.S. 31.

# FORT VALLONIA — VALLONIA, INDIANA

The name "Vallonia" is very likely derived from the French word "un vallon," which means a small vale or valley. The community of Vallonia is one of the oldest in Jackson County, and dates from 1810. In 1811 a stockade was constructed here to protect settlers from hostile tribes of Shawnee, Delaware, and Miami Indians. The stockade has been reconstructed in the centre of town, and a stone memorial and small museum are on Main Street nearby. Vallonia is southwest of Brownstown, Indiana off of SR 50, on SR 135.

# MISSISSINEWA BATTLEFIELD — MARION, INDIANA

After the fall of Michilimackinac and Detroit in the summer of 1812, it was clear that the Indian population of the old northwest, was disposed in favour of the British. A number of tribes, chiefly from the Miami and Delaware nations, began to assemble on the Mississinewa River, a tributary of the Wabash. Feeling that this gathering was a threat, William Henry Harrison, commander of the North Western Army, determined to strike first as he had done before at Tippecanoe. He directed Lieutenant Colonel John B. Campbell, with one company of the 19th Infantry and one company of the 2nd U.S. Light Dragoons, to move against these tribes.

Campbell's force numbered about six hundred men, and by the middle of December they had reached the vicinity of the Indian Villages. In their first attack they burned one of the villages to the ground, killing eight warriors and capturing thirty-two women and children. Moving on, they destroyed other Indian towns and captured some horses and corn. They then returned to the site of their first attack on the Mississinewa River and encamped for the night. Just before dawn on December 18th, they were attacked by an unknown number of Indians. The battle was short but brutal, and terminated at sunrise. Fifteen Indians were left dead on the field, while Campbell's force suffered eight killed and forty-two wounded. With his force badly shaken, and with rumours that Tecumseh himself was only eighteen miles away, Campbell's party quickly retreated from the field. The retreat, however, proved to be long, and the soldiers endured much hardship.

Before reaching Greenville, the men suffered horribly from the cold, with over three hundred men frostbitten and unfit for further service. Campbell was later congratulated by the Commander-in-Chief for what he considered a successful raid.

The raids on the Mississinewa were small, but would be bitterly remembered by the Indians, who would face the Americans at Frenchtown less than five weeks later. Today Mississinewa Battlefield is administered by the Mississinewa Battlefield Society Incorporated. The battlefield has two monuments: one is dedicated to the U.S. soldiers, and the other to native Indians who were killed in the conflict. There are also twelve grave markers. Mississinewa Battlefield is seven miles northwest of Marion, Indiana on State Road 15.

## TIPPECANOE BATTLEFIELD — LAFAYETTE, INDIANA

Tippecanoe has sometimes been called the first battle of the War of 1812, although it actually occurred before the formal outbreak of war. It was near here at the "Prophet's Town" that the great Indian leader Tecumseh and his brother "the Prophet" established a large Indian community composed of various tribes from the old northwest. Ever since the Council of Vincennes in August of 1810, it was inevitable that the two great personalities of William Henry Harrison and Tecumseh would clash. With the establishment of the large Indian community on the frontier, Harrison as territorial governor felt threatened, and determined to move against it.

Under orders from the Secretary of War, Harrison's mixed force of regulars and militia left Vincennes, Indiana Territory, on September 26, 1811. His army numbered some 1,300 men and was composed of Indiana and Kentucky militia, and detachments of the 4th and 7th U.S. Infantry.

By November 5th, the army was within ten miles of "Prophet's Town" on the Tippecanoe River, which was a tributary of the Wabash. Tecumseh was not present as he was engaged in a great tour of the south, attempting to rally the tribes there to his cause. It is impossible to say what would have happened if he had been present, but he had warned his brother "the Prophet" not to engage the white soldiers until his great confederacy had been firmly established. Bowing to pressure from Chief Winnemac of the Potawatomi, "the Prophet" decided to attack Harrison's column before it could approach the village.

In the pre-dawn hours of November 7th, the Indian forces from Prophet's Town struck Harrison's encamped army. The success of the confederacy is indicated by the number of tribes who were present at the battle. The Miami, Potawatomi, Wyandot, Kickapoo, Winnebago, Chippawa, Sac, and Shawnee. The number of warriors

Tippecanoe Battlefield as sketched by Benson Lossing in the autumn of 1860

Tippecanoe Battlefield today.

is difficult to determine, but estimates are that they numbered at least seven hundred. "The Prophet" had assured his warriors that his "magic" would make them invincible to the white man's bullets.

The Indians attacked valiantly, and at one point Harrison's lines were nearly broken. But as daylight approached, it was becoming quite evident that the "magic" was not working. More and more warriors were being killed, and finally the breaking point had been reached. The Indians left the battlefield, bringing away as many of their dead as they could carry. For Harrison's army, the remainder of the day was spent in caring for the wounded and preparing for another assault, which they believed would come. The assault never materialized, and on the next day the army moved on Prophet's Town, burning it to the ground. Many British rifles were found in the town, and this only confirmed in Harrison's mind that the Indian Confederacy was being fed by the British.

Today the battlefield of Tippecanoe is commemorated in the ninety-acre Tippecanoe Battlefield Park, which has a large monument that was dedicated on November 7, 1908. The park features a museum, with displays on the battle, and the well-maintained grounds have numerous markers and scenic trails. The battlefield is located at Tippecanoe and Railroad Street, seven miles northeast of Lafayette on SR 225, off SR 43 exit of I-65.

## PROPHET'S TOWN — LAFAYETTE, INDIANA

This was the site of a large Indian community, composed mainly of tribes from the northwest. It was at this site that Tecumseh, and his brother "the Prophet" tried to organize a great Indian Confederacy to combat the encroachment of white settlement.

After the Battle of Tippecanoe, Prophet's Town was burned by General Harrison's victorious army. Today there are no above-ground remains of the village, and the site is mainly in forested terrain. A plaque placed by the Battleground Historical Corporation is southeast of the battleground.

# OLD FORT WAYNE — FORT WAYNE, INDIANA

A number of forts were constructed in the immediate vicinity of present-day Fort Wayne and sorting them all out can lead to confusion. The first Fort Wayne was constructed by General "Mad" Anthony Wayne in October of 1794. This fort would have been at the approximate location of Clay and Berry streets in the modern city of Fort Wayne. In the winter of 1815–1816 a more substantial work was constructed, designed to resist artillery. This fortification, a much larger work, would have been on what is now the corner of Main and Clay streets. The present "Old Fort Wayne" is a reconstruction of this particular fort, and is located less than a quarter mile from its original site.

The 1812 fort had four cannons, and was garrisoned by seventy soldiers under Captain James Rhea. In August of 1812, hostile bands of Indians began attacking settlers in the vicinity, and on the evening of September 5th they began a series of attacks on the fort, but with little effect. After the surrender of Hull's army at Detroit, the British organized a small expedition to cooperate with these Indians in the hope that Fort Wayne itself may be taken. The expedition, which included British regulars and Indians, was under the command of Major Muir, and it was hoped that he would reach Fort Wayne by September 1st.

The column's progress was delayed, and at the site of old Fort Defiance, Muir learned that an American relief column had already reached Fort Wayne. With vastly superior numbers between him and his objective, Muir re-embarked the expedition on bateaux and returned to Fort Malden. This was the only serious threat against Fort Wayne for the remainder of the war.

The present Old Fort Wayne has been reconstructed to the period 1816, but gives an excellent interpretation of garrison life just after the war. Old Fort Wayne is located in the modern city of Fort Wayne and is administered by the city.

# CHAPTER 5
## LAKE ERIE

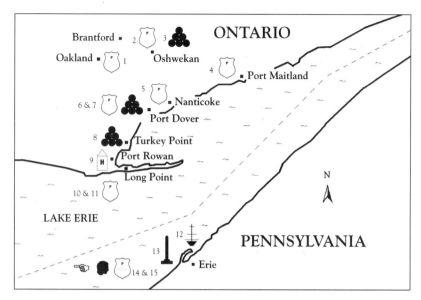

1. Battle of Malcolm's Mills
2. Captain John Brant
3. The Six Nations
4. Grand River Naval Depot
5. Skirmish at Nanticoke
6. Brock's Embarkation
7. Campbell's Raid
8. Fort Norfolk
9. Backhouse Mill
10. Long Point Settlement
11. Long Point Portage
12. The Brig *Niagara*
13. Presque Île Naval Base
14. Perry Statue, Cleveland, Ohio
15. Fort Huntington, Cleveland, Ohio

## BATTLE OF MALCOLM'S MILLS — OAKLAND, ONTARIO

In the late fall of 1814, the British and American armies were in a stalemate position on the Niagara Frontier. In order to help relieve pressure on General Brown's army, and remove the possibility of a counter-raid against Detroit, the Americans planned a raid into western Upper Canada.

The raid was to be under the command of Brigadier General Duncan Macarthur, and was organized at Detroit with 750 mounted

Kentucky and Ohio volunteers. Performing a diversionary move around Lake St. Clair, the column crossed the St. Clair River into Upper Canada on October 26th.

Moving rapidly through the Thames Valley, Macarthur's column caused much destruction and confusion, although his main objective was to destroy the mills that were supplying the British Army. As the column approached the Grand River, he found it overflowing from recent rains, so he decided to turn south and disperse a party of Canadian militia, which he knew had gathered at Malcolm's Mill.

On November 6th, he successfully outflanked and defeated the militia, losing only one man killed and six others wounded, while the Canadians suffered eighteen men killed and twelve wounded. Since Macarthur was paroling prisoners as he moved through the district, he claimed in his official report the capture of 108 prisoners. With the passage of the Grand River too risky, Macarthur's force returned to Detroit via the Talbot Road and the Thames Valley.

The raid had been very successful, for with the burning of five valuable mills the British Army had suffered a severe setback to their supply network, and the economy of Upper Canada had been hurt. Macarthur's troops had behaved fairly well to the civilian population, and receipts were given for commandeered private property. An Ontario Provincial Plaque is located in the Community Park, Oakland, Brant County near the site of the engagement.

## CAPTAIN JOHN BRANT — OSHWEKAN, ONTARIO

John Brant (Ahyouwaighs) was the son of the famous Chief Joseph Brant, who had fought the Americans during the Revolutionary War. After the Revolution Brant and his people settled on the Grand River in Upper Canada, and it was here on September 27, 1794, that John was born. He was educated at Ancaster and Niagara and upon the death of his father in 1807 became Chief of the Six Nations. The Brant Clan had a long history of loyalty to the crown, and it was only natural that they would align themselves with the British at the commencement of the War of 1812.

John Brant led Indian units at the battles of Queenston Heights and Beaver Dams and later became a Captain in the British Army. He was eventually appointed Superintendent of the Six Nations. During a cholera epidemic in 1842, John Brant died at the Mohawk Village on the Grand River, and he is buried alongside his famous father at the Mohawk Chapel near Brantford. An Ontario Provincial Plaque commemorates the many services of John Brant to the crown. The plaque is in front of the Indian Council house on the Mohawk Reservation, Oshwekan.

## THE SIX NATIONS — OSHWEKAN, ONTARIO

At the commencement of the War of 1812, the policy of the Six Nations was officially to remain neutral, however some of the more zealous did participate in the Battle of Queenston Heights on October 13, 1812. The success of the British on that day was partially attributable to the timely arrival of the Indian warriors, who prevented the Americans from consolidating their position on the heights.

In November of 1812, Indians from the Six Nations assisted the British in foiling American attempts to cross the Niagara River near Frenchman's Creek. During the crucial second year of the war, Six Nations Indians participated in the battles of Fort George and Beaver Dams, and in 1814 they participated in the Battle of Chippawa where they took significant casualties.

After the losses suffered at Chippawa, the Six Nations participation in the war was minimal, but their role during the first two years of the War of 1812 was critical. The Historic Sites and Monuments Board of Canada has commemorated their valuable assistance in the Seven Years' War, the American Revolution, the War of 1812, and the Rebellions of 1837. The commemorative plaque is mounted on a stone base, and is located in a small park opposite the Indian Council house at Oshwekan.

# GRAND RIVER NAVAL DEPOT — PORT MAITLAND, ONTARIO

The Grand River Naval Depot was not operational during the War of 1812, but its creation in 1815 was a direct result of the war. Initial plans called for a garrison of one thousand men and a naval force of three frigates, but the Rush Bagot agreement of 1817 limited the size of naval forces on the lakes and prevented the depot from being a major centre. There are no traces of the Naval Depot today, but there is an Ontario Provincial Plaque dedicated to the depot in Esplanade Park in the town of Port Maitland.

# SKIRMISH AT NANTICOKE — NANTICOKE, ONTARIO

After the Battle of the Thames on October 5, 1813, most of the western portion of the province was left undefended, and as a result, many raiding parties operating out of Buffalo slipped across the border and struck the isolated settlements. Determined to put an end to these raids, a group of Norfolk Volunteer militia and civilians, under the command of Lieutenant Colonel Henry Bostwick, decided to take direct action. Bostwick's plan was to strike the raider's rendezvous point at the home of John Dunham just east of Nanticoke.

On November 13, 1813, Bostwick's militia surrounded the house, but some of the defenders opted to make a fight of it, and some musket fire ensued. Three of the raiders and one Canadian were killed, and although a few managed to escape, the rest were captured. The prisoners were taken to Ancaster, since it was the only place that had a building secure enough to hold them. In the famous "Ancaster Assizes" they were put on trial for their life, and eight of the prisoners were eventually hanged.

The skirmish at Nanticoke, though small even by 1812 standards, restored the confidence of the local population at a time when it was badly flagging. A plaque, placed by the Historic Sites and Monuments Board of Canada, is affixed to the public school at Nanticoke. (see also Ancaster Assizes)

## BROCK'S EMBARKATION — PORT DOVER, ONTARIO

On August 5, 1812, Major General Isaac Brock left York to begin his campaign for the relief of Amherstburg. Landing at Burlington and passing through the Grand River settlements of the Six Nations, he proceeded to Dover, arriving on August 7th. Here he reviewed the militia while the bateaux that were to carry them were prepared for the long lake voyage.

On the afternoon of August 8th, he embarked with forty men of the 41st Regiment, and 260 men of the York, Lincoln, Oxford, and Norfolk militia. There was not enough transportation for about one hundred men, and these troops eventually marched overland. The little flotilla arrived at Amherstburg near midnight of August 13th, after a grueling journey enduring heavy rains, rough water, fatigue, and hunger. A cairn placed by the Historic Sites and Monuments Board of Canada commemorates the embarkation site. The cairn is located in the city park in the town of Port Dover.

## CAMPBELL'S RAID — PORT DOVER, ONTARIO

On May 14, 1814, Lieutenant Colonel John Campbell, with eight hundred American regulars and Pennsylvania militia, disembarked from six schooners near the mouth of Patterson Creek, and began a destructive raid through Norfolk County. They took possession of Dover, and after carrying off all movable provisions set the town ablaze and then moved on to Port Ryerse, which they also destroyed.

In a deposition made by Mathias Steele, a local citizen, Colonel Campbell, stated that the purpose of the raid was retaliation for the British attacks against Havre de Grace, Maryland and Buffalo, New York. In a letter dated June 16, 1814, and addressed to British Major General Riall, Campbell took complete responsibility for the raid. On June 20, 1814, a court martial was held at Buffalo, New York, with Brigadier General Scott, Major Wood, and Major Jessup attending.

These officers arrived at the conclusion that Campbell was fully justified in burning the mills in the vicinity, since they were a source of supply to the British Army, but they completely disavowed Campbell's destruction of private property and homes. Campbell later died of wounds suffered at the Battle of Chippawa on July 5, 1814.

Campbell's raid brought retaliation from the British when Commander-in-Chief Sir George Prevost contacted Vice Admiral Alexander Cochrane at Halifax. In this communication, he asked the Admiral to retaliate on the east coast of the United States. This policy led to the raid on Stonington, Connecticut, and the raids in Chesapeake Bay. Ultimately, the raids escalated to the point where the public buildings in Washington were burned on August 25, 1814. An Ontario Provincial Plaque, on the outskirts of Port Dover, on County Road 5, describes the raid. (see Mississinewa Battlefield)

## FORT NORFOLK — TURKEY POINT, ONTARIO

The British began to take notice of Turkey Point after the Battle of the Thames, which lost for them most of western Upper Canada. On March 5, 1814, Lieutenant General George Gordon Drummond wrote to Sir George Prevost, informing him that he intended to leave military posts at Turkey Point, Point Ryerse, and Dover. From these posts British troops could be alerted, should the Americans descend from the lake or from the west. In October of 1814, Drummond suggested to Prevost that Turkey Point be considered for the site of the new naval base.

During the winter of 1814–1815, Lieutenant Wilson and soldiers of the 37th Regiment of foot commenced a blockhouse here designed for three hundred soldiers. The navy yard was never constructed, since Penetanguishene on Lake Huron was chosen as the new naval base. It was a moot point, since the end of the war made both sites unnecessary, and soon after the site was abandoned. A report that was made in 1825 stated that the buildings were in a complete ruin, and there are no traces of the establishment today. A cairn placed by the Historic Sites and Monuments Board of Canada commemorates the site, and is located on Turkey Point, Lake Erie.

## BACKHOUSE MILL — PORT ROWAN, ONTARIO

Flour Mills were essential to the economy of Upper Canada, and critically important for maintaining the British Army. Because of this, they were legitimate military targets. The Backhouse Mill, constructed in 1798, was lucky enough to avoid destruction from the enemy, especially the Macarthur raid in October of 1814. The mill still stands today, and is one of the oldest in the province that still produces flour. An Ontario Provincial Plaque is located at the Old Mill, and an agricultural museum nearby features period farm implements. The mill is located in the Backus Conservation Area on County Road 42, northwest of Port Rowan, Ontario.

## LONG POINT SETTLEMENT — LONG POINT, ONTARIO

During the War of 1812, the settlement known as Long Point encompassed more than just the peninsula of land that now juts out into Lake Erie, and included the territory east of the peninsula. The farms and mills of Long Point were an important source of supply for the British forces during the war and General Brock, when passing through the settlement, recruited volunteers here for his campaign against Detroit. An Ontario Provincial Plaque on Long Point gives a history of the settlement and its role in the War of 1812.

# LONG POINT PORTAGE — LONG POINT, ONTARIO

In the nineteenth century, bateaux traffic used to hug the north shore of Lake Erie, but since Long Point juts fifteen miles out into the lake, it was easier to portage across the isthmus, which saved time and avoided the open waters of the lake. During the War of 1812, water communication was essential, and traffic across the portage increased accordingly. By 1833, natural erosion caused the lake waters to break through, and this destroyed the portage. Even today, Long Point wrestles with the continuing problem of lake erosion. The Ontario Archaeological and Historic Sites Board has erected a plaque commemorating the historic portage near the community of Long Point.

# PRESQUE ÎSLE NAVAL BASE — ERIE, PENNSYLVANIA

When war was declared in June of 1812, the United States was woefully unprepared for fighting a naval war on the Great Lakes. Erie, Pennsylvania was an excellent harbour, although it had the peculiarity of having a sand bar that barred its entrance to heavier draft vessels. Daniel Dobbins, a skilled navigator and seaman, had gone to Washington in September of 1812 to plead his case for a lake navy to be based at Erie.

Presque Îsle was eventually chosen, for the only other contender was Black Rock, but its position relative to the British guns at Fort Erie made it unsuitable. On September 15, 1812, Dobbins finally received from Secretary of the Navy, Paul Hamilton, the permission to construct four gunboats at Presque Îsle. Dobbins chose Ebenezer Crosby, a master shipwright, to build the vessels. Oliver Hazard Perry, the new commander of the American Navy on Lake Erie, arrived at Presque Îsle on March 26, 1813 and proceeded to put the base in a defensible condition while the vessels were being constructed.

In April of 1813, the gunboats *Tigress* and *Porcupine* were launched, and the following month, the gunboat *Scorpion*. The sister ships, *Niagara* and *Lawrence*, both twenty-gun brigs, slid down the ways at the end of June, and in early July the gunboat *Ariel* was added. Four converted merchant ships, *Somers*, *Trippe*, *Ohio*, and *Caledonia*, later joined from the small base at Black Rock. Except for the *Ohio*, this was the fleet that Perry commanded when he defeated the British at the Battle of Lake Erie on September 10th. Presque Îsle Naval Base no longer exists, but in Presque Îsle State Park there is a commemorative monument to Oliver Hazard Perry near the spot where he took command of his fleet.

## BRIG NIAGARA — ERIE, PENNSYLVANIA

The brig *Niagara* became Commodore Oliver Hazard Perry's flagship during the decisive Battle of Lake Erie. In the battle Perry's first flagship, the *Lawrence*, had been battered to a wreck by the guns of H.M.S. *Detroit* and *Queen Charlotte*. In a bold move, Perry transferred his flag to the *Niagara* during the action, and regained the initiative from British Commodore Robert Heriot Barclay. Perry went on to capture the entire British squadron, making the Battle of Lake Erie one of the most decisive battles of the war.

The *Niagara* was raised from the bottom of the lake in 1913 for the one-hundredth anniversary commemoration. (Recent scholarship has shown, that this vessel might actually have been her sister ship Lawrence.) The *Niagara* has undergone many restorations in her long history, the last one taking place in 1984. A reconstructed *Niagara* is now birthed at its own dock in the city of Erie, Pennsylvania. The ship is a working vessel, and roams the lake during the summer months. Visitors should confirm the *Niagara*'s schedule. A small museum is at the site.

# OLIVER HAZARD PERRY STATUE — CLEVELAND, OHIO

Oliver Hazard Perry was born on August 23, 1785, in South Kingston, Rhode Island. His naval career began when he entered the United States Navy as midshipman at age fifteen and his first service was under Commodore Preble at Tripoli, in the war with the Barbary Pirates. In 1802 he received his lieutenant's commission, and command of the schooner *Revenge*, which was attached to Commodore John Rogers' squadron, operating from Long Island, New York.

At the commencement of the War of 1812 he was in command of a gunboat flotilla based at Newport, Rhode Island. Given the opportunity to take command of the Lake Erie squadron, which had yet to be built, Perry gladly accepted the assignment. His supervision of the construction of the fleet and his brilliant conduct at the Battle of Lake Erie are in the public record.

Perry was a magnanimous man, and his handling of British officers and seamen after the Battle of Lake Erie reflect credibly on him. He was made post captain after his great victory, and after the war was given command of the frigate *Java*. In *Java* he joined Stephen Decatur's squadron, which at that time was operating in the Mediterranean. In 1819 he was given command of his own squadron, with the *John Adams* as his flagship. Unfortunately he contracted yellow fever, and died in Venezuela. There are many memorials to Perry, including this statue to him in Fort Huntington Park in downtown Cleveland.

# FORT HUNTINGTON — CLEVELAND, OHIO

The National Society, United Daughters of 1812, has erected a plaque, mounted on a boulder, commemorating old Fort Huntington, which was constructed in May of 1813. Fort Huntington was named after Samuel Huntington, who was governor of the State of Ohio from 1808–1810. During the War of 1812 he served as paymaster. The fort saw no action during the war, but on June 19, 1813, the British Squadron under Commodore Barclay appeared off of Cleveland. Barclay's intention was to scout out the place, but winds forced him to withdraw. The plaque is situated near the Oliver Hazard Perry Statue in Fort Huntington Park in downtown Cleveland.

# CHAPTER 6
## THE THAMES VALLEY

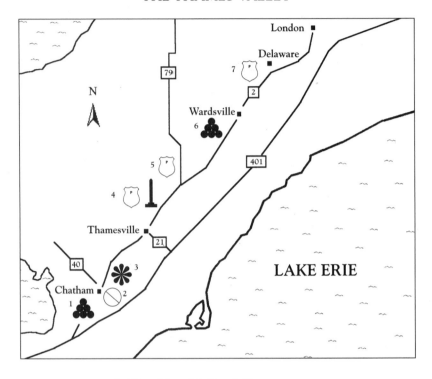

1. Skirmish at McCrae's House
2. Skirmish at the Forks
3. Salute Gun
4. Battle of the Thames
5. Fairfield on the Thames
6. Battle of the Longwoods
7. Ebenezer Allan

## SKIRMISH AT McCRAE'S HOUSE — CHATHAM, ONTARIO

After the Battle of the Thames, American forces were in control of most of the region west of Moraviantown. At the house of Thomas McCrae, they posted a small detachment of forty soldiers under Lieutenant Larwell of the 26th Regiment. Larwell and McCrae were responsible for administering an oath of neutrality to the local inhabitants, most of whom took the oath within a few days.

Later on, a small party of thirty-four men of the Kent Militia was sent from Delaware to gather cattle in the Thames Valley. Learning of the presence of Larwell's detachment, the commander, Lieutenant Henry Medcalf, determined to capture it.

On the morning of December 15, 1813, Medcalf's men surrounded the house and fired a musket volley into it. The surprise volley killed one American and wounded three others, but the rest surrendered immediately. One of the men stationed here was a prominent Canadian merchant from Ancaster named Abraham Marcle. Marcle was the owner of the Rousseau Grist Mill in Ancaster, but he had now sided with the Americans. In the confusion of the moment he managed to escape, and was never heard from again in Upper Canada.

Five days later, three hundred American militia and regulars arrived, only to find the house deserted and Medcalf's detachment gone. A cairn commemorating the event has been placed by the Historic Sites and Monuments Board of Canada. It is located four miles west of Chatham on the south side of the Thames River, on County Road 36, in Raleigh Township.


## SKIRMISH AT THE FORKS — CHATHAM, ONTARIO

During General Proctor's retreat from Amherstburg, a small rear guard action was fought near here, at the mouth of McGregor's Creek. Near the old mill and bridge, Tecumseh and two hundred warriors contested the crossing for two hours. The American advance guard, which was under the command of Colonel Whitley, eventually brought up cannons and shelled the position. The British and Indians soon retired, but not before burning a schooner that lay in the Thames. Two Indians were killed in the action and several wounded. Tecumseh also received a slight bullet wound in his left shoulder. American losses were two men killed and three wounded.

The next day, General Proctor's army was defeated at the Battle of the Thames, where the great Tecumseh was killed. Urbanization has all but absorbed the historic site, but the ground where the skirmish took place is now called Tecumseh Park, in downtown Chatham. Presently the "Skirmish at the Forks" is unmarked.

## SALUTE GUN — CHATHAM, ONTARIO

In Tecumseh Park, there is a small signal cannon with a plaque which reads "This Gun was used Niagara Peninsula Canadians War with the Americans 1812–1814." Tecumseh Park is by the river, in downtown Chatham, Ontario.

## BATTLE OF THE THAMES — THAMESVILLE, ONTARIO

On the morning of October 5, 1813, General Proctor deployed the 41st Regiment, which consisted of less than 297 men rank and file, across the main road to Burlington. Tecumseh, with eight hundred Indians, was deployed in the woods on the British right. It was here, near the Moravian village, that they would try to stop the American advance.

When the American Army, three thousand strong under Major General Harrison approached, Harrison noted that the British line looked rather thin. He decided to charge with his mounted infantry, and the attack succeeded beyond his wildest dreams. After one ragged volley, the British line went to pieces under the impact of the charge. On the right, the Indians fought with great tenacity, but when Tecumseh was killed they lost heart and retired from the battlefield. The Battle of the Thames was small, but it was one of the most decisive of the war, although never properly exploited. The British were never able to field an army in the western half of the province for the entire war.

Thamesville would hardly be remembered today but for the death of the great Tecumseh. In more recent times, a small park dedicated to his memory has been laid out on the ground near where he was killed. The Historic Sites and Monuments Board of Canada and the citizens of Thamesville have both placed their own historic markers at the site, and there is a monument to Tecumseh. The battle site is located on Highway 2, about four kilometres east of Thamesville.

View looking up the Thames River as sketched by Lossing.

A similar view of the Thames today

# FAIRFIELD ON THE THAMES — FAIRFIELD, ONTARIO

At this site stood the village of Fairfield, or Moraviantown, consisting of about sixty dwellings. It was constructed by peaceful Delaware Indians and missionaries of the Moravian faith. After the Battle of the Thames, the remnants of General Proctor's army retreated through the village on their way to Burlington. Just north of the village, adjacent to a ravine, six brass cannons were captured by the rapidly advancing Americans.

On the evening after the battle, Colonel Johnson's men encamped around the village, and next day looted over five tons of hay and two thousand bushels of corn. General Harrison then ordered the town burned, ostensibly to prevent the British from using it as their winter quarters. After the War of 1812, the village relocated to the other side of the Thames River. Today the site has a few restored buildings and a museum dedicated to the Moravian missionaries. A plaque placed by the Historic Sites and Monuments Board of Canada commemorates the site.

# BATTLE OF THE LONGWOODS — WARDSVILLE, ONTARIO

After the capture of the American outpost at McCrae's house on December 15, 1813, the commanding officer at Detroit, Lieutenant Colonel Butler, determined on a counter measure. Captain Andrew Hunter Holmes of the 24th Tennessee Regiment was dispatched on a raid into the British Western District. His objective was to capture the British post at either Port Talbot or Delaware. Holmes' force numbered about 180 men, and consisted of a detachment from his own regiment and soldiers from the 26th Vermont, 27th New York, and 28th Kentucky. Accompanying the force were two light pieces of artillery.

The "Longwoods" was the heavily forested tract of country that lay between the present towns of Thamesville and Delaware. On

March 3rd, Holmes' rapidly moving force, which was entirely mounted, approached within fifteen miles of Delaware, where a British force was stationed. From a local settler, he learned that the British had left Delaware and were on their way to intercept him. Holmes' force fell back to Twenty Mile Creek, and after crossing took up a strong position on the west side. This is the site now known as Battle Hill.

The British force sent to capture Holmes was under the command of Captain James Lewis Basden. Basden had under his command the light companies from the Royal Scots and 89th Regiment, a detachment of Kent militia, a company of rangers, and some native warriors: in all about three hundred men.

Morale in the American force was not high, but after a brief council of war it was determined to remain in position and meet the British. On the late afternoon of March 4th, Basden's small contingent arrived opposite Battle Hill. The American position, naturally a strong one, was enhanced by an abatis that had been constructed the evening before. The sides of the ravine were also very slippery, the Americans having watered the position down, and the surface was now frozen.

Basden decided to have the Kent Militia, under Captain Caldwell, outflank the position to the north. The forty Indian warriors would engage the American right flank. Basden himself, not utilizing great judgement, would lead the flank companies of regulars on a frontal assault. What occurred was hardly surprising, as Basden's men were cut down mercilessly by the rifle fire from above. Basden himself received a fatal wound in the right thigh. As darkness fell, the British retired from the position and retreated east. Considering the numbers engaged, the British suffered greatly. Official reports state fourteen men killed, fifty-two wounded, and one missing. American losses were light, with four men killed and three wounded.

Despite their successful defence, Holmes now knew he could not take the British post at Delaware, and the same evening they began their retreat to Detroit, which they reached unhindered. The Historic Sites and Monuments Board of Canada has commemorated the action with a cairn and plaque, which is located on Highway 2, west of Delaware, Ontario.

## EBENEZER ALLAN — DELAWARE, ONTARIO

New Jersey-born Ebenezer Allan fought for the British during the American Revolution, but after the war he settled in this vicinity, and the community of Delaware grew up around his holdings. Bitter disputes over his land claims disaffected him, and during the War of 1812 he espoused the American cause. He was later arrested by the authorities and released in 1813. He died shortly thereafter. An Ontario Provincial Plaque to him is located in the municipal park in Delaware, Ontario.

# CHAPTER 7
## NIAGARA-ON-THE-LAKE

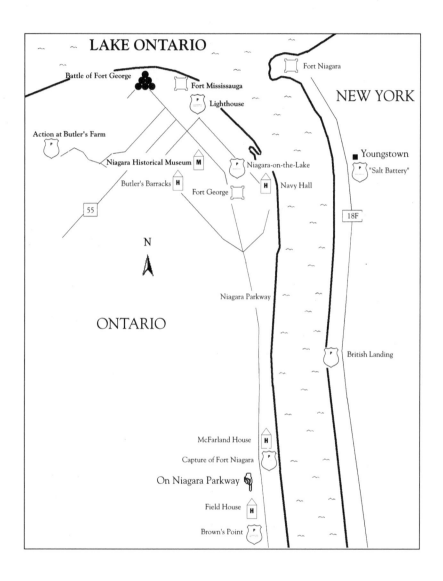

LAKE ONTARIO

Battle of Fort George

Fort Niagara

NEW YORK

Fort Mississauga

Lighthouse

Action at Butler's Farm

Youngstown

"Salt Battery"

Niagara Historical Museum M

Niagara-on-the-Lake

Butler's Barracks H

Fort George

H Navy Hall

55

18F

N

Niagara Parkway

ONTARIO

British Landing

McFarland House H

Capture of Fort Niagara

On Niagara Parkway

Field House H

Brown's Point

# TOWN OF NIAGARA-ON-THE-LAKE

At the time of the War of 1812, Newark (Niagara-on-the-Lake) was a pleasant little town consisting of about three hundred buildings. A former capital of the province, the town was largely a commercial centre. After the Battle of Fort George on May 27, 1813, the town was occupied by American troops under the command of Brigadier General George McClure. Acting under loosely interpreted orders from Secretary John Armstrong, McClure had the town put to the torch on the evening of December 10, 1813.

McClure perpetrated this cruel act in the dead of winter, and gave the townspeople only thirty minutes to evacuate. He later defended his actions with the absurd defence that he was denying the British the use of the town as their winter quarters. Strangely, in the conflagration which followed, Butler's Barracks, which were the winter quarters, went unharmed. After this incident the war on the Niagara entered a much tougher phase where retaliation was commonplace. General Drummond's winter campaign which followed ended with the burning of Buffalo.

Today the picturesque town of Niagara-on-the-Lake has many historic buildings built on the same site as their 1812 predecessors. Examples of these are the old courthouse, McClelland's west end store, and St. Mark's Anglican Church. The town of Niagara-on-the-Lake is located at the mouth of the Niagara River, adjacent to Lake Ontario.

# POINT MISSISSAUGA LIGHTHOUSE — NIAGARA-ON-THE-LAKE

Under the orders of Lieutenant-Governor Peter Hunter, a stone lighthouse was constructed here in 1804. At the commencement of the War of 1812 the lighthouse keeper, Dominick Henry, and his wife were living in a small wooden house adjacent. On May 27,

1813, the Battle of Fort George raged all around the lighthouse while the couple assisted British soldiers who were wounded in the fight.

In 1814 the lighthouse was purposely destroyed to make way for Fort Mississauga and material from the lighthouse was utilized in the construction of the new fort. An Ontario Provincial Plaque is located at Fort Mississauga on the golf course grounds in the town of Niagara-on-the-Lake.

## FORT MISSISSAUGA — NIAGARA-ON-THE-LAKE

In their evacuation of Niagara in December of 1813, the American Army destroyed Fort George. When the British took possession of the site soon after, they were left with no major fortification on the Canadian side of the river. In early 1814, it was decided to construct Fort Mississauga.

Utilizing material from the lighthouse that had stood here, they sited the fort closer to the lake shore, and in this respect it was superior to Fort George, for it controlled the entrance to the Niagara River. The fort remained in British hands until the end of the war, and was never seriously threatened. Presently, visitors may tour the grounds, but the blockhouse is not open to the public. The fort is located on the grounds of the golf course, in the town of Niagara-on-the-Lake.

Fort Mississauga as sketched by Lossing

Fort Mississauga today

# BATTLE OF FORT GEORGE — NIAGARA-ON-THE-LAKE

On May 27, 1813 at about 9:00 am, the battle for Fort George began in earnest. After a two-day bombardment from the guns of Fort Niagara and batteries along the Niagara River, the advanced guard of the American Army landed near this point. The first assault wave of eight hundred men was under the command of Lieutenant Colonel Winfield Scott, and opposed to the landing were about 550 British regulars and militia.

Ably supported by the guns of Commodore Chauncey's fleet, the continued waves of American infantry forced the British to retreat after suffering heavy casualties. Rallying between the town and the fort, they were joined by other British forces that had been stationed up river. After a pause Commodore Chauncey's flagship, the *General Pike*, with twenty-eight 24-pound cannons, anchored in the river opposite the fort. The vessel then began a devastating bombardment of the fort.

When General Vincent observed more American troops embarking at Youngstown, he knew it was time to retreat. Sending a messenger off to notify Colonel Bishop to abandon Fort Erie, he began his retreat to Burlington to link up with General Vincent. Colonel Bishop left a small party to destroy Fort Erie, and then began his march to the Burlington rendezvous. The forces engaged in the Battle of Fort George were about 4200 Americans and about 1500 British. In proportion to the numbers engaged, the contest resulted in severe British casualties. The Battle of Fort George was serious and decisive, for it left the American Army in possession of the entire Niagara region.

A cairn has been placed by the Historic Sites and Monuments Board of Canada near the landing place of the Americans. The cairn is located at the extreme western edge of the golf course, in the town of Niagara-on-the-Lake. (see next entry)

## FORT GEORGE — NIAGARA-ON-THE-LAKE

After the signing of Jay's Treaty in 1796, the British were forced to give up Fort Niagara on the American side of the river. This necessitated the construction of a new fort on the left bank. The first fort was constructed between 1796 and 1799 under the orders of Lieutenant-Governor John Graves Simcoe, and was named after the King. It was a simple work, consisting of six earth bastions connected by a picketed fence. The fort's location was poor, since it neither commanded the river nor protected the town of Niagara. Despite these glaring faults, the fort was in continuous use until the outbreak of the War of 1812.

At the commencement of the war, Major General Isaac Brock made the fort his headquarters. During the Battle of Queenston Heights, which was fought just upriver, the fort's batteries were engaged with the guns of Fort Niagara, just across the river. The garrison of Fort George under Roger Hale Sheaffe marched to Queenston that very morning, and were instrumental in winning the battle there.

On May 27, 1813, the fort was the object of a large amphibious attack that resulted in its loss to the Americans. In their retreat, the British destroyed most of the fort's buildings, leaving only the powder magazine intact. In the weeks that followed the American troops repaired the fort, and constructed extensive fortifications around the perimeter. After the decisive battle of Stoney Creek, and the skirmish at Beaver Dams in June, the American Army spent the rest of the summer bottled up inside the fortifications.

During the winter, the American Army realized it was unproductive to remain on the Niagara frontier, and so they left Fort George in December, destroying the buildings and also burning the town of Niagara. The British repossessed Fort George and it remained in their hands until the end of the war.

In 1937 the fort was restored to the period 1796–1813. The only remaining original structure is the powder magazine, but there are over nine replicated historic buildings. Fort George has been declared a National Historic Site, and is administered by Parks Canada. In the summer months guides in period dress perform musket firing demonstrations. (see previous entry)

## BROCK'S BASTION — FORT GEORGE

Major General Isaac Brock was killed in the early stages of the Battle of Queenston Heights on October 13, 1812. His aide-de-camp John Macdonell was also killed in that engagement. Both men were buried in what is now called "Brock's Bastion" inside Fort George. Twelve years later on October 13th, 1824, their bodies were removed from this location, and re-interred in a moving ceremony at the large monument on Queenston Heights. Brock's Bastion is inside Fort George, Niagara-on-the-Lake, and has been marked by Parks Canada. (see Queenston Heights Battlefield)

# NAVY HALL — NIAGARA-ON-THE-LAKE

During the American Revolution, a naval establishment was set up across the river from Fort Niagara. The site was chosen away from the fort, because it offered superior shelter from the lake. The establishment eventually became the headquarters of the Provincial Marine, whose function was to transport and supply the British Army in Canada. After the Revolution the site was abandoned, and by 1788 Navy Hall, which was the principal building, was in very poor shape.

Deputy surveyor General John Collins, in that same year, mentioned that the site could not be protected if batteries were placed on the east side of the river, a comment that turned out to be rather prophetic later on. Navy Hall was unused until the arrival of Lieutenant-Governor John Graves Simcoe in July of 1792. That summer it was renovated as the Governor's personal residence. In 1797, when the seat of government was moved to Toronto, Navy Hall once again came under the control of the military.

While Fort George was under construction, the building was used as a barracks, and after 1800 it functioned as a storage area and unloading platform for the fort. During the War of 1812, the building appears to have functioned as a mess hall for the garrison of Fort George. Navy Hall did not survive the War of 1812. Soon after the Battle of Queenston Heights, it was consumed by fire from heated shot, fired from Fort Niagara.

The present structure dates from August of 1815, and was also known as Navy Hall. Parks Canada has placed interpretive markers at the site, and although the building is not open to the public, visitors may tour the grounds. Navy Hall is located on the Niagara Parkway, in the town of Niagara-on-the Lake. (see next entry)

# BUTLER'S BARRACKS — NIAGARA-ON-THE-LAKE

During the War of 1812 the barracks had been destroyed by gunfire from Fort Niagara, so Butler's Barracks was constructed soon after, on a site located further back from the river. The present structures range in date, from post-1812 to the Korean War, and are maintained by Parks Canada. Historical markers are located at this well-maintained site, and guide visitors through various periods in the barracks history. Butler's Barracks is located on John Street in the town of Niagara-on-the-Lake. (see prior entry)

# ACTION AT BUTLER'S FARM — NIAGARA-ON-THE-LAKE

On July 8, 1813 Major General Francis Baron De Rottenburg ordered a small detachment to proceed to the house of a Mr. Cassel Chorus, located at Two Mile Creek near Fort George.

The purpose of the movement was to recover a large quantity of medical supplies that had been buried during the army's retreat from the Battle of Fort George. The detachment consisted of soldiers of the 8th Regiment, some provincial dragoons, and a body of Indians. The farm was located very close to the American picket lines, and although they managed to reach the farm without detection, they were detected by American pickets while loading the supplies onto wagons. A skirmish soon erupted with the American pickets and the Indians under Captain Norton, who were covering the operation.

The skirmish lasted until afternoon, when several hundred men of the 13th U.S. Infantry arrived, and Norton was forced to retire. At this point in the battle, a party of about forty U.S. soldiers rashly moved ahead, under the command of Lieutenant Eldridge, and were ambushed by the Indians, who were concealed in a ravine. In the first volley alone, about eighteen American soldiers were hit, and the rest retreated. Lieutenant Eldridge himself was killed, and ten soldiers were taken prisoner, while the Indians suffered only three wounded. An Ontario Provincial Plaque commemorating this action is located at Butler's Burying Ground, Butler Street in the town of Niagara-on-the-Lake.

## NIAGARA HISTORICAL MUSEUM — NIAGARA-ON-THE-LAKE

The Niagara Historical Museum features artifacts and displays from the Loyalist period to the Victorian era, with emphasis on the town's role during the War of 1812. Featured in the collection is the cocked hat owned by Major General Isaac Brock, who was killed at the Battle of Queenston Heights. The hat passed into the possession of Mr. George Ball, who was given it by General Brock's cousin, James Brock. The hat was used at the funeral arrangements of 1824 and 1853, and at that gathering many War of 1812 veterans requested to "try it on." The museum is located at 43 Castlereagh Street in the town of Niagara-on-the-Lake.

## McFARLAND HOUSE — NIAGARA PARKWAY

This red brick Georgian style house was built by John McFarland in 1800. During the War of 1812, a British battery was located behind the house, overlooking the river. The house was used by both American and British soldiers as a hospital during the war. The Niagara Parks Commission restored the house in .1959 to its 1800 appearance, and in 1973 further restoration was done.

Just to the south of the house is the ravine where British forces embarked for the taking of Fort Niagara in 1813. The house is open to the public, and the grounds are a popular picnic area during the summer months. The house is located on the Niagara Parkway just south of Fort George.

# CAPTURE OF FORT NIAGARA — NIAGARA PARKWAY

At the close of navigation in the fall of 1813, the American Army transferred most of their regular troops from Fort George to Sackets Harbor in order to join General Wilkinson's campaign against Montreal. On December 10, 1813, they abandoned Fort George and burned the town of Newark before crossing over to Fort Niagara.

Determined to avenge the senseless burning of the town, Colonel Murray of the 100th Regiment presented to Lieutenant General William Drummond a plan to capture Fort Niagara. With great difficulty, boats were hauled from Burlington, over fifty miles away, to the embarkation point. On the evening of December 18th, the troops assembled at St. Davids for the march to Longhurst Ravine, just south of McFarland House, on the Niagara River. The troops under Murray consisted of detachments of the 100th and 41st regiments, Royal Artillery, and some Canadian militia: in all about 550 men. By midnight all of the assault troops had embarked, with each soldier instructed to unload his musket and rely solely on the bayonet.

The troops landed south of the fort and, moving forward, bayoneted the American pickets that had been stationed at a tavern. Having obtained the countersign from the pickets, the British moved confidently forward. Now armed with the element of surprise, there was little chance of a successful American defence. The British stormed the fort at bayonet point, and the defenders were forced to surrender.

The taking of Fort Niagara was an important strategic coup for the British, for it influenced American strategy and remained in British hands until the end of the war. The embarkation point of the expedition has been marked with an Ontario Provincial marker and is located on the Niagara Parkway just south of the McFarland House. (see also British Landing)

# FIELD HOUSE — NIAGARA PARKWAY

This red-brick classical villa was built by Gilbert Field in 1800. In 1812, General Brock rented the house as a barracks to quarter British regulars and Canadian militia. It was here that General Brock was said to have uttered the statement "Push on York Volunteers," on his fateful ride to the Battle of Queenston Heights. The story does have some foundation, as Captain Duncan Cameron's company, of the 3rd York Militia, was stationed near the house.

However, another company of the Yorkers, Captain Heward's 2nd York Militia, was also posted at Brown's Point nearby, and this has led to some confusion. Regardless, if Brock did tell the York Volunteers to "push on," it was very likely here, rather than at Queenston Heights, where some say the story occurred.

After the Queenston campaign, the house was damaged by American batteries from the opposite shore, but in 1962 it was fully restored, and is now owned by the Ontario Heritage Foundation. Presently the house is not open to the public. Field House is located on the Niagara Parkway, about halfway between the town of Niagara-on-the-Lake and Queenston Heights. An Ontario Provincial Plaque is located in front of the house. (see next entry)

# BROWN'S POINT — NIAGARA PARKWAY

The present day Niagara Parkway follows the old military road of 1812, which connected Fort George to points south on the Niagara River. At various spots along the road, defences had been placed to guard the frontier. Here at Brown's Point, a battery and military camp were located, and an old stone marker at the site perpetuates a Canadian legend. The marker simply reads "Here Gen. Sir Isaac Brock called out on his way to Queenston Heights 13th Oct. 1812 Push on York Volunteers."

The story has many variations, but General Brock did meet a

dispatch rider from the York Volunteers near here. This was Lieutenant S.P. Jarvis, who was riding from Queenston to warn the general that the Americans had crossed the river. Brock instructed him to ride on to Fort George, and ordered General Sheaffe to bring up the reserves. While on his way there, Jarvis met Brock's aide, Colonel Macdonell, who was riding after the general. In his haste, Macdonell had forgotten his sword and he quickly borrowed Jarvis'. Lieutenant Jarvis arrived safely at Fort George, where he delivered Brock's message. Both Brock and Macdonell were killed at Queenston Heights, just hours later. Brown's Point is located on the Niagara Parkway, about halfway between Fort George and Queenston Heights. (see prior entry)

## BRITISH LANDING — YOUNGSTOWN, NEW YORK

At this spot, the British troops under Colonel Murray landed on December 19, 1813 preparatory to their taking of Fort Niagara. A New York State plaque marking the site is located on Highway 18F just south of Youngstown, New York. (see Fort Niagara and Capture of Fort Niagara)

## THE "SALT BATTERY" — YOUNGSTOWN, NEW YORK

A battery was placed here in 1812 for the defence of the Niagara River. The nickname "Salt Battery" arises from the fact that salt bags were used in its construction. A New York State marker is located on Main Street in Youngstown, New York.

# FORT NIAGARA — YOUNGSTOWN, NEW YORK

The history of Fort Niagara dates back to the early French exploration period, and a series of forts has existed on the site since 1682. Just prior to the Seven Years' War, the French commenced strengthening the fort by adding earthworks, a powder magazine, moats, and additional batteries, but despite these efforts, the fort fell to the English on July 25, 1759. During the American Revolution, the fort was the main British base on the Niagara, and the staging area for many of the Indian and Tory raids on New York and Pennsylvania.

The fort that existed during the War of 1812 was essentially the French fort of 1726 that had been constructed by Gaspard Chaussegeros de Lery, but the fort's defences had been added to over the years. In the Queenston Heights campaign, Fort Niagara exchanged fire with British-held Fort George, located just across the river, and part of its garrison participated in the Battle of Queenston Heights.

In May of 1813, American forces captured Fort George and later advanced towards Burlington, but after the decisive battles of Stoney Creek and Beaver Dams they were confined to the vicinity of Fort George. During the winter they destroyed Fort George and the town of Newark before moving back to Fort Niagara. In retaliation, the British determined to capture Fort Niagara, and then lay waste the American side of the river.

On the night of December 19, 1813, a British force under the command of Colonel Murray took the fort by surprise, and after this action it remained in British hands until after the war. Fort Niagara today has been fully restored, and is a part of Fort Niagara State Park. The fort's most notable feature is the "French Castle," which is constructed of stone, and is the only structure of its kind in North America. The fort is opened year round, and in the summer months guides are dressed in period uniform. The fort emphasizes its history under three flags, French, British, and American. Fort Niagara is located just to the north of Youngstown, New York.

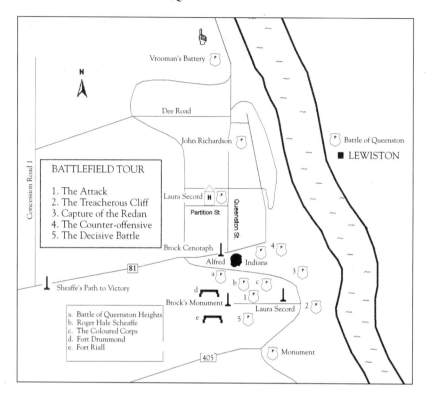

VROOMAN'S BATTERY — NIAGARA PARKWAY

Vrooman's battery was constructed in 1812, and consisted of a twenty-four-pound cannon, mounted in a crescent shape earthwork, that overlooked the river near this site. During the Battle of Queenston Heights the battery was manned by a company of the 5th Lincoln Militia under Captain Hatt. The battery fired continually at the American troops as they crossed the river, and aided materially to the success of that day. A plaque commemorating the battery has been placed by the Historic Sites and Monuments Board of Canada, and is located on the Niagara Parkway, 2.1 kilometres north of the intersection with York Road.

# LAURA INGERSOLL SECORD — QUEENSTON

In 1812, Laura Secord (maiden name Ingersoll) was living in the village of Queenston with her husband James and their five children. During the Battle of Queenston Heights, the Secord home was in the line of fire, and Laura and her children were forced to evacuate. Unfortunately when they returned, the house had been plundered. James was a sergeant in the 1st Lincoln Militia and also fought in the battle, where he was wounded. When Laura first heard of his injuries, she rushed to the battlefield where she found her husband and nursed his wounds. Convalescing at home, James eventually recovered.

It was during the summer of 1813 that the events unfolded that were to make Laura famous. After the Battle of Fort George on May 27th, the American Army was in possession of most of the Niagara frontier, with their pickets based at Fort George and stationed several miles into the country. The British, who were now based at Burlington, observed American movements through the use of small scouting parties. One of these was under the command of Lieutenant James FitzGibbon of the 49th Regiment. FitzGibbon had been particularly troublesome to the Americans, and they determined to capture him. FitzGibbon's company of thirty picked volunteers was based at De Cew's house, a strategic crossroads at the time, seventeen miles from Fort George. General Dearborn gave orders to Colonel Charles Boerstler, of the 14th United States infantry to march on De Cew's house and capture the whole of FitzGibbon's party.

The exact sequence of events is unclear, and accounts vary, but somehow Laura learned of the American plans, and resolved to carry the news to FitzGibbon. Leaving her still-convalescing husband and children, she embarked on a twenty-mile journey in the dead of night on June 22nd. The journey itself was fraught with danger, for enemy pickets controlled the main roads, and a large swamp lay between her and FitzGibbon. She finally encountered a party of Indians, whom she convinced to take her to the British, and at De Cew's she met FitzGibbon and told her story. Based on Laura's information, FitzGibbon was able to lay his own trap, and the battle that resulted, now known as the Battle of Beaver Dams, ended with the capture of the entire American detachment of over five hundred men and three cannons.

After the War of 1812, Mrs. Secord's contribution to the victory at Beaver Dams was forgotten, and it was not until 1860, when the Prince of Wales was touring Canada, that the story re-emerged. Niagara veterans of the War of 1812 had arranged to meet the Prince, and to sign an address to him. Laura also applied for this honour and when the Prince was informed of her story, he later rewarded her services with a gift of one hundred pounds. In 1863 Colonel FitzGibbon gave Laura Secord a deposition, fully vindicating her actions, which had led to the victory at Beaver Dams. Today there are numerous memorials and references to her. On September 8, 1992, Canada Post acknowledged her services to the country with a commemorative stamp. An Ontario Provincial Plaque dedicated to her is in front of the Laura Secord house, in the town of Queenston. (see Beaver Dams, Laura Secord House)

## LAURA SECORD HOUSE — QUEENSTON

This simple frame house was the home of David and Laura Secord during the War of 1812. In the Battle of Queenston Heights it was damaged by gunfire and looted. It was restored in 1971, and is a memorial to the heroism and courage of Laura Secord. The house is open to the public and has exhibits on the Secord family and a gift shop. The house is located at Partition and Queen streets in Queenston.

The stamp issued by Canada Post on September 8, 1992 to Laura Ingersoll Secord

## LAURA SECORD MONUMENT — QUEENSTON HEIGHTS

This cut stone memorial to Laura Secord was dedicated in 1911. It acknowledges her contribution to the saving of her husband's life at the Battle of Queenston Heights, and her part in the British victory at Beaver Dams. The memorial is located on the site of the first monument to General Brock, on the crest of Queenston Heights.

## MAJOR JOHN RICHARDSON — QUEENSTON

John Richardson, one of the province's early historians and authors, was born in Queenston in 1796. At the commencement of the War of 1812, he joined the 41st Regiment as a gentleman volunteer, and served on the Detroit frontier, where he participated in many of the battles and skirmishes fought by the British Right Division. He was present at the battles of Brownstown, Maguaga, Frenchtown, Fort Meigs, and the surrender of Detroit. He was captured at the Battle of Moraviantown on October 5, 1813.

His eyewitness account of the War of 1812 was published in 1842, and here he vividly describes his life as a common soldier, and as a prisoner of war in Kentucky. Richardson is also know for his epic poem, *Tecumseh*, and his novel of the Pontiac uprising, *Wacousta*. Unfortunately, financial success eluded him, and he died in 1852 in complete poverty.

The Historic Sites and Monuments Board of Canada has dedicated a plaque to him at Amherstburg, Ontario, where his regiment was based during the War of 1812. Another plaque to him has been placed by the provincial government, and is located in front of the Laura Secord Memorial School in Queenston.

## FORT DRUMMOND — QUEENSTON HEIGHTS

This earthwork fortification was built by the British Army in June of 1814, and was named for the commander of the army on the Niagara frontier, Sir Gordon Drummond. After the Battle of Chippawa on July 5, 1814, the British were forced to abandon Queenston Heights, and they dismantled the fort on July 10th and retreated to Fort George. Following the Battle of Lundy's Lane on July 25th, the Americans were forced to retreat in turn from the vicinity, and the British reoccupied the fort, subsequently holding it for the remainder of the war.

In the 1920s the site was a favourite place for picnickers, and the Niagara Parks Commission used the inside of the fortification as a wading pool for children. In 1967, Canada's Centennial year, a modern spray pool was added, replacing the earlier wading pool. The remains of Fort Drummond's earth walls can still be seen today, and they are located in Queenston Heights Park, not far from Brock's Monument. (see next entry)

## FORT RIALL — QUEENSTON HEIGHTS

Large stone letters, marked "FORT RIALL" are imbedded in an earthwork fortification just yards away from Fort Drummond. Named after Major General Phineas Riall, it is a sister fortification to Fort Drummond and shares a similar history. The fort is located near Brock's Monument on Queenston Heights. (see prior entry)

## SIR ROGER HALE SHEAFFE — QUEENSTON HEIGHTS

Roger Hale Sheaffe was an experienced officer who had fought in the American Revolution and the Napoleonic wars, but was not a popular commander with the common soldier. As early as 1800 this character trait was emerging, and in that year he was acting Lieutenant Colonel of the 49th Regiment, stationed on the Isle of Jersey.

During the leave of absence of the regular commander, Major Isaac Brock, Roger Sheaffe made himself very unpopular with the men. When Brock returned, Sheaffe paraded the regiment for his benefit. When the soldiers caught sight of Brock, they gave three hearty cheers for their returning commander. This was considered a gross impropriety at the time, and was taken as a slight for Sheaffe, rather than a compliment to Brock. Brock had the regiment confined to quarters for "this most unmilitary conduct."

A more serious instance occurred in the summer of 1803 when Sheaffe was once more left in command of the 49th Regiment, stationed at Fort George. Exasperated at Sheaffe's command style and sense of discipline, some of the soldiers plotted mutiny, which included the murder of Sheaffe. Isaac Brock was informed of the plan while engaged in his civil duties at York, and acting immediately, he boarded a schooner bound for Fort George. Again, to the embarrassment of Sheaffe, Brock practically put down the mutiny single-handed, for the ring leaders were promptly arrested and sent to trial at Quebec.

Roger Hale Sheaffe was to have his shining hour, and this was at the Battle of Queenston Heights. On the morning of October 13, 1812, Major General Brock had been killed while trying to retake the heights from the Americans. Gathering up all of his reinforcements, Sheaffe rejected a frontal assault, and took a flank march that gained the heights in the rear of the American Army. By late afternoon, Sheaffe with all of his forces in position, attacked and drove the Americans from the cliff. Their defensive position was hopeless and the Americans were forced to surrender. For this magnificent action, Sheaffe received a baronetcy.

In April of 1813, he was the commanding officer at York when the Americans made their amphibious assault. Sheaffe was in a bad position both militarily and politically, for his regular soldiers were badly outnumbered, and he was at odds with the civil administration. Even worse, the local militia was not supportive, and were more interested in parole than in fighting. The American Army, through the use of Chauncey's fleet, could choose their point of attack, and Sheaffe was unable to oppose their landing. After a half hearted defence, where everything seemed to go wrong, his regular soldiers blew up the powder magazine and retreated to Kingston.

After the fiasco at York, and his continued unpopularity with the local government, he was recalled back to England. He eventually reached the rank of General, and he died in 1851 at Edinburgh, Scotland. Under Brock's shadow, Sheaffe never achieved the recognition he deserved, even though he won one of the most decisive battles of the War of 1812. A plaque dedicated to him is adjacent to Brock's monument, at the site where he won his greatest victory.


## THE COLOURED CORPS — QUEENSTON HEIGHTS

During the War of 1812, a small company of about thirty soldiers of African descent was formed under the command of white officers. The company served well at the battles of Queenston Heights and Fort George, and after the war was disbanded. An Ontario Provincial Plaque, dedicated to the "Coloured Corps," is located in front of Brock's Monument on Queenston Heights.

# BATTLE OF QUEENSTON HEIGHTS

The Battle of Queenston Heights, fought on October 13, 1812, was one of the first major battles of the War of 1812. The decisive victory for the British was offset by the loss of General Brock, who was killed near the beginning of the engagement. The site is administered by Parks Canada, and features a pamphlet walking tour of the battlefield, which may be obtained from guides stationed at Brock's Monument. The plaque placed by the Historic Sites and Monuments Board of Canada is at the base of the monument, located on the crest of Queenston Heights.

# BROCK'S MONUMENT — QUEENSTON HEIGHTS

The foundation stone for the first monument dedicated to the memory of Sir Isaac Brock was laid on the first of June, 1824. William Lyon Mackenzie, editor of the radical newspaper "The Colonial Advocate," was a resident of Queenston, and was present at the ceremony. He hid a copy of his newspaper inside the hollow corner block of the monument, but when Sir Peregrine Maitland, Lieutenant-Governor of Upper Canada, heard of this, he ordered the paper removed, and Mackenzie was forced to comply.

The first monument was a Tuscan column, 130 feet high, crafted from Queenston limestone. On October 13th, over five thousand people gathered at the monument for the dedication ceremonies. On this occasion the bodies of General Brock and his aide de camp, Lieutenant Colonel Macdonell, which had been buried at Fort George, were re-interred in a vault under the monument. Visitors could ascend to the top by way of an internal staircase for a magnificent view of the surrounding countryside, and for years it was a popular tourist attraction.

On April 17, 1840, a wanton act of destruction took place, when one of Mackenzies's rebels set a charge of gunpowder under the monument, and damaged it severely. The bodies of Brock and Macdonell were removed from the site and re-interred in a cemetery at Queenston. Almost immediately there was universal condemnation on both sides of the river for this act of destruction. On July 30th, there was a huge gathering of over eight thousand people on Queenston Heights to form plans to erect a new monument to the fallen hero. Among the attendees at the gathering were Lieutenant-Governor Sir George Arthur, Sir Allan McNab, Sir John Beverley Roberston, and William Hamilton Merritt.

Over a decade passed while plans were made, tenders sent out, and money gathered through contributions. On October 13, 1853, the cornerstone of the present monument was laid. The bodies of Brock and Macdonell were re-interred a final time in the vault below, and among the attendees was the brother of Lieutenant Colonel Macdonell. The monument was completed in 1856, and is one of the tallest in the world at 190 feet.

At the top of the monument is a likeness of General Brock, his right arm extended with a baton in his hand. Brock's Monument is the centre piece for Queenston Heights Park, and each year it is attended by thousands of visitors. The monument, which can be seen for miles, is located at the crest of Queenston Heights, above the town of Queenston.

## BROCK'S MONUMENT PLAQUE — QUEENSTON HEIGHTS

The Niagara Parks Commission has placed a plaque describing "Brock's Monument," which dominates the Queenston Heights Park. The plaque is mounted on a small stone base, and is located on the walking paths adjacent to the Niagara Parkway, just south of the parking area.

The stamp issued by the Canadian government to Sir Isaac Brock

## QUEENSTON HEIGHTS BATTLEFIELD TOUR

Parks Canada has placed five bronze markers, which are part of a walking tour, outlining various highlights of the Battle of Queenston Heights. The tour entails walking over terrain that varies greatly in height, and is not recommended for the infirm. The next five sites are part of the battlefield tour.

### Stop 1 — "Attack"

The first marker describes the initial American assault from boats launched from Lewiston, just across the river. Crossing under fire from the batteries at the redan and Vrooman's point, some of the boats drifted out of control due to the swift current, and ended up at the foot of Queenston village where they were captured. Others made it to the shore near the landing, but were pinned down by musket fire from British infantry. At this phase of the battle, Major General Isaac Brock was on his way to Queenston, riding swiftly from Fort George.

Stop 2 — "The Treacherous River Cliff"

The second marker, which overlooks the high cliff over the Niagara River, describes the little-known pathway where a party of Americans under Captain John E. Wool eventually gained the crest of Queenston Heights.

Stop 3 — "The Capture of the Redan and Death of Brock"

Marker number three describes the American capture of the Redan Battery, and Brock's unsuccessful attempt to retake it. The marker is located at the site of the Redan Battery. Although the site where Brock was killed is not part of the battlefield tour, it is located just northwest of the Redan Battery.

Stop 4 — "The Counter-offensive Takes Shape"

Marker number four describes the brief lull in the fighting that occurred after the death of Isaac Brock, and the measures taken by Roger Sheaffe to regain the initiative and counter-attack. It also mentions the participation of the Indian forces at the battle under John Norton. At this phase of the battle, the Indians kept up a steady skirmishing with the Americans, and prevented them from consolidating their position on the heights.

## Stop 5 — "The Decisive Battle"

The final marker describes how Sheaffe gained the heights by a flank march to the west and defeated the Americans on the crest. With their backs to the river and both flanks turned, the American army was forced to surrender.

Brock's Cenotaph sketched in the summer of 1860

# BROCK'S CENOTAPH — QUEENSTON

This stone cenotaph was placed by Albert Edward, Duke of Wales on September 18, 1860, and is close to the location where General Brock was killed. Eyewitnesses claimed that he was killed approximately fifteen yards to the west of the cenotaph. In the early phases of the Battle of Queenston Heights, General Brock had ridden to the Redan Battery, located about three hundred yards up the slope from here. Soon after his arrival, the American Army gained the heights from an obscure path located to the southeast. Spiking the gun with a ramrod to make it unusable for the Americans, Brock and the gunners ran down the slope of the hill, Brock leading his horse "Alfred" by the reins.

Rallying at the Hamilton house in the village of Queenston, Brock lead the Grenadier Company of the 49th Regiment and Captain Chisholm's company of the York Volunteers forward. At a stone wall near the south end of the village, he paused and told his men, "Take breath boys you will need it in a few moments." Viewing the steep ascent of Queenston Heights today, one can well understand this statement.

The two companies began their attack up the slope. They had not gone far when an American rifleman stepped out from under cover and took deliberate aim at the General. Some members of the 49th who saw the action quickly fired, but it was too late; Brock was hit squarely in the chest and fell immediately. A young gentleman volunteer, George Jarvis, was the first to reach the general, saying "Are you much hurt sir?" Brock was unable to reply: the rifle bullet had killed him almost instantly.

The gallant band retreated down the hill, taking the body of their beloved general with them. In a vain attempt to regain the heights and avenge the fallen general, Brock's aide de camp, John Macdonell, led another charge up the steep slope. Mounted, and also a very conspicuous target, he was hit, and the entire force retreated to the Durham farm, near Vrooman's Point. After the deaths of Brock and Macdonell, there was a lull in the battle, and a deep rooted feeling that all was lost. It was late afternoon when General Roger Hale Sheaffe counter-attacked, bolstered with

Brock's Cenotaph at Queenston Heights today

reinforcements from Fort George, and finally won the battle of
Queenston Heights. The stone cenotaph is easily located at the
south end of the village of Queenston.

## MONUMENT TO "ALFRED" — QUEENSTON

This bronze statue of General Brock's horse "Alfred" was officially
dedicated on October 3, 1976. Brock's aide de camp, John
Macdonell, was killed leading a second charge on the heights along
with "Alfred." The monument is located next to Brock's Cenotaph,
at the location where "Alfred" was tethered before the attack.

# INDIANS AT QUEENSTON HEIGHTS — QUEENSTON

The participation of Indian warriors in the Battle of Queenston Heights was important in the middle and latter phases of the battle. During the lull after the death of Brock, the Indian units harassed the American lines on the crest of the heights and prevented them from consolidating their position. With their war cries audible from the other side of the river, they frightened a great many of the New York Militia from crossing to aid the regulars.

Among the more notable Iroquois warriors who fought here were John Brant and John Bearfoot. The former was the son of the famous Chief Joseph Brant. The Indians were led by John Norton, himself an adopted Indian of Cherokee and Scottish descent. A plaque erected by the Niagara Parks Commission in 1980 commemorates the participation of the various native tribes who took part in the victory. The plaque is mounted on a boulder, just to the west of Brock's Cenotaph.

# SHEAFFE'S PATH TO VICTORY — QUEENSTON

A small stone marker simply states "Sheaffe's Path to Victory" at the location where the British Army, under Roger Hale Sheaffe, climbed the escarpment to attack the rear of the American Army to win the Battle of Queenston Heights. The marker is located 2.3 kilometres west of the Niagara Parkway on York Road.

## BATTLE OF QUEENSTON HEIGHTS —
## LEWISTON, NEW YORK

On Remembrance Day, November 11, 1994, a plaque was placed by the Veterans of Foreign Wars, dedicated to the American participation in the Battle of Queenston Heights. The plaque is not far from the location where the American Army embarked in boats to cross the Niagara River. The plaque is mounted on a boulder, and is located in a small park at the Lewiston waterfront.

## FORT GRAY — LEWISTON, NEW YORK

The guns of Fort Gray helped support the American crossing of the Niagara River during the Battle of Queenston Heights on October 13, 1812. Fort Gray was located at the crest of the hill, directly opposite the highest point of Queenston Heights. Presently the site is unmarked, and is remembered only by "Gray Drive," which passes near the site.

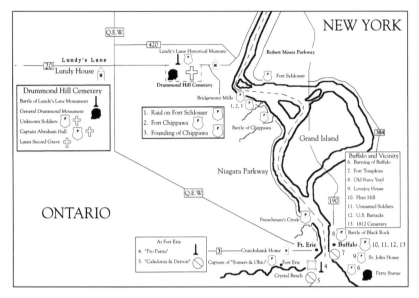

DRUMMOND HILL CEMETERY,
NIAGARA FALLS, ONTARIO

Battle of Lundy's Lane

One of the most fiercely contested battles of the War of 1812 was fought on this site, in the quiet country lane of William Lundy. In the early evening hours of July 25, 1814, the advanced guard of the British army, under Lieutenant General Gordon Drummond, posted itself on this hill overlooking the Portage Road. Just to the south of this position was Brigadier General Scott's brigade of American Regulars. Scott believed that he was opposed by only a small portion of the British Army, and decided to advance. He was completely unaware that the British offensive on the American side of the river had been cancelled, and that the bulk of their army was once again on Canadian soil. At around 7:15 pm, Scott's brigade advanced towards the high ground over Lundy's Lane, and the battle began.

The heavy firing drew units from both armies, and soon they were locked in a "meeting engagement," with both commanders calling for reinforcements. The American Army under General Jacob Brown reinforced Scott from the south, while British units arrived from the north and west. With darkness falling, the battle became confused, with neither side being able to properly identify friend or foe. At one point, the 25th U.S. Infantry Regiment under Major Jesup gained the rear of the British left flank. In the confusion the British second in command, Major General Phineas Riall who had been wounded, was captured.

At around 9:00 pm of this hot summers evening, both armies paused while new units arrived on the field. By this time it was completely dark, and the only illumination was from the full moon. Fifteen minutes later, a dramatic change occurred in the battle when Colonel Miller, in command of the 21st U.S. Infantry, attacked and captured the British guns located in the cemetery. In a counter move, the 89th Regiment under Colonel Morrison, the victor of Crysler's Farm, opened up a destructive flank fire on Miller's men at point-blank range. Despite this destructive fire, the 21st held on, and the British retired down the rear slope of the hill.

During this phase of the battle, the British engaged in a series of desperate frontal attacks in order to win back their artillery. By midnight, both armies had been completely exhausted, with some of the bloodiest hand-to-hand fighting yet seen in the war. Though he was still in possession of the hill, General Brown's army was too badly mauled to hold the position, and he ordered a withdrawal to Chippawa. Thus ended the battle of Lundy's Lane; tactically a stalemate, but a strategic victory for the British, for after this battle, the Americans never launched a major offensive on the Niagara Frontier again.

The battlefield itself has had a fascinating history and at one time it was one of the most visited tourist attractions in Ontario. Located not far from Niagara Falls, thousands of visitors came to see the historic ground each year. At different times in its history, five different observation towers have stood on the crest of Drummond Hill, overlooking the battlefield. It was not until 1895 that a dignified monument honouring the fallen soldiers was erected. Due to the efforts of the Lundy's Lane Historical Society and the Dominion Government, the monument was unveiled on July 25, 1895. Attending the ceremonies were over two thousand people.

Gradually tourism declined at Lundy's Lane, especially after the American Civil War, when American visitors found it more convenient to travel to those battlefields. With the decline of the tourist dollar, maintenance of the cemetery and the battlefield suffered greatly. In 1911, during a restoration of the cemetery, nine skeletal remains were found. These proved to be American soldiers, and they were re-interred in a moving ceremony, with Canadian and American officials in attendance. As the village of Drummondville grew, soldiers' remains and other artifacts were often found, especially when digging foundations for new homes.

In 1914, for the one-hundredth anniversary, there was a renewal of interest in the Battle of Lundy's Lane. On that occasion, huge celebrations were put in motion and a medal struck commemorating the battle. Truly, July 25, 1914 was the battlefield's shining hour.

The events included a military parade, decorations of the soldiers' graves, guest speakers, the town decked out in banners, and a new plaque commemorating the event, but after 1914 interest in the battlefield waned quickly. World War I and the great events happening in Europe made the battle of Lundy's Lane seem a small affair.

Drummondville eventually became incorporated into the city of Niagara Falls. With no single organization in charge of the battleground, and no protection by the national government, it was eventually lost to developers. The quiet country lane of William Lundy is now a busy thoroughfare, leading through the heart of the city of Niagara Falls. Most of the battlefield remains are in Drummond Hill Cemetery, on the crest of Lundy's Lane. But all is not lost. Recently, through the contribution of Ruth Redmond, more of the battlefield is being reclaimed. An organization now exists called "Friends of the Lundy's Lane Battlefield" that is dedicated to preserving and restoring the historic ground. Through the heroic efforts of the Lundy's Lane Historical Society, a wreath laying ceremony is still held on July 25th every year. The monument to this most famous battle is located in Drummond Hill Cemetery.

## Battle of Lundy's Lane Plaque

A plaque placed by the Historic Sites and Monuments Board of Canada describes the decisive battle of Lundy's Lane, fought on these grounds July 25, 1814. The plaque is adjacent to the General Drummond monument in Drummond Hill Cemetery, city of Niagara Falls.

## General Gordon Drummond

This beautiful monument, sculpted by Ralph Sketch, was placed by the Niagara Parks Commission in 1989. It depicts Lieutenant General Sir Gordon Drummond, astride his horse on July 26, 1814. Drummond is depicted alertly awaiting a second American attack, which never materialized. The monument is located in Drummond Hill Cemetery.

## Unknown Soldiers

Over the years various remains of soldiers have been found on the battlefield of Lundy's Lane, and traditionally they have been reburied in Drummond Hill Cemetery. Four stone markers, with commemorative plaques, denote the resting places of these soldiers. Two plaques mark the site of nine U.S. soldiers interred below, while another marks the resting place of two unknown U.S. soldiers. One plaque marks the resting place of Abraham Fuller Hull, of the 9th U.S. Infantry, whose remains had been identified. The markers are located near the Lundy's Lane Monument in Drummond Hill Cemetery.

## Captain Abraham Hull

In 1907 the Niagara Frontier Monuments Association of Buffalo placed a monument to Captain Abraham Hull and unknown U.S. soldiers that had been recovered on the battlefield. Abraham Hull was the nephew of General William Hull, who surrendered Fort Detroit to General Isaac Brock, on August 16, 1812. Captain Hull was severely wounded in the struggle for the top of the hill in the latter stages of the battle. When the British Army took possession of the hill that evening, Lieutenant John Le Couteur of the 104th Regiment met Captain Hull and saw that he was mortally wounded. He offered the dying enemy some brandy and water, and conversed briefly with him. Upon returning to the scene the next morning, he found Hull's body stripped of its possessions. Thus ended the life of a brave American officer. The monument to Hull and the unknown soldiers is adjacent to Drummond Hill Church, in Drummond Hill Cemetery.

## Laura Secord Grave

The most famous heroine of the War of 1812 is buried here in Drummond Hill Cemetery. Her grave features a bust of the young Laura, and an inscription describing the part she played in the victory at Beaver Dams on June 24, 1813. Her grave is located near the battle monument, in Drummond Hill Cemetery.

# LUNDY'S LANE HISTORICAL MUSEUM — NIAGARA FALLS, ONTARIO

The Lundy's Lane Historical Museum is established in the old Stamford Township Hall, which was erected in 1874. The collection consists of pioneer, Indian, and military artifacts, and of particular interest is a display on the Battle of Lundy's Lane. Featured are artifacts recovered from the battlefield, and banners from the one-hundredth anniversary celebration in 1914. The uniform coat of Captain James Thompson is also on display. Thompson was a member of the 2nd Regiment of Lincoln Militia, and fought in the Battle of Lundy's Lane. At the visitors' request, a short video is shown on the Niagara Campaign of 1814. The museum is located at 5810 Ferry Street (an extension of Lundy's Lane) in the city of Niagara Falls.

# WILLIAM LUNDY HOUSE — NIAGARA FALLS, ONTARIO

In 1796, when William Lundy first arrived in this vicinity, he blazed a trail from his home to the main Portage Road to the east. It has been called Lundy's Lane ever since, although today it is a thriving commercial thoroughfare. Lundy was a Quaker and a United Empire Loyalist, who built this house in 1790. The home is still owned by the Lundy family, and not open to the public. The house is back from the road at 3478 Lundy's Lane, not far from the Queen Elizabeth Way. The grounds are private property, so visitor discretion is advised.

# BRIDGEWATER MILLS — NIAGARA PARKWAY, ONTARIO

In American history the Battle of Lundy's Lane has sometimes been called the Battle of Bridgewater, because of the nearby mills. Due to the swift current that existed here, it was an ideal site to take advantage of water power. The mill complex was constructed in the late 1790s, and included a saw mill, grist mill, and an iron foundry. The American Army burned the mills on July 26, 1814 during their retreat from the Battle of Lundy's Lane. A plaque, placed by the Niagara Parks Commission, is located on Burning Springs Hill Road, near the intersection with the Niagara Parkway, at Dufferin Island.

# FORT SCHLOSSER — NIAGARA FALLS, NEW YORK

During the Seven Years' War the French kept a small post here which they called "Little Fort Niagara," or "Fort du Portage." Its main purpose was to protect the Portage Road around Niagara Falls, but in 1759 the French destroyed the post to prevent its use by the British, who were at that time besieging Fort Niagara. In 1760, the British constructed a new fort on the site, and named it after its builder, German Captain Joseph Schlosser.

Fort Schlosser was much larger than the old French fortification, and consisted of a picketed earthwork with four bastions. By the time of the War of 1812, the fort was in disrepair, and was used only as a supply depot. In December of 1813 it was raided by British and Canadian forces and subsequently burned. There are no above-ground remains of the fort, but a metal sign marker has been placed at the site. (see next entry)

# RAID ON FORT SCHLOSSER — NIAGARA PARKWAY, ONTARIO

In the early morning hours of July 5, 1813, thirty-six militia and six privates of the 49th Regiment, under the command of Lieutenant Colonel Thomas Clark, assisted by Ensign Winder, crossed the Niagara River in three boats to Fort Schlosser. Surprising the garrison, which consisted of less than twenty men, they proceeded to capture a quantity of stores. They remained less than an hour, and returned without casualties to the Canadian shore. The raid was typical of similar incursions into American territory during the summer of 1813. An Ontario Provincial Plaque in Kings Bridge Park in the former village of Chippawa marks the spot of the embarkation.

# FORT CHIPPAWA — NIAGARA PARKWAY, ONTARIO

Fortifications were erected here in 1791 to protect the south end of the Niagara Portage, and during the War of 1812 they were upgraded and expanded. Major General Phineas Riall used this as his jumping-off point to move to the Battle of Chippawa, just south of this location. The fortifications also figured prominently as a rallying point for the British after their defeat at that battle. When the pursuing American Army, under General Brown, arrived here, they found the position too strong for a frontal attack. General Brown then outflanked the position to the west, and Riall was compelled to withdraw. The Ontario Provincial Plaque to Fort Chippawa is located on the north bank of the Welland River (former Chippawa River), in Kings Bridge Park.

# FOUNDING OF CHIPPAWA — NIAGARA PARKWAY, ONTARIO

An Ontario Provincial plaque describes the founding of the village of Chippawa, which grew up around Fort Chippawa in 1792. The village was largely destroyed during the War of 1812, as it was under British and American control numerous times. The plaque is located on the south side of the Welland River (former Chippawa River) in the town square in the former village of Chippawa. (see prior entry)


# BATTLE OF CHIPPAWA — NIAGARA PARKWAY, ONTARIO

At this spot on July 5, 1814, one of the major battles of the War of 1812 was fought. The British were under the command of Major General Phineas Riall and the American Army was commanded by General Jacob Brown. Two days before, Brown's army had crossed into Canada and captured ill-defended Fort Erie.

Following the river road north, his army of approximately 3500, effective troops encamped here at Usshers Creek (formerly Streets Creek). Upon learning of the American invasion, Riall decided to counter-attack the rear of the American Army, which he believed was still besieging Fort Erie. While awaiting the arrival of reinforcements, he moved his army to the fortified position at Chippawa, and on the morning of July 5th, his skirmishers were in contact with the American pickets, posted north of Usshers Creek.

When Riall's reinforcements reached him that morning, he still believed he was facing only a small portion of the American Army. He decided to attack, and his army, now numbering about two thousand effective troops, moved out onto the plain south of Chippawa Creek. Noting the advance of the British, General Brown ordered Scott's brigade to form up in the fields and engage the enemy. The American Army that now faced Riall, however, was quite a different one than the British had faced a year before. Under the leadership of Brown and Scott, it was now a highly trained and disciplined force.

Even though slightly outnumbered, Scott's brigade drove Riall's forces from the field, and won the battle. Some American historians have called the Battle of Chippawa, the "real birth of the American Army," for it was here that the American Army proved that it was now every bit as good as the British in field manoeuvres and discipline. Though Chippawa was a major battle, there is little to be seen at the site today, although there are plans to develop the field. A marker has been placed by the Historic Sites and Monuments Board of Canada, and is located north of Streets Creek, opposite Navy Island.

## FRENCHMAN'S CREEK — NIAGARA PARKWAY, ONTARIO

On November 28, 1812, an American force composed of detachments from the 12th, 13th, 14th, 20th, and 23rd U.S. regiments, crossed the Niagara River and landed at this point. Their purpose was to interrupt the communications between Fort Erie and Chippawa, and to destroy a battery of guns that was mounted here. Lieutenant Lamont, and his thirty soldiers stationed at the battery, were badly outnumbered and forced to retreat. Spiking the cannons, they fell back and waited for reinforcements from Fort Erie. When the reinforcements did arrive, the Americans in turn were forced to withdraw, and forty U.S soldiers were taken prisoner. A plaque, placed by the Historic Sites and Monuments Board of Canada, commemorates the small action, and is located at Frenchman's Creek on the Niagara Parkway, just north of Fort Erie, Ontario.

# OLD FORT ERIE — FORT ERIE, ONTARIO

Three different forts, all named after the lake, have been constructed in this immediate vicinity. The first Fort Erie was constructed in 1764 under the direction of British engineer John Montressor. With its close proximity to the lake, the fort was often damaged by storms, and in March, 1779, one such storm damaged the fort so badly that it had to be reconstructed the next summer.

In 1803 another severe storm, this time accompanied by ice, once again damaged the fort, and this led to the approval of construction of a new solid masonry fort on January 9, 1804. Under this plan the fort was constructed further back from the river. But construction work was sporadic, and by the time of the War of 1812 the fort was still incomplete. In the first year of the war no serious effort was made by the Americans to capture Fort Erie, but on November 28th a party of U.S. soldiers landed at Frenchman's Creek, just to the north, and tried to destroy the battery there. British reinforcements eventually drove them off.

After the fall of Fort George on May 27, 1813, the British were forced to evacuate most of the Niagara Peninsula and retreat to Burlington. At that time Fort Erie and the nearby batteries were held by Lieutenant Colonel Cecil Bisshop, with two companies of the 8th Regiment. Bisshop's regulars joined in the retreat to Burlington, while detachments from the Lincoln Militia remained to destroy the fort.

The destruction by the militia was very thorough, and when the American Army occupied the site they found it in a "heap of ruins." The U.S. Army did not hold the fort long, and just three days after their defeat at the Battle of Stoney Creek on June 6th they concentrated their forces at Fort George. In General Drummond's "Winter Campaign" the British retook Fort Erie, and by the spring of 1814 a larger garrison was placed there. Once again, work was begun on repairing the fortifications.

On July 3, 1814, General Jacob Brown and his army crossed the Niagara River and invested Fort Erie. With no hope of defence, Major Buck, with less than 150 soldiers, was forced to surrender. For the duration of Brown's campaign the fort was used as his main base on the Canadian shore. After the Battle of Lundy's Lane on July 25th, Brown's army fell back to the fort, where it was put under siege by the British under Lieutenant General Gordon Drummond.

While in possession of the fort, the American Army had not been idle, and the fortifications were greatly extended and improved. On the evening of August 15th, Drummond ordered a general assault on the fortifications. Troops under his nephew, Lieutenant Colonel William Drummond, temporarily succeeded in occupying the northeast bastion, but somehow during the confusion the magazine exploded, and the assault was repulsed. On September 15th, Brown launched his own counter-attack against Drummond's positions, and this resulted in the destruction of many of his batteries. Now Drummond had no hope of retaking Fort Erie, and withdrew his forces to Chippawa on the evening of September 21st.

The siege, though unsuccessful, had contained the American Army on the Niagara Peninsula, and now they held only the fort itself. When Major General George Izard replaced Brown as commander of the army, he ordered the troops to blow up Fort Erie and retire to Buffalo. Old Fort Erie has been beautifully restored, and the well-maintained grounds are under the jurisdiction of the Niagara Parks Commission. The fort features period rooms, displays on the fort's history, a gift shop, and an audio tape tour. Old Fort Erie is located on the Niagara Parkway in the town of Fort Erie.

## FORT ERIE — FORT ERIE, ONTARIO

The plaque placed by the National Historic Sites and Monuments Board of Canada gives a brief history of Fort Erie, and is located at the entrance to Old Fort Erie.

The stamp issued by Canada Post to commemorate Old Fort Erie

## "PRO PATRIA " MONUMENT — FORT ERIE, ONTARIO

This impressive column is dedicated to the officers and men of the regular forces and militia who were killed during the siege of Fort Erie. Beneath the monument are the remains of soldiers, both British and American, who were discovered in 1939 during the restoration of the fort. The monument is located at the entrance to Old Fort Erie, in the city of Fort Erie.

## THE *CALEDONIA* AND THE *DETROIT* — FORT ERIE, ONTARIO

On the morning of December 8, 1812, two British vessels, the *Caledonia* and the *Detroit*, were anchored under the guns of Fort Erie. The *Caledonia* was a small schooner that had been pressed into service by Captain Roberts for the capture of Fort Michilamackinac. The *Detroit* was the former American brig *Adams*, which had been captured by Brock at Detroit.

Lieutenant Jesse D. Elliot, determined to capture the two

British vessels and add them to his own squadron, then fitting out at Black Rock, just across the river. Utilizing some sailors that had just arrived, and collecting some drafts from the army, Lieutenant Elliot soon had a force of about one hundred men. At 1:00 am on December 9th they left the American shore in two long boats carrying fifty men each. At 3:00 am they were alongside the two vessels, when they were met by a volley of musketry.

In a ten-minute boarding action at close quarters, the two vessels were taken. With great difficulty, the vessels were finally brought away, fighting the swift Niagara current, and under constant fire from British troops. The *Caledonia* eventually reached the safety of Black Rock, but the *Detroit* became unmanageable and ran aground on Squaw Island. Hit numerous times by artillery fire from both sides, she was finally set on fire by the Americans and destroyed. The *Caledonia* eventually became part of the American Lake Erie squadron, and participated in the Battle of Lake Erie in September of 1813. This daring "cutting out expedition," tipped the naval balance in favour of the Americans on Lake Erie. Presently, this small but important naval action is uncommemorated.

## CAPTURE OF THE *SOMERS* AND *OHIO* — FORT ERIE, ONTARIO

A plaque placed by the Historic Sites and Monuments Board of Canada is dedicated to the capture of the two American schooners *Somers* and *Ohio* on the night of August 12, 1814. The plaque is mounted on a wall inside Old Fort Erie, Niagara Parkway. (see next entry)

# CAPTURE OF THE *SOMERS* AND *OHIO* — CRYSTAL BEACH, ONTARIO

On the evening of August 12, 1814 in a daring cutting-out raid, a party of Royal Navy sailors under the command of Captain Alexander T. Dobbs managed to capture two American schooners that were anchored near Fort Erie. Of particular note was the method by which the boats arrived on the shores of Lake Erie. It was dragged twenty-five miles overland from Queenston, and then an additional eight miles of trail had to be blazed through the forest wilderness. This obscure but important operation was undertaken just to get one captain's gig and five bateaux onto Lake Erie near this spot.

After the capture of *Somers* and *Ohio*, the two vessels entered the British Navy establishment under their new names *Saulk* and *Huron*. This daring exploit was the last naval action fought on the Great Lakes during the War of 1812. A plaque placed by the Ontario Provincial Government is located in the traffic circle off of Derby Road in Crystal Beach, Ontario.

# ERNEST CRUIKSHANK HOME — FORT ERIE, ONTARIO

Ernest Alexander Cruikshank was one of Canada's most prolific historians. He is best remembered for his work as editor of the eight volume *Documentary History of the Campaigns Upon the Niagara Frontier*. He also wrote copious material on battles and campaigns of the War of 1812.

Cruikshank rose to the rank of Brigadier General in the Canadian army, and was later Director of the Historical Section, General Staff in Ottawa. He also was President of the Ontario Historical Society. As chairman of the Historic Sites and Monuments Board of Canada, he was active in marking a great number of the War of 1812 sites in Ontario. A plaque placed by the Bertie Historical Society stands in front of the home where Cruikshank was born in 1853. The house, which is not open to the public, is located at 848 Garrison Road, Bertie Township, Fort Erie, Ontario.

## BURNING OF BUFFALO — BUFFALO, NEW YORK

After the wanton burning of Newark by American forces in December of 1813, General George Gordon Drummond planned a counter move. "Drummond's Winter Campaign" began with the seizing of Fort Niagara on the night of December 18th. Plans were then set in motion to lay waste the American frontier on the Niagara River. This policy continued over the next few weeks, and eventually the villages of Manchester, Schlosser, Black Rock, and finally Buffalo were destroyed.

At Buffalo some resistance was offered to the British. General Phineas Riall had with him 965 regulars, 50 Canadian militia and about 400 Indians, and opposed to him were about 2000 New York militia under General Hall. At Black Rock, just to the north of Buffalo, about 500 of Hall's soldiers made a stand, but the rest retreated. Here, four of Perry's vessels were trapped in the ice and promptly burned. With no opposition and the Indians under little restraint, Black Rock and Buffalo were destroyed. Only three houses survived the conflagration. There is little to "commemorate" the burning of Buffalo today, but there is a "Seaway Trail" marker located at the Naval and Serviceman's Park in the city of Buffalo.

# FORT TOMPKINS — BUFFALO, NEW YORK

Fort Tompkins was one of the larger fortifications constructed to protect the town of Buffalo. When the American regular army was transferred to Sackets Harbor in the autumn of 1813, Buffalo was left defenceless. This was demonstrated when General Riall's British forces burned the town on December 29, 1813. Without a garrison, the usefulness of Fort Tompkins was questionable. The fort was abandoned after the war, and the growing city of Buffalo eventually obliterated all remains. The Niagara Frontier Landmarks Association has placed a plaque at 1010 Niagara Street in the city of Buffalo near the site of the fort.

# OLIVER HAZARD PERRY STATUE — BUFFALO, NEW YORK

The monument to Oliver Hazard Perry was erected by the State of New York to commemorate his victory at the Battle of Lake Erie in September of 1813. This impressive monument is located in Front Park in the city of Buffalo. (see also Perry's Victory, South Bass Island, Lake Erie)

# BATTLE OF BLACK ROCK — BUFFALO, NEW YORK

On the early morning of August 3, 1814 a force of some six hundred British regulars from the 41st and 104th regiments, under the command of Lieutenant Colonel John Goulston Tucker, landed about two miles below the village of Black Rock. Their intention was to raid the depot which was supplying American-held Fort Erie, then under siege by the British. Approaching Conjocheta Creek, they found the bridge destroyed and, on the opposite side, about 250 riflemen under Major Lodowick Morgan. In repeated attempts to cross, the British were foiled by Morgan's riflemen, and after three hours retreated. The British lost eleven soldiers killed, seventeen wounded, and four missing. The city of Buffalo has completely absorbed the site of the battle, but it has been commemorated by the Niagara Frontier Landmarks Association. A plaque placed in 1902 is affixed to the side of a building at Niagara and Tonawanda Street in the city of Buffalo.

## OLD NAVY YARD — BUFFALO, NEW YORK

Black Rock was the site of a small navy yard during the War of 1812, but because it was in range of British cannons from Fort Erie, it proved to be an inferior location. The Niagara current is also strong here, and vessels had to wait for favourable winds, or be warped out of the harbour. Because of these disadvantages, Erie, Pennsylvania eventually became the main base. Five of Captain Oliver Hazard Perry's vessels were outfitted here before they joined the fleet. These were the schooners *Somers*, *Amelia*, *Ohio*, the brig *Caledonia* and the sloop *Trippe*. Presently the site is unmarked, but the navy yard was located in the vicinity of 1700 Niagara Street in the modern city of Buffalo.

## ST. JOHN HOUSE — BUFFALO, NEW YORK

The St. John house was one of only three structures that escaped the burning of Buffalo in December of 1813. At the time of the raid, the widow Mrs. Martha St. John lived here with her children.

The house is no longer standing but the site has been marked by the Niagara Frontier Landmarks Association. The marker is at 460 Main Street in downtown Buffalo.

## LOVEJOY HOUSE — BUFFALO, NEW YORK

Mrs. Sarah Lovejoy was the only civilian killed in the December 1813 raid on Buffalo. The Buffalo and Erie County Historical Society has marked the site of her residence, which was at 465 Main Street in the city of Buffalo.

## FLINT HILL — BUFFALO, NEW YORK

"Flint Hill" was the site of a large encampment during the War of 1812, and over three hundred soldiers died here of disease. The site of "Flint Hill" has been marked at 2064 Main Street in the city of Buffalo. The site is now occupied by Mount Saint Joseph's Academy. (see next entry)

## UNNAMED SOLDIERS — BUFFALO, NEW YORK

Three hundred soldiers who died of disease at "Flint Hill" are buried at this location. A boulder and cannon are at the site, which is in the centre of Delaware Park in the city of Buffalo. (see previous entry)

# WAR OF 1812 CEMETERY — WILLIAMSVILLE, NEW YORK

After the Battle of Lundy's Lane on July 25, 1814, wounded soldiers were sent here to a temporary military hospital. To the west of this location is the cemetery for the hospital where over two hundred American and Canadian soldiers lie. The Erie County Sesquicentennial Committee has marked the site on Garrison Road and Route 5 at Williamsville, New York.

# U.S. BARRACKS — CHEEKTOWAGA, NEW YORK

General Smyth's soldiers were quartered in log barracks at this site during the first winter of the war. The buildings were later used as a hospital. The New York State Education Department has placed a plaque marking the site at Transit Road and Aero Drive in the city of Cheektowaga.

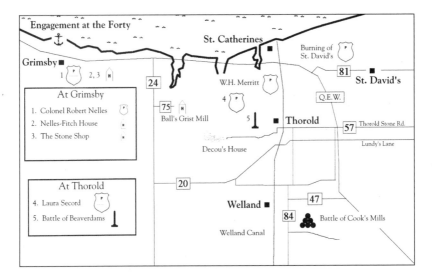

## ENGAGEMENT AT THE FORTY — GRIMSBY, ONTARIO

After their defeat at the Battle of Stoney Creek, the American forces, now under the command of General Lewis, regrouped here at Forty Mile Creek. On the morning of June 8, 1813, the British squadron under Commodore Yeo appeared about one mile off shore from Lewis's position. With continual harassment from small bands of British forces on land, and now confronted with an enemy squadron on his flank, Lewis prepared to retreat to Fort George.

Yeo attempted to have the squadron bombard the American camp, but because of the light winds, his vessels could not close on the shore. Exercising his own initiative, Captain Francis Spilsbury of the schooner *Beresford* had the vessel towed closer inshore, where he could now fire at the American camp.

Quickly setting up a makeshift furnace, the Americans returned fire with four field guns throwing heated shot. At about the same time, a party of Indians appeared overlooking the camp, and harassed the Americans with musket fire. The Indians were driven off by light infantry, and the *Beresford* bore away with the rest of the squadron. Later on in the afternoon the wind freshened, and Yeo landed two companies of the 49th and 41st regiments, with two light field guns, under the command of Major Dennis.

Dennis's force pursued the Americans by land, while the guns of the fleet harassed them from the water. In this confused retreat, the *Beresford* managed to capture twenty of the American bateaux, which contained hospital stores and supplies. General Lewis's army retreated so rapidly, that Major Dennis's party never caught their rear guard. A plaque commemorating this small affair has been placed by the Historic Sites and Monuments Board of Canada. It is located in the waterworks park on the shore of Lake Ontario at the foot of Elizabeth Street in the town of Grimsby.

## COLONEL ROBERT NELLES — GRIMSBY, ONTARIO

An Ontario Provincial Plaque honours Colonel Robert Nelles, one of Grimsby's first settlers. Nelles was a United Empire Loyalist, and during the War of 1812 he was the commanding officer of the 4th Lincoln Militia. The Ontario Provincial Plaque is located in front of his stone manor at 126 West Main Street in the town of Grimsby.

## NELLES FITCH HOUSE — GRIMSBY, ONTARIO

United Empire Loyalist Robert Nelles built this house in 1791. During the War of 1812 it was used primarily as a barracks, and the basement was altered to hold cells for prisoners. The house is located at 125 Main Street West in the town of Grimsby, across from the Grimsby Museum.

## THE STONE SHOP — GRIMSBY, ONTARIO

This old stone building was built in 1800 as a farm shop, and in 1812 was used by the local blacksmith. Local tradition has it that he "pricked" the hooves of American horses that he was forced to shoe. Currently the building is privately owned and not open to the public, but the Ontario Heritage Foundation has marked the site with an oval plaque attached to the building. The Stone Shop is located in the town of Grimsby on Regional Road 81, a little west of the Grimsby Museum.

## BALL'S GRIST MILL — VINELAND, ONTARIO

Grist mills became targets for enemy raids during the war, since they provided flour for the British army. Fortunately Ball's Mill was one of the few to survive, and is a four-storey structure that was built by John and George Ball in 1809. Today the mill can be seen in the Ball's Falls Conservation area, located on Regional Road 24 near Vineland, Ontario.

## DE CEW HOUSE — DE CEW'S FALLS

Captain John De Cew was a militia officer during the war, and lived here with his wife Catherine and eleven children. He was captured in 1813, but made his escape the next year, and later fought in the Battle of Lundy's Lane. The nearby De Cew Mill was owned and operated by him until 1834, when he sold the property. John De Cew lived until 1855 and is buried at Decewville, another community named after him.

De Cew's house is more famous than the man himself, for it was to this place that Laura Secord made her famous journey on June 24, 1813, to warn the British of an American attack. At that time the house was the headquarters of a British detachment under Lieutenant James FitzGibbon. The information that Laura related to FitzGibbon was directly responsible for the victory at the Battle of Beaver Dams. In this affair the entire American column — over five hundred men under Colonel Charles Boerstler — was forced to surrender.

Unfortunately De Cew House, which had stood for over one hundred years, has been destroyed. In 1950 the unoccupied house was burned down under mysterious circumstances. The above-ground remains are located on De Cew Road, not far from the De Cew Falls, in the Regional Municipality of Niagara.

The site of De Cew House today

De Cew House as sketched by Lossing

# BATTLE OF BEAVER DAMS — THOROLD, ONTARIO

After the Battle of Fort George on May 27, 1813, the American Army was in control of a large portion of the Niagara Frontier. But after their defeat at the Battle of Stoney Creek on June 6th, they were unable to extend their influence as far as Burlington Heights. During this period, they controlled primarily the area around Fort George and Queenston. At the same time the British maintained a number of outposts close to the American lines.

One of these outposts was stationed at the De Cew house under the command of Lieutenant FitzGibbon of the 49th Regiment. FitzGibbon's party had been particularly troublesome in harassing the American pickets, and a plan soon emerged to capture his entire party. On June 24th an American column under the command of Colonel Charles Boerstler consisting of five hundred infantry, one troop of dragoons, and two field guns, advanced on FitzGibbon's position.

Forewarned of the American advance by Laura Secord, a young settler, FitzGibbon was able to lay a trap for the U.S. column. At the "Battle of the Beechwoods" or "Beaver Dams," the entire American column was surrounded by native forces under the command of Dominique Ducharme and William Kerr. Lieutenant FitzGibbon arrived towards the close of the action, but he decided on a ruse to bluff Colonel Boerstler into surrender. He sent a messenger to inform Boerstler that he was surrounded by greatly superior forces. FitzGibbon also suggested that a capitulation would be in order. The American commander pondered the fact that his reinforcements were over eighteen miles away. Having no idea that he was actually surrounded by an inferior force, Boerstler surrendered his whole command.

Captain Norton of the Indian Department observed wryly, "The Cognawaga Indians fought the battle, the Mohawks or Six Nations got the plunder, and FitzGibbon got the credit." The victory at Beaver Dams was of strategic importance, for after this battle the Americans could no longer afford to send out small parties into the Niagara countryside, and they were now hemmed in to the immediate vicinity of Fort George. A monument to the victory at

Beaver Dams was erected by the Historic Sites and Monuments Board of Canada in 1923. For decades it stood near the spot where Boerstler's troops surrendered, but in a move of questionable intelligence the monument was moved from its original site to "Battle of Beaver Dams Park" in the city of Thorold. (see next entry)

## BATTLE OF BEAVER DAMS — ACTUAL SITE

The Battle of Beaver Dams, which had been a "marked" site for over fifty years, now has the embarrassing distinction of being an "unmarked" site. The actual battlefield is at the intersection of Thorold Stone Road and Davis Road, in the Regional Municipality of Niagara. The old monument, which was dedicated in 1923, was placed at the approximate centre of the battlefield. Today, although the terrain has changed considerably, and the famous Beechwoods are now gone, certain landmarks can still be located.

The place where the Indians encamped would have been at the present site of the cemetery on Davis Road, just to the north of the Welland Canal branch. The site of Boerstler's surrender was in the vicinity of the east entrance to the Welland Canal tunnel. The old 1813 road used by Boerstler's troops no longer exists. However, if one stands at the intersection of the two roads mentioned above and faces northeast, the line of sight would follow the trace of the old road. Unfortunately, the old monument of 1923 is no longer on the battlefield, and was moved into "Battle of Beaver Dams Park" in the city of Thorold. (see prior entry)

## LAURA SECORD — BEAVER DAMS PARK, THOROLD, ONTARIO

Second only to General Isaac Brock, Laura Secord is the most known personality of the War of 1812. A plaque, commemorating her arduous nineteen mile journey to warn the British of an American attack, is located in "Battle of Beaver Dams Park" in the city of Thorold. (see previous three entries)

## WILLIAM HAMILTON MERRITT — ST. CATHARINES, ONTARIO

William Hamilton Merritt served as Lieutenant in the Provincial Light Dragoons during the War of 1812. He later rose to the rank of Captain. He was a dispatch rider in the Battle of Fort George, and was responsible for the reconnaissance of Mr. Cassel Chorus's farm, which resulted in the skirmish at Butler's Farm on July 8, 1813.

Although his surviving letters give us an insight into what it was like to raise a corps of volunteers during the war, he is primarily remembered for his role in the construction of the first Welland Canal. The Ontario Provincial Plaque to him is located in Memorial Park in the city of St. Catharines. (see Action at Butler's Farm)

## THE BURNING OF ST. DAVID'S — ST. DAVID'S, ONTARIO

On July 18, 1814 a small party of American Militia, under the command of Lieutenant Colonel Isaac W. Stone, marched from Queenston to St. Davids. They soon engaged a detachment of the 1st Lincoln Militia who were stationed at the town. Unable to hold, the 1st Lincoln fell back, and Stone's troops proceeded to loot the town and set it aflame. Stone was later officially censured for this cruel action and was dismissed from the service. An Ontario Provincial Plaque describing the incident is located in front of the St. David's Public School.

# BATTLE OF COOK'S MILLS — WELLAND, ONTARIO

After Sir Gordon Drummond's unsuccessful siege of Fort Erie, his army fell back to the prepared positions at Chippawa. During October of 1814, his far right flank faced south at Cook's Mills, and his left flank rested at the mouth of the Chippawa River. His opponent was now Major General George Izard, who had replaced General Jacob Brown. With the British in command of Lake Ontario, Izard saw little point in commencing a general offensive, and was content in sending out raiding parties against the British Army's food supply.

One of these raiding parties was under the command of Brigadier General Daniel Bissel, and was ordered to march to Cook's Mills on October 18th to destroy the grain there. Bissel's troops consisted of detachments from the 5th, 14th, 15th, and 16th U.S. infantries, with some light dragoons and a company of rifleman — in all about nine hundred men. After arriving at Cook's Mills they destroyed about two hundred bushels of wheat.

The next morning, a British column under the command of Lieutenant Colonel Christopher Myers arrived. Myers had about 750 men, consisting of the 82nd Regiment, detachments of the Glengarry Light Infantry, the flank companies of the 100th and 104th regiments, and a detachment of Royal Artillery. After a sharp skirmish the American force was finally compelled to withdraw. In the subsequent reports filed by each officer, both sides claimed a victory. A cairn commemorating the skirmish has been placed by the Historic Sites and Monuments Board of Canada, and is located at the corner of Matthews Road and East Main Street in east Welland.

# CHAPTER 11
## HAMILTON AND VICINITY

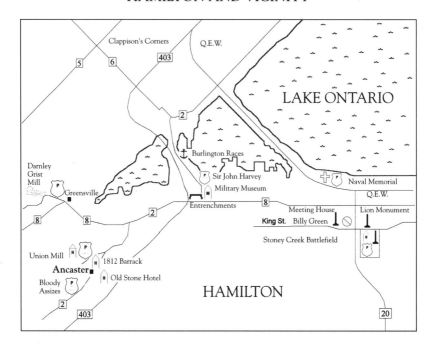

## STONEY CREEK BATTLEFIELD — STONEY CREEK, ONTARIO

After the fall of Fort George on May 27, 1813, Brigadier General John Vincent's army retreated to Burlington Heights, just west of present-day Hamilton. The American Army under Brigadier General John Chandler slowly followed to Stoney Creek, where on the evening of June 5th they encamped. Chandler's army numbered over three thousand men, and included field artillery and some dragoons. General Vincent had with him about seven hundred regulars from the 8th and 49th regiments. The situation was grim, for if the British retreated any further, the whole of the Niagara Peninsula would be under American control. There are several stories concerning Stoney Creek. One concerns the scouting of the American camp and the other with the obtaining of the password.

The reconnaissance story was told by Mary Agnes FitzGibbon in 1894 and concerns her grandfather, Lieutenant FitzGibbon of the 49th Regiment. In this story, FitzGibbon disguised himself as a farmer selling butter, and made his way into the American camp where he studied the dispositions and noted their weaknesses. He later returned to Colonel Harvey, and based on FitzGibbon's report, General Vincent approved the night attack.

The obtaining of the password to the American lines was an incredible piece of luck, which so often occurs in war. Young "Billy Green" had obtained the password from his brother-in-law Isaac Corman, who had been briefly held in the American camp. Corman in turn had obtained it from a gullible U.S. soldier. Billy went on to Burlington Heights where he related the information to Colonel Harvey. FitzGibbon's reconnaissance of the enemy camp had shown that the American positions were scattered about and not in supporting distance of each other. Now armed with the American countersign, Harvey urged General Vincent to launch a night bayonet assault on the American positions.

With a hand picked force of seven hundred regulars, Harvey moved towards the American lines at about 11:00 pm. With flints removed from their muskets to prevent premature firing, the British troops bayoneted the American sentries who were posted at a meeting house just to the west of the main position. Past midnight, the British hit the American main line, and in a nightmarish action of bayonet thrusts and musket shots at close range, the American forces were thrown into confusion. In the general melee, the two senior ranking American generals, Winder and Chandler, were captured near the Gage House. After that, the American command system broke down, and unaware of the size of the force opposing them, they retreated, taking the road to Fort George. The British also decided to leave the field, lest daylight should expose their inferior numbers. Colonel Harvey had become separated from the rest of his men, and when the British left the vicinity, they assumed he had been captured. The next morning, he was found miles from the battlefield by the famous Mohawk John Brant, son of Chief Joseph Brant.

Stoney Creek was one of the most decisive battles of the War of 1812. It yielded important results far out of proportion to the size of the forces engaged and it affected the entire American strategy for 1813. After Stoney Creek, the American Army abandoned its offensive against Burlington, and were content with defensive measures in the vicinity of Fort George.

Over the past one hundred years, the Stoney Creek battlefield has been slowly absorbed by the growing city of Hamilton, but some of the historic ground is still preserved. The American generals, Chandler and Winder, pitched their headquarters' tents by the Gage House, which still stands today. The Stoney Creek Monument was dedicated on the one-hundredth anniversary of the battle, on June 6, 1913. The monument was unveiled by Queen Mary, who pushed a button in England and electronically opened the ceremony. This impressive monument towers above the ridge, where the American Army encamped over 180 years ago. Gage House is open to the public and features tour guides in period dress and a small display area on the Battle of Stoney Creek. An Ontario Provincial Plaque dedicated to the battle is located on the grounds near the house.

## LION MONUMENT — STONEY CREEK, ONTARIO

This impressive monument marks the resting place of soldiers, both British and American, who were interred here during the War of 1812. The monument is located on a small knoll where the American cannons were posted during the battle. In 1972 the American Legion placed a marker at the site, which honours U.S. soldiers killed in the War of 1812. The monument is located on King Street near the intersection of Battlefield Drive in the town of Stoney Creek.

## BATTLEFIELD HOUSE — STONEY CREEK, ONTARIO

This house, constructed in 1795, was inhabited by the Gage family during the War of 1812. On the evening of June 5, 1813, the American Army under generals Chandler and Winder encamped in this vicinity, both generals pitching their tents close by the house. During the ensuing Battle of Stoney Creek the house was hit numerous times by musket balls. After the War of 1812 the Gage family continued to live in the house. James Gage eventually expanded the structure, and by the 1830s it was considered a spacious and moderately elegant home.

Today the house is called "Battlefield House" and is administered by the Niagara Parks Commission. In July and August, guides in period dress take visitors on a guided tour of the house. Featured also is a small museum, with an audio-visual presentation on the Battle of Stoney Creek, and a small gift shop is located in the basement. "Battlefield House" is located in the town of Stoney Creek, at the intersection of King St. and Highway 20. The one-hundred-foot monument dedicated to the battle is immediately in front of the house.

## OLD MEETING HOUSE SITE — STONEY CREEK, ONTARIO

On the evening of June 5, 1813, the American Army encamped around the home of James Gage. At an old "meeting house," which used to stand at this site, they posted sentinels. When the British forces under Colonel Harvey advanced against the American position, they bayoneted the American pickets that were located here. The old meeting house was torn down in 1871, and presently a modern church and cemetery occupy the site. The meeting house site is not marked, but there is a monument to the scout "Billy Green," who was instrumental in the British victory, in the cemetery. They are located near the corner of King Street and Centennial Parkway in the town of Stoney Creek. (see next entry)

# BILLY GREEN MONUMENT — STONEY CREEK, ONTARIO

A gravestone-type monument honours General Harvey, Billy Green, and Isaac Corman for the part they played in the Battle of Stoney Creek. The inscriptions reads "In Memory of General Harvey British Gen. who had command at Battle of Stoney Creek June 6 1813. In Memory of Billy Green the Scout who led British troops in surprise night attack winning Decisive Battle of Stoney Creek born Feb. 4 1794 Died Mar. 15 1877. In Memory of Isaac Corman who gave the password to Billy Green who in turn gave it to Gen. Harvey camped at Burlington Heights." The monument is in the cemetery near the corner of King Street and Centennial Parkway, in Stoney Creek, Ontario.

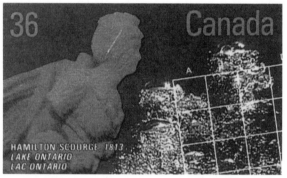

The *Hamilton — Scourge* stamp issued by Canada Post on August 7, 1987

## *HAMILTON– SCOURGE* MEMORIAL — HAMILTON, ONTARIO

On the evening of August 7, 1813, two American schooners, *Hamilton* and *Scourge*, capsized suddenly in a gale on Lake Ontario. There were only sixteen survivors out of a combined crew of over one hundred. The exact location of the vessels and their condition was unknown for over 160 years. But in 1973 both vessels were discovered by utilizing side-scan sonar. Amazingly, the fresh water and intense cold have kept the vessels perfectly preserved.

The Hamilton–Scourge Foundation hopes one day to raise the vessels for public display. For the present, they have erected a memorial garden, dedicated to those who lost their lives in the tragic accident. The memorial garden features a tombstone for each sailor who lost his life, a plaque, and a full-size replica of the foremast of the *Scourge*. The memorial garden is located in Confederation Park in the city of Hamilton.

## BURLINGTON HEIGHTS — HAMILTON, ONTARIO

Burlington Heights overlooks Lake Ontario on the outskirts of present-day Hamilton. On the evening of May 29, 1813, the British, under Brigadier General John Vincent, arrived here in their retreat from Fort George. A depot was constructed, and three fortified lines were erected, with the left flank resting by the lake. It was here that Vincent had an ominous decision to make. Should he make a stand against the more numerous American Army, or retreat? If he retreated, the entire Niagara Peninsula would be under the control of the enemy.

His final decision was suggested by Lieutenant Colonel Harvey. Based on intelligence received from Lieutenant FitzGibbon, and having been informed of the American password from scout Billy Green, Harvey advocated a night bayonet attack. Vincent approved the plan, and this resulted in the decisive battle of Stoney Creek, which completely reversed the strategic picture, and put the American Army on the defence.

Burlington Heights is now a pleasant park and there are several markers indicating the importance of the position. The Wentworth Historical Society has marked the spot of the first fortified line with a stone marker and cannon. The plaque placed by the Historic Sites and Monuments Board of Canada is located in Harvey Park. A small marker, which commemorates United States soldiers who died in the

War of 1812, has been placed by the American Legion. Across the road in the Hamilton Cemetery are some outstanding remains of the fortifications erected by the British, and these are indicated by a large stone marker imbedded in the earth. Burlington Heights is easily reached from York Boulevard in the city of Hamilton.

## SIR JOHN HARVEY — HARVEY PARK, ONTARIO

On the afternoon of June 5, 1813, Sir John Harvey, with the light companies of the 8th and 49th regiments, reconnoitered the American positions at Stoney Creek. After his reconnaissance, he suggested to General Vincent that an attack on the American camp would be feasible. Under Harvey's leadership, the resulting Battle of Stoney Creek was a turning point in the war. An Ontario Provincial Plaque, located on Burlington Heights in Harvey Park, describes the battle and the later career of this daring soldier.

## THE BURLINGTON RACES — HARVEY PARK, ONTARIO

In 1813, the Lake Ontario British squadron was under the command of Sir James Lucas Yeo, and the U.S squadron was commanded by Commodore Isaac Chauncey. In September, both fleets moved back and forth the length of the lake in a series of manoeuvres that became known as "The Burlington Races."

On September 28th, the two fleets came within cannon range of each other. In the light winds that prevailed, the fleets did not close to point-blank range, but Yeo's flagship *Wolfe* lost her main and mizzen top masts to American long-range gunfire.

With his flagship damaged, James Yeo retired the fleet to the protection of the batteries on Burlington Heights. Chauncey's flagship *General Pike* sustained some underwater damage, and parts of her crew were forced to man the pumps. With the east wind freshening, Chauncey could not afford to risk his fleet in the confined area at the head of the lake. He therefore put about and bore the fleet away. An Ontario Provincial Plaque located in Harvey Park, city of Hamilton, describes the action.

## HAMILTON MILITARY MUSEUM — DUNDURN PARK, HAMILTON, ONTARIO

The Hamilton Military Museum highlights the role played by Hamilton's citizens in various military conflicts. There are displays on the War of 1812, and a period map shows the positions of the British forces on Burlington Heights. The museum is located in Dundurn Park, next to Dundurn Castle, in the city of Hamilton.

## DARNLEY GRIST MILL — GREENSVILLE, ONTARIO

Grist mills were of great importance to the British Army during the war, and as a result they were important military targets. The Darnley Grist Mill managed to survive the War of 1812, although it is in ruins today. The walls still stand, but a sign warns that they are unstable, and should be explored with caution. A marker, placed by the Hamilton Region Conservation Authority, tells the mills history. The ruins are in the Crooks Hollow Conservation Area, on Crooks Hollow Road, one-half mile west of Greensville, Ontario.

# UNION MILL — ANCASTER, ONTARIO

This old grist mill, built in 1790, housed condemned prisoners for the Ancaster Assizes in 1814. The mill was the only place in Ancaster where the prisoners could be held with any security, and they were kept in a stone chamber beneath the main floor. The mill was rebuilt again in 1863, and now houses a trendy restaurant. The building is located on Mill Street, just off the old Dundas Road, in Ancaster, Ontario.

# ANCASTER ASSIZES — ANCASTER, ONTARIO

On June 7, 1814, a series of trials began for nineteen condemned Upper Canadians accused of treason. Two weeks later, fifteen of the prisoners were condemned to death.

Seven of the condemned men had the death penalty waived, but on July 20th, the other eight were hanged at Ancaster. An Ontario Provincial Plaque in front of the Ancaster Memorial School on Wilson Street in Ancaster describes the trials.

# 1812 BARRACKS — ANCASTER, ONTARIO

Local tradition says that the building was used as a barracks during the War of 1812. However, it seems more likely that soldiers may have billeted here in an earlier structure that once stood on this site. The building still remains, although now it is used as a commercial structure. A wooden sign on the front of the building simply indicates "1812 Barracks." The building is located at 423–425 Wilson Street in the town of Ancaster.

# OLD STONE HOTEL — ANCASTER, ONTARIO

The old Rousseau Hotel has had a long association with the town of Ancaster. It was constructed by one of the town's first settlers, Jean Baptiste Rousseau, in 1797. The first structure was made of heavy logs, and stood across the street from the present site. The hotel was rebuilt, and later leased to one Plumer Burleyn, the owner of the local stage coach line. Under Mr. Burleyn's proprietorship, the front of the hotel was redone in stone, which is what we see today.

During the War of 1812 the hotel was used as a hospital for British soldiers, but General Vincent had it cleared temporarily for the "Ancaster Assizes Trials" in 1814. The hotel was chosen since it was the only building large enough to hold the crowd, and it was close to Vincent's army based at Burlington Heights.

Over the years, the hotel has been owned by various families, and as with most structures of this vintage, two fires are of note. The fire of January, 1878 destroyed only the stable, but a second fire that summer gutted the interior. What remains today are the exterior stone walls of the structure. The hotel is now a commercial building, and is located at the 380–386 block on Wilson Street in the town of Ancaster.

# CHAPTER 12
## TORONTO AND VICINITY

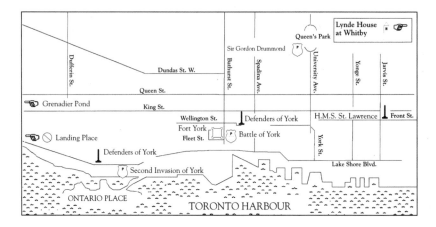

Dufferin St.

Dundas St. W.

Bathurst St.

Spadina Ave.

Sir Gordon Drummond

Queen's Park

University Ave.

Yonge St.

Jarvis St.

Lynde House at Whitby

Queen St.

Grenadier Pond

King St.

Wellington St.

Defenders of York

H.M.S. St. Lawrence

Front St.

Landing Place

Fort York
Fleet St.

Battle of York

York St.

Defenders of York

Second Invasion of York

Lake Shore Blvd.

ONTARIO PLACE

TORONTO HARBOUR

## THE BATTLE OF YORK — FORT YORK

On April 27, 1813, the American squadron under Commodore Chauncey appeared off of York harbour. On board was an army under Major General Henry Dearborn numbering some 1700 troops. Chauncey's intention was to land the troops at the site of old Fort Rouille, now on the grounds of the Canadian National Exhibition. However, adverse winds blew the boats further west, and the first troops ashore landed near present-day Sunnyside Beach. These troops were Major Forsyth's veteran riflemen, forming the advanced guard under General Zebulon Pike. At this spot they encountered a small party of British regulars and Indians, and after a thirty-minute skirmish, they forced the British to retreat.

At the western battery, about one-half mile west of Fort York, the British rallied, and it was here that a dreadful accident occurred. The battery's travelling magazine accidentally exploded, and the grenadier company of the 8th Regiment was practically wiped out. Not long after, the American fleet moved closer inshore and began to bombard the British. With his outnumbered regulars in an untenable position, and unable to hold the town, General Sheaffe decided to retreat to Kingston. His last order was to blow up the magazine of Fort York, but in the confusion of the hour, the fort's flag was left flying.

The Americans still believed the British were inside and lingered in the vicinity. When the magazine did explode the effects were frightening, as tons of earth, stone, timber, and debris rained down on the Americans. General Pike, along with a British sergeant he was interrogating, was crushed by a huge rock. On learning of Pike's death General Dearborn was rowed ashore from the fleet, and began negotiations for the surrender of the town. The American Army remained in York for six days, and were quite an annoyance to the civilian population. The American military freed the prisoners from the jail and much looting took place. The Provincial Parliament buildings were burned, an act that was to be remembered by the British in 1814.

The raid on York was an important American success, but its full impact was not appreciated until later. This was because valuable naval stores, destined for Lake Erie, had been destroyed in the raid. When Captain Barclay eventually fought the Battle of Lake Erie that September, he did so at a great disadvantage. His fleet was in sore need of those naval stores, and his flagship's main armament was missing. As a result, the flagship *Detroit* finally sailed with a variety of cannons taken from the ramparts of Fort Malden!

The destruction of the new corvette *Isaac Brock*, which was burned on the stocks by the American Army, was another grave setback for the British. The loss of even this single vessel affected the delicate naval balance on Lake Ontario. The Ontario Provincial Plaque commemorating the raid is located at the entrance to Fort York.

## THE SECOND INVASION OF YORK — CORONATION PARK

On July 31, 1813, the American fleet returned to York, but this time the invasion was unopposed, for the British forces had marched to Burlington. Commodore Chauncey landed some infantry and marines, who proceeded to look for military stores. They eventually discovered several hundred barrels of flour and provisions, five artillery pieces, and eleven boats, which they destroyed or carried off. On August 1st they burned the barracks and public store house before embarking on their fleet, and then proceeded to Niagara. The Ontario Provincial Plaque, commemorating the second raid on York, is located in Coronation Park, east of the Canadian National Exhibition grounds.

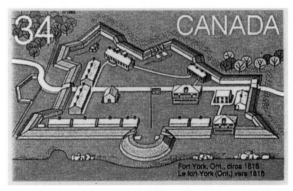

The stamp issued by Canada Post dedicated to Fort York

## FORT YORK — TORONTO

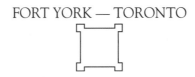

Fort York was constructed by the Queen's Rangers in 1796 under the direction of Lieutenant-Governor John Graves Simcoe. Just prior to the War of 1812, it was strengthened by Major General Isaac Brock. On April 27, 1813, during the Battle of York, the grand magazine was exploded by the retreating British, and when the American forces vacated York on May 2, they burned the fort.

During the second occupation of the town on July 31, the American forces destroyed the barracks and blockhouses on Gibraltar Point at the entrance to the harbour. In the fall of 1813, the fort was reconstructed and strengthened under the orders of Major General Baron de Rottenburg, who had new barracks, blockhouses, and earth fortifications added. Presently, eight of the original buildings remain. Guided tours of the fort are offered by guides in 1812 uniform. The fort is located on Garrison Road, off of Fleet Street, near the grounds of the Canadian National Exhibition.

## EXPLOSION OF THE GRAND MAGAZINE — FORT YORK

A marker inside Fort York is located near the site of the Grand Magazine, which exploded during the Battle of York, April 27, 1813.

## LANDING PLACE OF THE AMERICANS — SUNNYSIDE BEACH

Sunnyside Beach is the location where the American Army landed on April 27, 1813. Pushing aside the outnumbered defenders, they took the town of York, which they held for six days. Presently the site is unmarked.

## "GRENADIER POND" — HIGH PARK, TORONTO

During the first Battle of York, the grenadier company of the 8th Regiment and a party of Indians were deployed in this vicinity to harass the American landing. As successive waves of U.S. soldiers came ashore, they were forced to fall back. A local myth relates that in the retreat two grenadiers drowned when the ice cracked beneath them, hence the name. Historian Carl Benn has pointed out that the name likely comes from the fact that the garrison used to fish from the pond during their leisure time. Though a sign identifies Grenadier Pond, there is no historical marker located at the site. The pond is located at the south end of High Park, not far from Sunnyside Beach.

## TWIN LION MONUMENT — EXHIBITION GROUNDS, TORONTO

A plaque placed by the Chapters of the Imperial Order Daughters of the Empire is fixed to a monument with two Lions that face Lake Ontario. It is dedicated to those defenders of York who lost their lives on April 27, 1813 during the Battle of York. The monument is located on the grounds of the Canadian National Exhibition, adjacent to Lake Shore Boulevard.

## SIR GORDON DRUMMOND — PARLIAMENT BUILDINGS

Gordon Drummond was one of the first native-born Canadians to achieve high rank in the British Army, and in the fall of 1813 he assumed the civil and military command of Upper Canada. His winter campaign at the end of 1813, which was in retaliation for the burning of Newark, resulted in the capture of Fort Niagara and the destruction of Buffalo. In 1814 he commanded the troops at the Battle of Lundy's Lane, the Siege of Fort Erie, and the raid on Oswego. An Ontario Provincial Plaque, dedicated to this gallant officer, is located inside the entrance to the main Parliament building in Toronto.

## H.M.S. ST. LAWRENCE — ST. LAWRENCE MARKET, TORONTO

This monument is dedicated to two famous vessels in Canadian history, Lasalle's *Griffon*, which was launched in 1679 and mysteriously lost, and *St. Lawrence*, the only Ship of the Line to ever sail Lake Ontario. *St. Lawrence* was launched September 10, 1814, from the Kingston navy yards, and became the flagship of Commodore Sir James Lucas Yeo. The huge vessel carried 104 guns, and with her launching, the British held undisputed command of Lake Ontario until the end of the war.

This odd medallion-type monument was originally located in the memorial arch at Clifton Gate in Niagara Falls. When the gate was demolished in 1967, the stone medallions were preserved by the Niagara Parks Commission. The monument is now located at the northeast corner of Front and Jarvis Streets, across from the St. Lawrence Market in downtown Toronto.

## DEFENCE OF YORK — VICTORIA SQUARE, TORONTO

This monument commemorates those who lost their lives for the defence of Canada during the War of 1812. The monument was erected by veterans of the British army and navy and the citizens of York on July 1, 1902. The monument features a soldier of the War of 1812, his cap removed and eyes looking pensively towards heaven.

Four bronze plaques are affixed to the monument and list the various engagements of the war, the regiments that served, and a special plaque recalls defence of York. At the base of the monument are headstones from the old garrison cemetery. This simple but impressive monument is located in Victoria Square, near Bathurst Street, in downtown Toronto.

## JABEZ LYNDE HOUSE — WHITBY, ONTARIO

United Empire Loyalist Jabez Lynde built this two-storey clapboard house between 1812 and 1814, but the exact date of construction is unknown. The 1812 date seems more probable, as the house was financed by proceeds from the British Army. The war brought boom times to some settlers, and the location of Mr. Lynde's tavern, on the main road to York, made it an ideal place of commerce.

Horses were kept here for the use of dispatch riders, and Mr. Lynde's own sons, Sylvester and Hawkins, were employed as such during the war. At various times General Brock's officers were entertained at the house, and Brock himself visited the tavern in the winter of 1811 on his way to York. On this occasion Mr. Lynde guided Brock and his aide Colonel Drummond to York, and it was recorded that the journey took three hours and five minutes to the doorstep of Government House.

The house originally stood on the corner of Dundas and D'Hiller Streets in Whitby. In 1988, it was faced with destruction from a local developer, and the house was moved to its present location in Cullen Gardens. The house has been lovingly restored, and depicts life as it would have been for the Lynde family in the 1850s. The house features animated creations and sounds, which make the old Georgian house come alive once more. A heritage building plaque, dedicated by the town of Whitby, is located just outside the house. In the yard is an inscribed boulder dedicated to the memory of Jabez Lynde, who first settled here in 1800. The house is located at the entrance to the Cullen Gardens at 300 Taunton Road West near Whitby, Ontario.

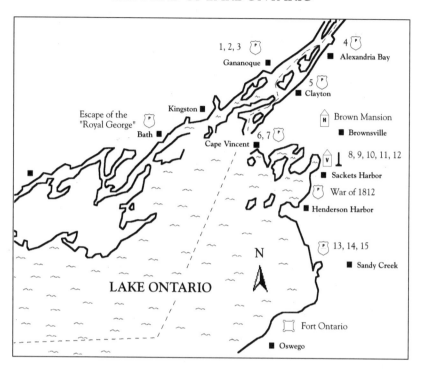

1. Gananoque
2. Raid on Gananoque
3. Colonel Joel Stone
4. Battle at Cranberry Creek
5. Action at French Creek
6. 1812 Barracks
7. Fort Haldimand
8. Sackets Harbor Battlefield

9. War of 1812 Monument
10. Sacket Mansion
11. Military Cemetery
12. Fort Chauncey
13. Battle of Sandy Creek
14. Carrying of the Cable
15. Hospital

## THE ESCAPE OF THE *ROYAL GEORGE* — BATH, ONTARIO

On the morning of November 9, 1812 the British corvette *Royal George* was intercepted by the brig *Oneida* and six schooners, under the command of Commodore Chauncey. The *Royal George*

managed to escape her pursuers by entering the Bay of Quinte, but the next day she was again spotted by the American squadron and chased into Kingston Harbour. Chauncey's schooners proceeded to engage the Kingston shore batteries, in an attempt to get into the inner harbour and destroy the *Royal George*. The long-range barrage continued for a few hours, but when the wind freshened, Chauncey bore the squadron away, sustaining some minor damage. For the *Royal George* it had been a close call.

The *Royal George* went on to participate in more naval actions than any other British vessel during the war. She was renamed *Niagara* by admiralty order on January 22, 1814. After the war she served as a transport vessel, and after her sale in 1837 she disappears from the navy list. An Ontario Provincial Plaque, adjacent to Highway 2 west of Bath, Ontario, describes the escape of this heroic vessel.

## GANANOQUE, ONTARIO

Gananoque was the last staging point for convoys of bateaux entering Lake Ontario, and as a consequence was an important point on the supply route linking Upper and Lower Canada. After Forsyth's raid, British authorities were alerted to its vulnerability, and a blockhouse was constructed there which was garrisoned by various regiments during the war. A plaque placed by the Historic Sites and Monuments Board of Canada is located on Stone Street in Gananoque. (see next entry)

# RAID ON GANANOQUE — GANANOQUE, ONTARIO

On the early morning of September 21, 1812, Captain Benjamin Forsyth, with one company of the United States Rifle Regiment and thirty militia, crossed the St. Lawrence River from Cape Vincent, New York. Landing two miles west of Gananoque at Sheriff's Point, their objective was to destroy a quantity of ammunition and other supplies that were rumoured to be there. Previous intelligence disclosed that Gananoque was lightly defended, but when they moved towards the village they were spotted by two British dragoons who gave the alarm. The flank companies of the Leeds Militia tried to oppose them, but they were no match for Forsyth's disciplined corps.

Upon entering the town, they destroyed foodstuffs and other property, and ransacked the home of Joel Stone, the commander of the Leeds Militia. At the Stone residence, a stray musket ball hit Mrs. Stone in the hip, a wound from which she never fully recovered. After seizing the arms and ammunition the raiding party retreated

Forsyth's raid was small but significant, for it alerted the British to the vulnerability of their supply lines, and from then on Gananoque was fortified and convoys were escorted. An Ontario Provincial Plaque describing the raid is on the grounds of the Gananoque Power company in the town of Gananoque.

# COLONEL JOEL STONE — GANANOQUE, ONTARIO

Colonel Joel Stone was born in Connecticut and served with the loyalist forces during the American Revolution. Having lost everything in his home state, he moved to Canada in 1786, and by the time of the War of 1812 he was Colonel of the 2nd Leeds Militia. During the raid on Gananoque in September of 1812, he commanded two companies of the militia, but was unable to hold off the invaders. An Ontario Provincial Plaque dedicated to him is located in front of the town hall in Gananoque.

# FORT HALDIMAND — CARLETON ISLAND, NEW YORK

In 1778 the new Governor-in-Chief of Canada, Frederick Haldimand, directed that a new fort be constructed in the vicinity of Cataraqui (present day Kingston). Buck Island, renamed Carleton Island, was chosen as the site, and the new fort was named for the governor. By the end of the American Revolution it was a substantial work, with barracks, bastions, and blockhouses. Under the terms of Jay's Treaty, the fort was to have been ceded to the Americans, but in 1812 it was still occupied by the British.

Upon the declaration of war, a local tavern keeper from New York named Abner Hubbard decided he would seize the fort from the British. Gathering up a few neighbours they rowed out to the fort and took possession. But this was in no way comparable to Ethan Allan's dramatic capture of Fort Ticonderoga in 1776, for the garrison of Fort Haldimand consisted of only three soldiers and two women! Fort Haldimand remained in American hands throughout the War of 1812, but served no useful function. It was formally annexed in 1817 and has been a part of the United States ever since.

Presently the fort site is on private lands and may not be visited. Some earthworks remain at the western extremity of the island. A "Seaway Guidebook" marker is located on the west side of town in Cape Vincent, New York.

# 1812 BARRACKS — CAPE VINCENT, NEW YORK

A New York State Historical Plaque simply states that a barracks was erected here during the War of 1812. The marker is located near the ferry landing in Cape Vincent.

The Brown Mansion and vicinity as Lossing sketched it in 1867

## BROWN MANSION — BROWNVILLE, NEW YORK

General Jacob Brown, a successful commander during the War of 1812, was born in Bucks County, Pennsylvania in 1775. He had a varied career teaching school, surveying lands, and studying law, and in 1799 had purchased a tract of land that would eventually become the small settlement of Brownville. In 1809 he received a commission as Colonel in the New York State Militia, and the following year was promoted to Brigadier General.

At the commencement of the War of 1812, he was given command of the district covering the south shore of the St. Lawrence River and the eastern frontier of Lake Ontario. It was not long before he attracted the favourable notice of the administration, and was given command of a regular regiment in the U.S. Army. For his successful defence of Sackets Harbor on May 29, 1813, he was promoted to Brigadier General of Regulars. During General Wilkinson's autumn campaign to capture Montreal, he was in command of the advanced guard. But in an oddity of the campaign, it was the rear guard that fought the main action, where it was defeated at the Battle of Crysler's Farm on November 11th.

Fortunately for Brown's career he was not present, he being with the head of the army at the Long Sault Rapids. With the "illness" of General Wilkinson, Brown was promoted to Major General, and given command of the army.

Acting under ambiguous orders from Secretary of War John Armstrong, Brown marched his troops to the Niagara Frontier in the spring of 1814. Once there, he embarked on a rigorous training programme to bring his regulars "up to par."

At the beginning of July, his army crossed the Niagara River and captured Fort Erie. On July 5th, he defeated the British under General Riall at the Battle of Chippawa, and twenty days later fought the bloodiest battle of the war at Lundy's Lane, where he was wounded twice. Though both sides claimed the victory, Brown had to withdraw to Fort Erie, where his army was later besieged by General Drummond. Brown was convalescing from his wounds, and did not sally forth from Fort Erie until September 17th. On this occasion, a number of British batteries were captured and this raised the siege. When General Izard took command of the army, Brown saw no further action in the war and after the Treaty of Ghent, quietly retired to his home at Brownville. In 1821 he was called to Washington as General in Chief of the Army, and he served in this capacity until his death in 1828.

The Brown Mansion as it appears today.

Construction of the Brown Mansion, built principally of blue limestone, was started in 1814 and completed the next year. Several important people have stayed at the mansion, including President Monroe, Joseph Bonaparte, Oliver Hazard Perry, and General Winfield Scott. The General Brown Mansion is operated by several organizations, among them the Village of Brownville, the Committee for the Restoration of the Brown Mansion, and the General Jacob Brown Historical Society. There are two historic plaques at the locatio., One gives a history of Brown's career and is affixed to the house. The other is the State Historical Marker and is located in front. The building is in the village of Brownville about four miles northwest of Watertown, New York. The home has limited hours of operation, but is open to the public.

## SACKETS HARBOR BATTLEFIELD — SACKETS HARBOR, NEW YORK

The town of Sackets Harbor was the main naval base for the American Navy on Lake Ontario, and every major war vessel that sailed the lake was constructed here. As a result it became the target of two British attacks. The first was on July 19, 1812 when the Provincial Marine arrived off of the harbour. This squadron was under the command of Lieutenant Hugh Earle, and he had with him the *Royal George*, *Earl of Moira*, *Prince Regent*, and *Duke of Gloucester*. The real objective of the raid was to capture the brig *Oneida*, which had just fled from Earle's squadron that morning.

At one point, the *Oneida* decided to make a run for it, but Earle's squadron cut the brig off and forced it to retreat into the harbour. The *Oneida*'s crew then landed some of the vessel's guns, and with a large thirty-two pound-cannon, began firing at Earle's flagship, the *Royal George*. But the *Royal George* was armed with only short-range carronades, and in this unequal contest the British fleet bore away.

The second attack of May 29, 1813 was a much more formidable affair whose objective was to destroy the base. This venture was under the command of the General in Chief, Sir George Prevost and was accompanied by part of the Lake Ontario squadron under James Yeo. At the time of the attack the American squadron was away, supporting the army's assault on Fort George, at the mouth of the Niagara River. With Chauncey's fleet absent, it was an excellent opportunity to strike the harbour.

The expedition, consisting of the corvettes *Wolfe*, *Royal George*, the brig *Earl of Moira*, two armed schooners, two gunboats, and thirty bateaux arrived off the harbour on May 28th.

On board the fleet were 750 troops from the 8th, 100th, 104th, Royal Scots, Glengarry Light Infantry, Canadian Voltigeurs, and the Royal Artillery. Vacillating until the morning of the 29th, Prevost landed the troops on nearby Horse Island which was connected by a ford to the mainland.

General Brown arrayed his militia to resist the British attack, but as he surmised they broke at the first volley. Rallying them, he then deployed them on the British right flank as they pushed east towards the town. Unfortunately for Prevost, Yeo's squadron was unable to give him the close support he needed due to contrary winds. When the militia began to work around his right flank and rear, Prevost lost his nerve and decided to call the attack off.

The British retired to their fleet unmolested, but the engagement was far from conclusive. The only benefit gained for the British was the loss of American military and naval supplies when one of the buildings caught fire. British losses, however, were considerable, considering that the objective of the raid was not met. The attack had one benefit that no one at the time could appreciate, and that was that it undoubtedly unnerved Commodore Chauncey, who feared another attack on his base, and subsequently it affected his strategy.

Sackets Harbor Battlefield is now a State Historic Site which is marked with fifteen interpretive displays, highlighting various phases of the battle. Some of the more prominent themes are: the two battles of Sackets Harbor, Fort Kentucky, Smith's Cantonment, Fort Tompkins, and Navy Point. The Commandant and the Lieutenant's house have been restored and are open to the public. The battlefield is administered by the State of New York, Office of Parks and Recreation and is located in the town of Sackets Harbor. The Official Visitor Centre for the town of Sackets Harbor has displays on local history and a very informative video presentation on the harbour's role in the War of 1812. The visitor centre is located in the old Sacket Mansion on West Main Street.

## 1812 MONUMENT — SACKETS HARBOR, NEW YORK

A small granite monument honours the officers and men who served on the northern frontier during the War of 1812, and commemorates the Battle of Sackets Harbor fought on May 29th, 1813. The monument was erected by the National Society of the United States Daughters of 1812, State of New York, Northern Frontier Chapter of Jefferson County. The monument is located on the battlefield near the Commandant's house.

## SACKET MANSION — SACKETS HARBOR, NEW YORK

The Sacket Mansion was built by Augustus Sacket in 1802, and was used as an officer's quarters and a hospital during the war. During the British raid on July 19th, 1812 a thirty-two-pound ball fired from the corvette *Royal George* plowed its way up to the door of the mansion.

The ball was picked up by the American artillery under Capt. Vaughan and fired back at the British! The Sacket Mansion is currently the visitor centre for the town of Sackets Harbor. A New York State plaque is located in front of the mansion on West Main Street.

## FORT VIRGINIA — SACKETS HARBOR, NEW YORK

A New York State Marker identifies the site of Fort Virginia, which was part of the main defences of the town in 1813. The fort was a square work, complete with bastions and mounted sixteen guns, though there are no traces of the fort today. The marker is located on Washington Street near the corner of General Smith Drive.

## BLOCKHOUSE SITE — SACKETS HARBOR, NEW YORK

A New York State Marker identifies the site of an 1812 blockhouse, which along with nearby Fort Virginia, protected the southwest section of the town. There are no traces of the blockhouse today, but a photograph of it is on display in the Sacket Mansion. The marker is located on Washington Street just in front of the George Tisdale House.

## FORT CHAUNCEY — SACKETS HARBOR, NEW YORK

Fort Chauncey was a minor fortification constructed in 1812, and featured a loopholed circular tower, which was built to withstand small arms fire. After the war the fortification was abandoned, and eventually the expanding town of Sackets Harbor absorbed the site. There are no above-ground remains today, but a New York State Marker is located on North Broad Street in the town of Sackets Harbor.

## WOOLSEY HOUSE — SACKETS HARBOR, NEW YORK

Lieutenant Melanchton Woolsey commanded the brig *Oneida* during the War of 1812. He participated in the defence of Sackets Harbor in July of 1812, and was present for Commodore Chauncey's attack on Kingston Harbour in November 1812. He was also in the skirmish at Sandy Creek, and the raid on Oswego in 1814. He built this house, which was also known as "Camp Haven," in 1816. The building is privately owned and not open to the public, but is on the Walking Tour of Sackets Harbor.

## SACKETS HARBOR MILITARY CEMETERY

After the War of 1812, many soldiers who had been buried in unmarked graves were transferred to the cemetery at Madison Barracks in Sackets Harbor. In 1908 these remains were transferred to the military cemetery here.

One of the famous officers who lies buried here is General Zebulon Pike, who was killed in the Battle of York on April 27, 1813. Although he is usually remembered for the famous peak named after him in Colorado. There are two monuments in the cemetery which honour the fallen of the War of 1812. The cemetery is located on Dodge Avenue just opposite the village cemetery in Sackets Harbor.

## SAMUEL GUTHRIE HOUSE — SACKETS HARBOR, NEW YORK

Samuel Guthrie was a surgeon in the War of 1812 and built this Georgian-style brick house in 1818. Guthrie is more famous for his experiments with "chloric ether," which led to the discovery of "chloroform" in medical applications. A New York State Marker is located in front of his house on the old Watertown Road (Dodge Street), just outside of town.

## FORT VOLUNTEER — SACKETS HARBOR, NEW YORK

Fort Volunteer was part of the main defence work for the town of Sackets Harbor. It was also known as Fort Pike, for Zebulon Pike who was killed at the Battle of York. Its main function was to protect the north end of the harbour, overlooking Black River Bay, and during the second battle of Sackets Harbor its guns were actively engaged. The site today has remains of period earthworks and a state marker. The fort is located on the grounds of Madison Barracks, in the town of Sackets Harbor.

## CARRYING THE CABLE — SACKETS HARBOR, NEW YORK

In the naval convoy that left Oswego on May 28, 1814 was a cable weighing over nine tons, which was destined for the frigate *Superior*, then under construction at Sackets Harbor. After the successful defence of the convoy, which was attacked by the British the next day, the cable had to be carried overland to the harbour. An entire week was lost in trying to find a vehicle that was capable of carrying the immense cable, but none being available, volunteers from Colonel Allan Clark's militia regiment agreed to carry it on their shoulders. Two hundred men joined up for the arduous duty. Leaving at noon and taking rest stops every mile, they managed to bring the cable to Sackets Harbor the next evening. A monument to this amazing sidelight of the War of 1812 is located on State Route 75 at the intersection with Route 3, just outside Sackets Harbor. The route that the volunteers took has been marked with similar markers at three other locations.

## BARTLETT'S POINT — CLAYTON, NEW YORK

A New York State Historical Marker identifies Bartlett's Point as the site of a battery in November of 1813. The marker is located on Highway 37 just south of Clayton, New York.

# ACTION AT FRENCH CREEK — CLAYTON, NEW YORK

On October 29, 1813 General Jacob Brown's brigade, forming the advance guard of General Wilkinson's army, encamped for the night at French Creek (present-day Clayton). On November 1st a British squadron under the command of Captain William H. Mulcaster approached the mouth of French Creek with the brigs *Melville* and *Earl of Moira*, the schooners *Sydney Smith* and *Beresford*, and four gunboats.

Mulcaster's intention was to disrupt the American troops as much as possible in their descent on Montreal. In the confines of the bay he anchored three of his vessels, which began exchanging gunfire with two brass eighteen-pound guns which had been placed on the west side of French Creek. The gunfire lasted until some of his vessels had been hit between "wind and water," and with darkness approaching, Mulcaster called off the action.

The next morning he renewed the effort, but during the night General Brown had deployed more cannons and the results were inconclusive, so Mulcaster once again withdrew. In this small action the British lost one man killed and four men wounded. American losses were two killed and four wounded. The small action at French Creek is marked only with the "Seaway Trail" marker, which is located in Clayton, New York.

# ACTION AT CRANBERRY CREEK — ALEXANDRIA BAY, NEW YORK

The St. Lawrence River was the vital supply line for the British Army during the War of 1812, and large convoys of bateaux travelled this route from Montreal to Kingston. But the supply line was vulnerable to attack from many quarters, especially so in the Thousand Islands. On July 19, 1812 one of these convoys, consisting of fifteen bateaux and the gunboat *Spitfire*, was making its way through the Thousand Islands. At 4:00 AM they were surprised by two American privateers, *Neptune* and *Fox*, and the entire convoy of over two hundred and seventy barrels of pork and sea bread was taken.

Making their way here to Cranberry Creek, the two privateers unloaded the supplies and built a breast work with the captured barrels. On July 21st the British arrived with four gunboats and some infantry to recapture the valuable supplies, but after exchanging gunfire for over two hours with the "pork barrel fort," the British gave up the attempt and withdrew.

The brig *Earl of Moira* was then stationed off of the creek to blockade the vessels, but the wily privateers managed to evade the *Moira* and safely deliver the supplies. It was small actions like this that caused the British to tie up valuable men and resources in securing the supply line on the St. Lawrence. Presently this action is commemorated only with the "Seaway Trail" marker, which is located near the shore at Alexandria Bay, New York.

## WAR OF 1812 — HENDERSON HARBOR, NEW YORK

A large plaque near Henderson Harbor outlines the major campaigns of the War of 1812 fought in the State of New York. A "Seaway Trail" marker dedicated to Naval Operations on the lakes is also located there. The plaque is located at the Henderson Harbor Overlook on Route 3.

## BATTLE OF SANDY CREEK — SANDY CREEK, NEW YORK

On the evening of May 28, 1814, a convoy of naval supplies left Oswego under the command of Captain Melanchton Woolsey and was accompanied by a detachment of 130 riflemen under Major Appling. The convoy was carrying thirty-five cannons and heavy cables, which were vital to the vessels being constructed at Sackets Harbor. Hugging the shore to avoid British patrols, they rendezvoused with a detachment of friendly Oneida Indians at the Big Salmon River.

The next morning one of the boats became lost in the fog and was captured by the British. From intelligence gained from the crew, Commodore James Yeo sent out two gunboats, two cutters, and a gig to intercept the convoy. These were put under the command of Captain Popham and Captain Spilsbury. On May 29th, the British vessels cruised the lake, looking for the American convoy, but all to no avail. The next morning, Captain Popham learned from a local woman that the convoy was up the Big Sandy Creek. In the meantime Commodore Woolsey had been reinforced by a detachment sent by General Gaines from Sackets Harbor. These consisted of a squadron of Cavalry, two light six-pound cannons, and some infantry, numbering about three hundred armed men.

Two miles from the mouth of the Big Sandy, the combined force waited in ambush for the British. When they sighted the convoy, the British began firing with their light cannons, but immediately afterwards were met by the fire from Major Appling's rifleman. The British were now in a trap, and surrounded by the riflemen on both banks of the creek, they were soon compelled to surrender. In the engagement the British lost eighteen men killed and their entire party captured. American losses were one rifleman killed and one Indian warrior wounded. The convoy was later unloaded near this spot and transported by land to Sackets Harbor. A metal plaque, part of the *Seaway Trail Guidebook to the War of 1812*, is located on Highway 3, between Pulaski, New York and Henderson, near Sandy Creek. (see next entry)

## CARRYING THE CABLE — SANDY CREEK, NEW YORK

This amazing little sidelight of the War of 1812 is mentioned on the same marker which commemorates the Battle of Sandy Creek. (see previous entry and Carrying the Cable, Sackets Harbor)

## HOSPITAL — SANDY CREEK, NEW YORK

A New York State plaque alongside Highway 3 near Sandy Creek points out the location of a period home that was used as a hospital after the Battle of Sandy Creek.

## FORT ONTARIO (OSWEGO) — OSWEGO, NEW YORK

The mouth of the Oswego River on Lake Ontario has been a strategic point since 1727, when the British built the first Fort Oswego on the western bank. By 1755 they had constructed a replacement fort on the east side of the river, and this was the fort that was attacked by the Marquis de Montcalm during the Seven Years' War and completely destroyed. In 1759 the British built a third fort and officially named it "Ontario," but period documents usually refer to it as "Oswego."

During the American Revolution, Barry St. Leger's expedition left here as part of Burgoyne's campaign, and the fort was later used as a base for numerous raids against the colonists. During the War of 1812 supplies moving up the Mohawk Valley, terminated at Oswego, and from there proceeded via Lake Ontario to Sackets Harbor. Oswego was an important supply depot and thus became a natural target during the war.

During the second week of June, 1813, the British naval squadron had been making sporadic raids on the south shore of Lake Ontario, and after the raid on Sodus, New York they appeared off of Oswego on June 20th. Sir James Lucas Yeo, the commander of the squadron, reconnoitred Oswego from the water, and believing it too strong to attack, bore the squadron away the next day.

On May 5, 1814 the entire British squadron once again appeared off of Oswego, but this time they came in force. It was hoped that by striking Oswego and destroying the naval supplies there, the American efforts on the lake would be crippled for the season. When the British squadron appeared, the schooner *Growler* under Captain Woolsey was moored in the Oswego River and, fearing its capture, Woolsey had the schooner sunk in the river.

The next day the British stationed the vessels to bombard the fort and landed about 1200 men under the command of General Drummond. The troops consisted of the flank companies of the De Wattville regiment, the light company of the Glengarry Fencibles, a battalion of marines, and two hundred seamen.

Fort Oswego was garrisoned by about three hundred regulars under Colonel Mitchell and mounted seven guns, but in the face of such numbers, Mitchell had little choice but to withdraw. Before retreating, his men inflicted eighteen men killed and seventy-three wounded on the British, while his losses were six killed, thirty-eight wounded, and twenty-five missing. The British captured 2,400 barrels of foodstuffs, seven cannons, and some ordnance stores. On May 7th, they dismantled the fort, burned the barracks, and departed in their squadron for Kingston.

Today Fort Ontario is administered by the New York State Office of Parks and Recreation and is open to the public. Most of the buildings and fortifications date from the American Civil War, but a portion of the wall between the New Hampshire Bastion and the Grenadier Bastion dates from 1812. The fort is located on the east bank of the Oswego River in the town of Oswego.

# CHAPTER 14
## KINGSTON

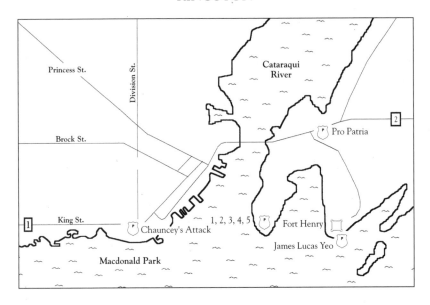

## CHAUNCEY'S ATTACK ON KINGSTON HARBOUR

After escaping from the American squadron by taking refuge in the Bay of Quinte, the British corvette *Royal George* continued her flight to Kingston Harbour. She anchored midway between the town and Point Frederick, opposite the point where the "Market Battery" marker is now located. In mid-afternoon of November 10, 1812 the American squadron under Commodore Isaac Chauncey bore down into the bay with the objective of destroying the *Royal George*. In the van were the schooners *Conquest*, *Julia*, *Pert*, and *Growler*.

Next in line was the brig *Oneida*, which was Commodore Chauncey's flagship, and following in the rear were the schooners *Hamilton* and *Governor Tompkins*. The American fleet was armed mainly with long guns except *Oneida*, which had only short-range carronades. The fleet directed their fire at the *Royal George* and the shore batteries that had been established at Point Frederick and Mississauga Point (presently the Market Battery site).

The *Royal George*'s main armament, much like *Oneida*'s, consisted of carronades, and she could do little in reply to the schooners which kept their distance and maintained a long-range cannonade. After an hour of receiving fire, the *Royal George* slipped her cable and moved further into the bay. Soon after the wind began to freshen towards shore, and with sundown approaching, the chances of destroying the *Royal George* were remote. Commodore Chauncey then hauled his wind and bore the squadron away.

Casualties for such a dramatic affair were light. One of the long guns on the *Pert* exploded, killing the sailing master and wounding four others, and on the *Royal George* only one man was killed. This engagement, though small, was important, for the *Royal George* was the largest vessel on the lake at the time, and her capture could have been serious. Nevertheless Commodore Chauncey had virtual command of Lake Ontario for the rest of the season, short as that may have been. A plaque erected by the Kingston Historical Society in 1953 commemorates the event and is located in Macdonald Park not far from Murney redoubt.

## POINT FREDERICK BUILDINGS

Point Frederick was the site of the main base for the British Navy during the War of 1812. A plaque placed by the Historic Sites and Monuments Board of Canada gives a history of the buildings that still stand on Point Frederick. Among these are the Naval Hospital, the Guard House and the Stone Frigate. The plaque is located at the entrance to the Royal Military College in Kingston.

## SIR JAMES LUCAS YEO

Following a distinguished career in the Royal Navy, thirty-one-year-old Sir James Lucas Yeo arrived in Canada on May 5, 1813. As

Commander in Chief of the Lake Squadrons, it would be his duty to win control of the Great Lakes and Lake Champlain. His position was difficult, for the American fleet under Commodore Chauncey virtually controlled Lake Ontario, as their raid on York had so recently demonstrated. The situation on Lake Ontario was unique, for if Chauncey lost control, it would have been an embarrassment and a setback, but if Yeo lost Lake Ontario, it would have meant the loss of the war. His position was much like that of Lord Jellicoe in World War I.

Of Jellicoe, Winston Churchill had said "he was the only man who could have lost the war in an afternoon" and this was exactly the position for James Yeo. Thus, from the outset he had a formidable task ahead of him, and the stakes were high. Yeo handled the Lake Ontario squadron creditably in all of its manoeuvres and actions. These included the battle on August 10, 1813, the Battle of Sackets Harbor, the Burlington Races, and the attack on Oswego. His career does not rest on a "Nelsonic" type battle as at Trafalgar, for he did not win a decisive naval victory over the American squadron. But with inferior resources and many disadvantages, he won the naval arms race on Lake Ontario by the fall of 1814. When his 104-gun ship of the line *H.M.S. St. Lawrence* was launched, Yeo had absolute and undisputed control of Lake Ontario.

Sir James' services were not forgotten by the people of Canada, and after the war the city of Montreal voted him a sword worth over five-hundred pounds sterling. He was also met by the magistrates of the city of Kingston and given a valedictory address. Sir James was curious to see what resources his late opponent had in the war, and on his way back to England he visited Sackets Harbor. Here he saw the hulls of two Ships of the Line that were meant to defeat his flagship *St. Lawrence* the next year. Fortunately these two leviathans were never completed, and with the coming of peace, the naval arms race on Lake Ontario was put to an end.

Sir James also submitted a detailed paper on why the British had successfully defended Upper Canada, and in it he candidly admits that much of it had to do with the ineptness of the American high command. In his report, he recommended that Kingston be properly fortified and that an alternate water route from Kingston to Montreal be surveyed. These suggestions were ultimately taken to heart as Fort Henry and the Rideau Canal demonstrate today. With Napoleon's final defeat at Waterloo in June of 1815, the long

Napoleonic Wars came to an end, and with this came reductions in the navy, and scores of officers were without work or put on half pay.

But the navy board had not forgotten him, and he was given command of the West African Squadron. But by August of 1818, the years of activity had taken their toll and Sir James died of "general debility and fever" on board his vessel en route to England. He was only thirty-six years old. The Historic Sites and Monuments Board of Canada has remembered this gallant officer by placing a commemorative plaque to him at the entrance to the Royal Military College of Canada.

## THE STONE FRIGATE

Years after the war, when vessels such as the *St. Lawrence* were placed "in ordinary" (a term used for vessels in storage), the cordage, spars, and masts were stored in the lofts of the "Stone Frigate." The building is one of the most historic of the old Naval Dockyard, and was built in 1820. The "Stone Frigate" can still be seen today and is part of the Royal Military College of Canada. A plaque placed by the Ontario Heritage Foundation, Ministry of Citizenship and Culture is attached to the front of the building.

## KINGSTON NAVY YARD

The ship yards for the Royal Navy were located here on Point Frederick and the yard was responsible for constructing many of the vessels that served in the war. Among these were *Earl of Moira*, *Duke of Gloucester*, *Royal George*, *Wolfe*, *Melville*, *Sir Sydney Smith*, *General Beresford*, *Prince Regent*, and *Princess Charlotte*.

The only Ship of the Line to ever sail Lake Ontario was built here: the *St. Lawrence* which was launched on September 10, 1814. A plaque placed by the Historic Sites and Monuments

Board of Canada is on the building known as "the Stone Frigate," located on the grounds of the Royal Military College in Kingston. (see next entry)

## POINT FREDERICK

The Naval dockyard, constructed in 1792 on the peninsula of land known as Point Frederick, was responsible for building many of the vessels that fought on Lake Ontario during the war. A battery was located here, and along with other batteries at Point Henry and Point Mississauga, helped repulse Commodore Chauncey's attack on the *Royal George* in November of 1812. During the Oregon Border Crisis in 1846 the point was greatly strengthened by the addition of a Martello Tower, which still stands today on the point. The grounds of Point Frederick and the Martello Tower are open to the public and may be visited. An Ontario Provincial Plaque is located in front of the Martello Tower on Point Frederick on the grounds of the Royal Military College. (see prior entry)

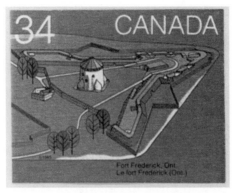

The stamp issued by Canada Post to Fort Frederick

## RUSH–BAGOT AGREEMENT

During the war both sides had spent prodigious amounts of money and resources to build fleets on the Great Lakes.

On Lake Ontario in particular, this "naval arms race" had reached epic proportions, especially when the 104-gun Ship of the Line *St. Lawrence* was launched, with a crew of over six hundred sailors! The Rush-Bagot agreement of 1817 came about as a direct result of the War of 1812, and is a treaty that is still honoured today. In essence it limits the United States and Canada from ever building warships on the Great Lakes and Lake Champlain. The treaty is named after the two dignitaries who signed the agreement, Richard Rush for the United States and Charles Bagot for Great Britain. An Ontario Provincial Plaque dedicated to this important treaty is located near the water on the grounds of the Royal Military College not far from the "Stone Frigate."

## "PRO PATRIA" 1812–1814

The Historic Sites and Monuments Board of Canada has placed a plaque honouring the soldiers and sailors of various units which served on Lake Ontario during the War of 1812. The plaque is mounted on a granite base with a large anchor beside it, and is located at the entrance to the grounds of Fort Henry off of Highway 2.

# FORT HENRY

Soon after war was declared in June of 1812, a blockhouse was commenced on Point Henry, on the land now occupied by Fort Henry. It was a small structure armed with only two light guns. Records are sketchy, but in all probability the blockhouse was completed by the time of Commodore Chauncey's attack in November of 1812. Early in 1813 it was decided to upgrade the fortifications, and by that summer two more cannons had been mounted here. An eighteen-pound cannon was later added at Murney Point.

In 1814 the fortifications were further upgraded, and this work went on until March of 1815, when news reached Kingston that the war was over. The present Fort Henry dates from 1832. Two plaques commemorate Fort Henry: an Ontario Provincial Plaque is located adjacent to the parking lot, and another, placed by the Historic Sites and Monuments Board of Canada, is at the entrance to the fort.

The present Fort Henry dates from 1832, although a fortification did exist there during the War of 1812. The commemorative stamp issued by Canada Post depicts the present structure.

# CHAPTER 15
## THE ST. LAWRENCE VALLEY

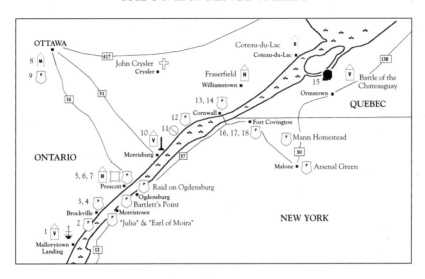

1. Brown's Bay Wreck
2. Chimney Island
3. Forsyth's Raid
4. Brock Monument
5. Stockade Barracks
6. Fort Wellington
7. Capture of Ogdensburg
8. Canadian War Museum
9. E.A. Cruikshank
10. Crysler Farm Battlefield
11. Hoople's Creek
12. Submerged Communities
13. Glengarry Fencibles
14. John Strachan
15. Charles de Salaberry
16. Funeral of Gen. Covington
17. Winter Quarters
18. Fort Covington

## BROWN'S BAY WRECK — MALLORYTOWN, ONTARIO

For decades after the War of 1812 the remains of an old wooden vessel could be seen in the bottom of Brown's Bay. Even in winter, under the right conditions, it was visible through the ice. In the mid-1960s the National Parks of Canada decided to survey the site, and early investigations determined that the vessel was from the period 1815. Very likely she was a gunboat or troop carrier, and over thirty years later she is still somewhat of a mystery.

Evidence indicates that she is the gunboat H.M.S. *Radcliffe* constructed at the Kingston Navy Yards in 1817, and if so, she is an exact copy of the gunboats that guarded the convoys of bateaux during the War of 1812. These sturdy little vessels which could be sailed or rowed, usually carried at least one cannon mounted in the bow.

The *Radcliffe* is an important find in marine archeology, for she is the only vessel of its kind that has been found in such a degree of preservation. When the *Radcliffe* was found preservation of large marine objects was still in its infancy and means of preserving the vessel had to be improvised along the way. The fascinating story of this gunboat and how it was preserved can be viewed at the "Brown's Bay Wreck" site in St. Lawrence Islands National Park. The gunboat is housed in a visitors centre off of the Thousand Islands Parkway at Mallorytown Landing, Ontario.

## BRIDGE ISLAND — MALLORYTOWN, ONTARIO

The problem of convoying supplies safely down the St. Lawrence River was never totally solved during the War of 1812, and at the start of the war the convoys were open to attack by American privateers and gunboats, especially among the Thousand Islands. At first soldiers accompanied the convoys, but this drained valuable manpower from the defence of the province. Allocating gunboats with the convoys was one solution, but even this was not infallible. The British finally decided to build a series of blockhouses which were constructed one-day's travelling apart, so that each night the bateaux would have a safe refuge.

One of these blockhouses was constructed here at Bridge Island in 1814. The small island as can be seen today is almost totally rock, but in 1812 a sand causeway could have connected it to the mainland, hence the name. There are no remains of the old fortification today, but a small chimney can be seen from the mainland, and because of this the island is often called "Chimney Island." A plaque placed by the National Historic Sites and Monuments Board of Canada is located opposite the island, just off of the Thousand Islands Parkway not far from Mallorytown Landing. (see also Battle at Cranberry Creek)

# FORSYTH'S RAID — BROCKVILLE, ONTARIO

In early February, 1813 Captain Benjamin Forsyth at Ogdensburg learned that a British raiding party had captured some Americans and carried them back to Elizabethtown (present-day Brockville), where it was rumoured they were to be tried for treason. Determined to attempt their rescue, on the evening of February 6, 1813 Forsyth moved two hundred of his men by sleigh to Morristown, just opposite Brockville. Although Forsyth knew a small party of Leeds militia held the town, he believed with his regulars he could defeat any militia force.

Leaving a small field piece in the middle of the frozen river, in case of retreat, the party surrounded the town by daybreak, without arousing suspicion. Moving boldly they captured about fifty-two soldiers of the garrison and released the prisoners. The barracks were set aflame and muskets and cartridges were carried off. Forsyth and his party escaped with only one wounded man.

Forsyth was a conscientious officer, and his arrival at Sackets Harbor in August of 1812 with his well-drilled rifle company was a great morale booster for the Americans. For this action he was breveted Lieutenant Colonel, and the commission was back-dated to the time of the Elizabethtown raid. The zeal that Forsyth showed did not win the approval of the local population, as they got along well with their cousins across the border.

The raid brought fear of retaliation, which was not long in coming, for the British struck back at Ogdensburg on February 22, 1813. Forsyth and his riflemen were present at the action but were forced to retreat. As a political move to keep the local populace happy, Forsyth was transferred to another front, and in June of 1814 he was killed in a small skirmish near Odeltown, Quebec. An Ontario Provincial Plaque dedicated to the raid is located on Blockhouse Island (now connected to the mainland) in the town of Brockville, Ontario. (see Skirmish at Odeltown)

# BROCK MONUMENT — BROCKVILLE, ONTARIO

Brockville, formerly Elizabethtown during the War of 1812, was named after the hero of the Battle of Queenston Heights, Sir Isaac Brock. A bust-type statue, erected by the General Brock Chapter, Daughters of the Empire, is located in front of City Hall Square in the town of Brockville.

# RAID ON OGDENSBURG — OGDENSBURG, NEW YORK

In retaliation for the American raid on Brockville, Sir George Prevost, who was then passing through Prescott on his way to Kingston, reluctantly approved a raid on Ogdensburg at the request of Lieutenant Colonel George Macdonell. On the early morning of February 22, 1813, Macdonell led about six hundred men across the frozen St. Lawrence River and attacked the town. Macdonell's troops consisted of detachments from the Glengarry Light Infantry, the Royal Newfoundland Regiment, the 8th Regiment, and militia from Glengarry, Stormont, Dundas, and Grenville. Three light cannons under the Royal Artillery accompanied the force

Advancing quickly, they were unable to bring up the guns, which got mired in the heavy snow. Splitting into two columns, the right was led by Captain Jenkins of the Glengarry Light Infantry while Macdonell led the left. In defence of the town was their old adversary Captain Forsyth, with his rifleman, some local militia, and a number of field pieces.

Macdonell's column had no trouble in capturing the redan battery located at the right end of the town, but Jenkins' men had a more difficult time near the site of old Fort La Presentation. Here the defenders were under Captain Forsyth with his disciplined rifle corps, and they put up a stubborn resistance around the old stone buildings. When Captain Jenkins' left arm was shattered by grapeshot, followed by another wound in his right arm, the command devolved upon Lieutenant Macaulay.

Macdonell's column eventually pushed through the town and formed up near the bridge over the Oswegatchie River. Forsyth was summoned to surrender, but he refused, and his men retreated down the road leading to Black Lake, eventually reaching Sackets Harbor. The British remained in the town for the rest of the day, carrying off much needed supplies. Before leaving they burned the barracks and two schooners that were trapped in the ice-bound river.

The twin raids of Brockville and Ogdensburg were small, but had far-reaching effects. When Macdonell announced to the people of Ogdensburg that the town would never be raided if it were not used as a military post, Ogdensburg was never garrisoned again. The war was very unpopular on the Northern Frontier, and rather than alienate the local population, the military presence was removed from Ogdensburg. This seemingly small effect had large repercussions for the British, for their supply line, which was critical to the entire war effort in Upper Canada, ran right past Ogdensburg.

Today the "Downtown Battlefield Committee" of the City of Ogdensburg has done much to commemorate this small skirmish. A pamphlet has been printed called "Ogdensburg's Downtown Battlefield" which takes visitors on a walking tour of the battle site, and there are a number of very informative plaques on the route. The majority of these are in a small park on Water Street and other plaques describe the Brockville Raid under Captain Forsyth and General Jacob Brown the commander of the U.S. forces on the northern frontier. The pamphlet may be obtained at the Chamber of Commerce in downtown Ogdensburg. (see next entry.)

## CAPTURE OF OGDENSBURG — PRESCOTT, ONTARIO

An Ontario Provincial Plaque describes the capture of Ogdensburg on February 22, 1813 by the garrison of Fort Wellington. The plaque is located in the town of Prescott in the Public Utilities Park. (see prior entry)

# FORT WELLINGTON — PRESCOTT, ONTARIO

When war was declared in 1812 a new fort was planned to guard the vital supply line linking Upper and Lower Canada. The first site considered was Windmill Point just to the east of Prescott, where General Amherst had his headquarters for the reduction of Fort de Levis in the Seven Years' War. But after some deliberation the present site was agreed upon. The original fort was constructed in the summer of 1812 by men from the King's German Legion under the direction of Frederic Baron de Gaugreben, and it was named after the Duke of Wellington, who had just achieved the great victory of Salamanca in Spain on July 22.

The fort is primarily constructed of earthworks and palisades, and the large stone blockhouse and barracks can house about 320 men. The fort was armed with four twenty-four-pound, two eighteen-pound, and three twelve-pound cannons, and a river battery was mounted near the shore of the St. Lawrence.

During General Wilkinson's campaign in the fall of 1813, the fort's strategic position influenced the American strategy. Wilkinson could not afford risking his army by running the fort's batteries by day, so on the evening of November 7, 1813, he debarked his troops on the south shore west of Ogdensburg. During the night his empty boats ran past the fort, while the troops marched over land and rendezvoused on the other side. The Fort Wellington garrison detected the movement and opened fire, but little could be done in the dark, and little damage was done to the flotilla.

The garrison of Fort Wellington was not inactive during the war, and they participated in the Ogdensburg Raid in February 1813 and a portion of them were at the Battle of Crysler's Farm on November 11th the same year.

The fort was never seriously threatened during the war, but its position aided in guarding the long supply route to Montreal. After the War of 1812 the fort fell into disrepair, but it was reactivated during the rebellion of 1837, when a detachment from Kingston restored the fortifications. The restored fort is what can be seen today in Fort Wellington National Historic Park in the town of Prescott, Ontario.

The stamp issued by Canada Post to Fort Wellington

## STOCKADE BARRACKS — PRESCOTT, ONTARIO

The Stockade Barracks is one of Ontario's oldest surviving military buildings, and was constructed by Major Edward Jessup in 1810. Architecturally, the building is classified as a two-and-one-half-storey Georgian stone house. In the autumn of 1812 it served as a barracks for the local militia.

During the war a stockade was built around the house and from this comes the name. In 1815 it functioned as a hospital and barracks store. Presently the building is used as a restaurant where groups may be served period meals by appointment. The building is located at 356 East Street in the town of Prescott.

## *JULIA* AND *EARL OF MOIRA* — MORRISTOWN, NEW YORK

When war was declared in June of 1812, eight civilian vessels of American registry were at the port of Ogdensburg. On June 29th they attempted to escape to Lake Ontario, but just above

Brockville they were intercepted by volunteers in bateaux from Maitland, Ontario. The *Sophia* and the *Island Packet* were taken, but the others managed to turn about and return to Ogdensburg. However, the Provincial Marine was not through with the vessels, and once more concentrated their efforts to capture them. The *Earl of Moira* and the *Duke of Gloucester* were moved to Prescott, opposite Ogdensburg, to observe the schooners.

American General Brown was also active, and on the evening of July 30th he dispatched the schooner *Julia* and sixty volunteers to Ogdensburg. The next afternoon they fell in with the *Earl of Moira* and the *Duke of Gloucester* near Morristown, eleven miles from Ogdensburg. The *Julia* set her anchor in order to give the vessel more stability, and thus greater accuracy, for her long thirty-two-pound cannon. The *Julia* and the two British vessels exchanged fire for over three hours, but when the *Earl of Moira* was hit several times, the British vessels bore away to the Canadian shore. The next morning, the *Julia* rendezvoused with the schooners in Ogdensburg, and taking advantage of a brief armistice, they escaped to Sackets Harbor, where they joined the rest of the squadron. This little sidelight of the War of 1812 is little remembered today and is not commemorated with any historical marker. However, the Seaway Trail has placed one of their markers overlooking the town of Morriston, New York.

## CRYSLER FARM BATTLEFIELD PARK

In the autumn of 1813 the American Army, under the command of General James Wilkinson, began its descent of the St. Lawrence River for the projected capture of Montreal. At about the same time another American Army, under the command of General Wade Hampton, began its march on Montreal, approaching it from the south. Wilkinson's army of seven thousand men and twenty-four guns slipped past Kingston in a great flotilla of boats. He bypassed the guns of Fort Wellington by landing his troops above the fort and marching down river on the American side while his boats ran past at night. By the evening of November

10th the bulk of his army had been concentrated at Cook's Point, about two miles east of the farm of John Crysler.

The brigade under General Brown had been detached previously to clear out a small party of militia that had been reported at the Long Sault Rapids. This left on shore about four thousand men under the command of Brigadier General Boyd. Wilkinson had excused himself and lay indisposed on board the flotilla. In the meantime a small British force, under the command of Lieutenant Colonel Joseph Wanton Morrison, had moved out of Kingston in pursuit of Wilkinson.

At Fort Wellington this small force, numbering about eight hundred men and officially designated a "Corps of Observation," was augmented by part of the garrison under Colonel Pearson. On the evening of November 10th, Morrison made his headquarters in John Crysler's House, just west of the American encampment.

The next morning Morrison sent his skirmishers, consisting of Voltigeurs and Indians, to scout the American camp. When the skirmishers began annoying his pickets, General Boyd determined to turn around and crush the British force that had been following them. Deploying his two brigades for the attack, the two forces met in the open fields of the Crysler Farm. Promising his men "a fair field and no favour," Morrison was sure that his well-disciplined regulars would prevail in an open-field European-style battle.

In a series of unco-ordinated manoeuvres, the American Army was unable to drive Morrison's force from the field. After a seesaw contest, Boyd ordered his dragoons to charge Morrison's right flank on the King's Road. When this charge was repulsed by a well-directed volley of musketry, the American Army began to lose heart. With his men now low on ammunition, and darkness approaching, Boyd's men quit the field. One of Wilkinson's brigade commanders, General Covington, was mortally wounded during the battle.

The next morning Wilkinson pushed forward to the Long Sault Rapids, only now he commanded a demoralized army. Soon after, Wilkinson received a message from General Hampton, which informed him that his army would not rendezvous with him at St. Regis as originally planned. In fact, Hampton had been turned back at the Battle of Chateauguay on October 26th, and now was in full retreat to Plattsburg. Wilkinson, who hated Hampton in the first place, now had the excuse he wanted, and he retired his army to winter quarters at French Mills, ending the entire campaign.

The failure of the Wilkinson-Hampton Campaign was a turning point. It represented one of America's last chances to win the war with a knockout blow. By 1814 it would be too late, for with the overthrow of Napoleon in Europe, Britain would be able to send enough soldiers for the proper defence of Upper Canada. The twin victories of Crysler's Farm and Chateauguay were truly decisive.

Most of the actual site of the Battle of Crysler's Farm now lies under the St. Lawrence River, a victim of the Seaway project in the late 1950s. The battle has been commemorated with the construction of a huge memorial mound, created from earth from the battlefield. The monument, which was dedicated in 1895, was moved from its original site to the top of the mound, where it can be seen today. Incidentally, the victor of the Battle of Crysler's Farm, Lieutenant Colonel Joseph Wanton Morrison, has been somewhat of a mystery. In 1960, when the St. Lawrence Development Commission was engaged in research on the battle, they did an extensive search for a portrait of Colonel Morrison.

But all efforts to secure a portrait failed. Even into the 1980s, no portrait of Colonel Morrison was thought to have existed. Reproduced below is an authentic portrait of Colonel Morrison, with grateful thanks to the McCord Museum.

The Battle Memorial Building features an audio-visual programme, a large mural painting by Adam Sheriff Scott, a display of the Crysler's Farm General Service medal, and other artifacts from the War of 1812. Several plaques honouring the various units

A portrait of Lieutenant Colonel Joseph Wanton Morrison, the victor at the Battle of Crysler's Farm, courtesy of the McCord Museum, Montreal.

that served in the battle are in the British and Canadian courtyards. The Crysler's Farm Battlefield Park is administered by the St. Lawrence Parks Commission, and is located east of Morrisburg, Ontario at Upper Canada Village.

The monument to the Battle of Crysler's Farm on its original location on old Highway 2

The Crysler's Farm monument as it looks today, on top of the Memorial Mound

# JOHN CRYSLER GRAVE — CRYSLER, ONTARIO

John Crysler, a prosperous Loyalist landowner, was a militia captain during the War of 1812. The famous Battle of Crysler's Farm was fought on his property on November 11, 1813 and his house was used as the British headquarters. John Crysler later returned to this location where he built a second home, and founded the town that now bears his name. His grave is a humble one, located in the Anglican cemetery, adjacent to the South Nation River in the town of Crysler, Ontario.

# BRIGADIER GENERAL ERNEST CRUIKSHANK — OTTAWA, ONTARIO

Ernest Cruikshank was one of Canada's foremost historians on the War of 1812 and his most famous work was as editor of the nine-volume series *Documentary History of the Campaigns on the Niagara Frontier*. He also wrote many detailed articles on the war such as "General Hull's Invasion of Canada 1812," "The Contest for Command of Lake Ontario in 1812 and 1813," "From Isle aux Noix to Chateauguay — A Study in Military Operations on the Frontier of Lower Canada in 1812 and 1813," and many others. An Ontario Provincial Plaque dedicated to this noted historian is affixed to a wall of the Canadian War Museum in Ottawa. (see Ernest Cruikshank Home)

# CANADIAN WAR MUSEUM — OTTAWA, ONTARIO

The Canadian War Museum, established in 1880, has been open to the public since 1942. It houses an extensive collection of war art, artifacts, and military memorabilia from a variety of periods, with emphasis on World War I and II. The first floor has displays on the War of 1812, and of special interest is the tunic worn by General Brock at the Battle of Queenston Heights, his telescope and watch. The museum is located at 330 Sussex Drive in the nation's capital.

# SKIRMISH AT HOOPLE'S CREEK — HOOPLE'S CREEK, ONTARIO

On November 10, 1813 a skirmish occurred between the advanced units of General Wilkinson's invading army and a small party of British posted at the Hoople's Creek Bridge. The lead units of the American force were under the command of Winfield Scott, and the British were commanded by Major James Dennis of the 49th Regiment. Scott and Dennis had faced each other before, just over one year ago at the Battle of Queenston Heights. In that battle the British emerged victorious, and Scott had been forced to surrender along with most of the American Army. After his parole, Scott was once more in command, but at this skirmish the shoe was on the other foot, for the advantage in numbers lay with the Americans. After a brief skirmish Dennis's force of regulars and Stormont militia were forced to withdraw.

The site of the skirmish at Hoople's Creek is now long gone, changed forever by the St. Lawrence Seaway, which inundated most of the site. Presently no historical marker commemorates the action, but the creek's name has been preserved with a metal marker, near the bridge on Highway 2, just west of Cornwall. (see next entry)

# SUBMERGED COMMUNITIES — CORNWALL, ONTARIO

With the building of the St. Lawrence Seaway in the late 1950s some of Ontario's most historic properties were lost. The villages of Mille Roches, Moulinette, Dickinson's Landing, Farrans Point, and Aultsville ceased to exist. The old Battlefield of Crysler's Farm, some old loyalist cemeteries, and portions of Morrisburg and Iroquois were also victims of the massive project, which included moving houses, relocating cemeteries, and establishing new communities. Upper Canada Village was created, and the old monument to the Battle of Crysler's Farm was placed on a newly created memorial mound. An Ontario Provincial Plaque describing these events is located in Lakeside Park, Highway 2 west of Cornwall.

# GLENGARRY FENCIBLES — CORNWALL, ONTARIO

Just prior to the War of 1812 the Reverend Alexander Macdonell helped raise the "Glengarry Light Infantry Fencibles," which were recruited from many of the veteran Scots that had accompanied him to Canada. In May of 1812 the regiment numbered four hundred strong, and saw action at York, Ogdensburg, Fort George, Sackets Harbor, Oswego, Lundy's Lane, and the siege of Fort Erie. The regiment was disbanded in 1816. An Ontario Historic Sites plaque dedicated to the regiment is located in front of the Armouries on 4th Street East in the city of Cornwall.

# REVEREND JOHN STRACHAN — CORNWALL, ONTARIO

The Reverend John Strachan was a man of many talents: clergyman, teacher, and legislator, he established a school for young boys at Cornwall which gained a reputation for high academic standards. At the commencement of the War of 1812 he was living in the provincial capital of York (Toronto), and was present during the two American attacks in April and July of 1813. He was highly critical of General Sheaffe's defence of the town, and when he acted as chief negotiator for the surrender, he blamed the regulars.

Because Strachan had shown a bold front to the American occupying army, he was remembered with great affection by the citizens of York in later years. He must have been a strong personality, for he even wrested an apology from Commodore Chauncey for some books that were stolen from the Public Library in the previous raid! Strachan's role in Ontario's history did not end with the war, for he later was one of the key players in the "Family Compact," and to the end of his days would help perpetuate the myth that it was the militia that saved Upper Canada during the War of 1812. There are two historic plaques to him in the city of Cornwall. The Ontario Provincial Plaque is in front of Bishop Strachan Memorial Church on Second Street West. The other is on the grounds of the Cornwall Collegiate and Vocational School.

# FRASERFIELD — WILLIAMSTOWN, ONTARIO

Alexander Fraser was the quartermaster for the Glengarry Light Infantry Regiment and commenced construction of this fine country residence during the first year of the war. He later became a colonel of the 1st Regiment, Glengarry Militia and served in that capacity during the rebellions of 1837. An Ontario Provincial Plaque dedicated to him is located three miles west of

Williamstown on Route 17 near the intersection with Highway 27. "Fraserfield" is presently a private residence and not open to the public, but the house with a cupola on top can be seen from the road across the open fields.

## FUNERAL OF GENERAL COVINGTON — FORT COVINGTON, NEW YORK

General Leonard Covington was mortally wounded at the Battle of Crysler's Farm on November 11, 1813. He accompanied the flotilla as it continued down the St. Lawrence, but two days later he died, and his body was taken to French Mills. He was buried near a blockhouse that used to stand at this site, and years later the old blockhouse was commonly called "Fort Covington." In 1820 his remains were removed to the cemetery at Sackets Harbor. There is no trace of the blockhouse today, but a New York State Plaque is located near the site of his funeral, in the town that bears his name.

## WINTER QUARTERS — FORT COVINGTON, NEW YORK

After the disastrous Battle of Crysler's Farm, Wilkinson's army headed for the old town of French Mills on the Salmon River, where it went into winter quarters. Wilkinson, of whom it has been said "he never won a battle but always won a court martial," retired to the village of Malone. His army spent two miserable months suffering for want of provisions and adequate winter clothing, and in February the War Department ordered the army to be broken up. A portion of it went with General Brown to Sackets Harbor, while the rest accompanied Wilkinson to Plattsburg. Before leaving, the army burned the barracks and flotilla to prevent them falling into British hands, and the hospital at Malone was abandoned. A New York State Plaque in the town of Fort Covington, New York marks the winter quartering site.

# FORT COVINGTON — FORT COVINGTON, NEW YORK

A New York State Plaque just west of Fort Covington on Route 37 states that the town is named after Brigadier General Leonard Covington killed at the Battle of Crysler's Farm.

# MANN HOMESTEAD — WESTVILLE, NEW YORK

The Mann brothers both served as officers in the War of 1812, and their house still stands about two miles east of Westville, on State Route 122. A New York State Plaque is located in front of the house.

# ARSENAL GREEN — MALONE, NEW YORK

In 1812 a stone arsenal was built here, and the green was used as a parade ground during the war. A New York State marker is located in a small park on Main Street in Malone, New York.

# FOOTE TAVERN — MALONE, NEW YORK

The Foote Tavern, built in 1807, was used as a hospital by the sick of General Wilkinson's Northern Army during the winter of 1813–1814. A New York State marker is located at the corner of Webster and Main streets in the town of Malone, New York.

# HARISON HOUSE — MALONE, NEW YORK

The Harison House was used as General Wilkinson's Headquarters during the winter of 1813–1814, while his army encamped at Fort Covington, New York. The house is located at 167 Webster Street in Malone and a New York State Plaque is located beside the house.

# FORT HICKORY — CHATEAUGUAY, NEW YORK

Descriptions of Fort Hickory are scarce, but it was very likely a simple fortification consisting of felled trees, or perhaps a blockhouse. It was constructed by troops from General Wade Hampton's army in the autumn of 1813. The troops called the

The stamp issued by Canada Post dedicated to Coteau du Lac

structure "Hickory" after their General, who was generally disliked and was a strict disciplinarian. A New York State Plaque at the site says that Samuel Hollenbeck once defended the fort single-handedly against the British. However, according to author John Bilow, the story seems a fabrication. Evidence seems to indicate that Hollenbeck was actually a double agent in the employ of the British! However that may be, the site of Fort Hickory is marked, and is located on the Earlville Road at the intersection of Smith Road northeast of Chateauguay, New York.

## COTEAU DU LAC BLOCKHOUSE — COTEAU DU LAC, QUEBEC

One of the first canals in North America to utilize a lock system was built here at Coteau du Lac. During the War of 1812, a new blockhouse was added to replace a former structure. By the summer of 1814, the site featured a clover-leaf bastion, barracks, bakery, guardhouse, magazine, cookhouse, and a hospital. The octagonal blockhouse is an unusual feature, and is one of the very few of its kind in North America. The 1845 Beauharnois Canal, and the Soulanges Canal of 1890, made the Coteau site obsolete, and over the years erosion had its effect on the fortifications. By the time restoration began in 1965 they were in pretty bad shape. Today the blockhouse and fortifications have been restored, and can be seen in Coteau du Lac National Historic Site, in the town of Coteau du Lac, Quebec. There is a visitors centre with displays that interpret the site's history.

## DE SALABERRY STATUE — VALLEYFIELD, QUEBEC

A statue honours Charles Michel de Salaberry, the victor at the Battle of Chateauguay on October 26, 1813. The statue is located at the end of the bridge connecting Coteau du Lac and Salaberry de Valleyfield.

The stamp issued by Canada Post to commemorate
Charles Michel de Salaberry

## BATTLE OF THE CHATEAUGUAY — ORMSTOWN, QUEBEC

In the autumn of 1813, General Wade Hampton, with an army of over 4,000 men, moved against the British defence system on the Chateauguay River. Opposed to him was the advanced guard under the command of Lieutenant Colonel Charles Michel de Salaberry, a French-Canadian from a proud military family. De Salaberry's force consisted of about 1,500 troops, mainly militia, from the counties of Beauharnois, Boucherville, and Chateauguay. Also with him were some Voltigeurs, Fencibles, and Indians.

De Salaberry arranged his defence in the wilderness terrain along the Chateauguay River. It would be a difficult position to outflank, but this was the tactic that was eventually chosen by General Hampton. On the evening of the 25th, he ordered a column of light troops, numbering about 1,500 men, to cross the Chateauguay River, and move against a ford in the rear of de Salaberry's position. The column was under the command of Colonel Purdy, and the plan called for his assault to begin at daybreak.

The next morning, the flanking column had not arrived at the ford, and in fact was hopelessly lost. At 10:30 AM, Hampton figured that too much time had been wasted, and ordered an assault against de Salaberry's main line. At about the same time, two companies of de Salaberry's militia collided with Purdy's column on the other side of the river. By noon Purdy's column, fatigued from an all-night march and now faced with brisk resistance, decided to retreat.

On Hampton's side of the river the battle was not going well either, for Izard's troops were having a tough time forcing the barricade. At one point, de Salaberry, to conceal his inferior numbers, decided on a clever ruse. He had his voltigeurs give a loud cheer and all bugles blown as if to advance. This tactic was echoed by Colonel Macdonell in the second line. The Americans now believed themselves outnumbered, and not long after, stragglers from Colonel Purdy's column appeared on the opposite bank of the river. A few bold soldiers swam across to inform Hampton that Purdy's column was in full retreat. Now Hampton believed he had justification to call off the battle and ordered his army to retreat. The Battle of Chateauguay, along with the victory at Crysler's Farm, prevented the capture of Montreal that year.

Today the battle is commemorated in "Battle of the Chateauguay National Historic Park." There is a visitors centre, with numerous exhibits, and an electric map presentation that explains the tactics used in the battle. A monument, erected in 1895, still stands at Allan's Corners at the place where the barricade was located. The terrain of the battlefield has changed considerably since 1813, for now the area is mainly farmland, though the Chateauguay River still winds its way peacefully through the countryside. The monument and visitors centre are located on Route 138 northeast of Ormstown, Quebec at Allan's Corners.

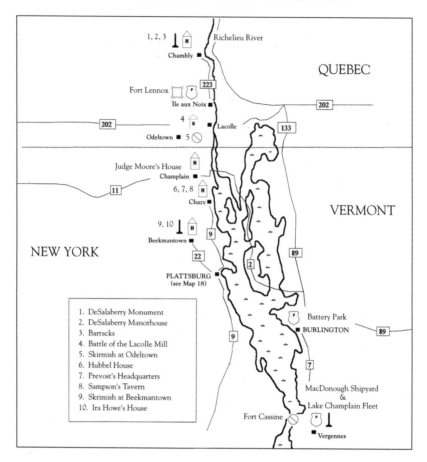

1, 2, 3   Richelieu River
Chambly

QUEBEC

223
Fort Lennox
Île aux Noix

202

202
4
Lacolle
133
Odeltown   5

Judge Moore's House
Champlain
6, 7, 8
Chazy

VERMONT

9, 10
Beekmantown
9

NEW YORK

22

89
2

PLATTSBURG
(see Map 18)

1. DeSalaberry Monument
2. DeSalaberry Manorhouse
3. Barracks
4. Battle of the Lacolle Mill
5. Skirmish at Odeltown
6. Hubbel House
7. Prevost's Headquarters
8. Sampson's Tavern
9. Skrimish at Beekmantown
10. Ira Howe's House

Battery Park
BURLINGTON
89

9

7

MacDonough Shipyard
&
Lake Champlain Fleet
Fort Cassine

Vergennes

## DE SALABERRY MONUMENT — CHAMBLY, QUEBEC

This impressive monument by sculptor Philippe Hebert was unveiled in 1881, and is dedicated to the memory of Charles Michel de Salaberry, the victor at the Battle of Chateauguay. On the sides of the monument are inscribed the words "Lacolle" and "Christler's Farm," two other battles of the War of 1812.

Charles de Salaberry was engaged in the skirmish at Lacolle but was not present at the Battle of Crysler's Farm. However, thirty of his French-Canadian voltigeurs were there. The monument to de Salaberry is in the public square in the town of Chambly.

## DE SALABERRY MANOR HOUSE — CHAMBLY, QUEBEC

De Salaberry Manor was built in 1814 and was the home of Charles Michel de Salaberry, the victor at the Battle of Chateauguay, on October 26, 1813. The house is privately owned and not open to the public and is located at number 18 rue Richelieu at rue Des Voltigeurs in the town of Chambly, Quebec.

## 1814 BARRACKS — CHAMBLY, QUEBEC

In 1814 many of the buildings in this vicinity were part of a vast military complex. This stone building, the Maison Vadenboncoeur, was used as a guard house and barracks during the war and was capable of housing four hundred men. Most of the other surviving buildings have been turned into private residences. The building is located at number 10 rue Richelieu in the town of Chambly.

## ÎLE AUX NOIX — RICHELIEU RIVER, QUEBEC

The Richelieu River–Lake Champlain corridor has been a historic invasion route to and from Canada for centuries, and because of this Île aux Noix occupies an important position in the Richelieu River. In two major wars Île aux Noix has been defended, first by the French, who fortified the island during the Seven Years' War and then by the British, who extended the fortifications to guard against attack from the colonists during the American Revolution.

For a brief time the island was occupied by American forces in 1776 where they suffered great privation and eventually had to give up the site.

At the time of the War of 1812 the fortifications were in very poor condition, and Sir George Prevost, the governor of Canada, did not even mention the island in a detailed defence report to the Earl of Liverpool. One of the reasons that Île aux Noix was ignored in the summer of 1812 was because the Americans had no navy on Lake Champlain. Also, since the Revolution new roads had been cut that bypassed the fort.

By the fall of 1812 this had all changed. When the Americans managed to put a small navy on to Lake Champlain, Sir George Prevost immediately declared Île aux Noix reactivated. The fortifications were restored, expanded, and a naval base was established with a permanent garrison. By the fall of 1814 the shipyards were in full production.

On July 3, 1813, the garrison aided in the dramatic capture of two American vessels, *Growler* and *Eagle*. Under the orders of Captain MacDonough, the two vessels had proceeded to the border where they blockaded the British gunboats in the river. Under assurances from the sailing master that the river was wide enough, the two vessels entered the mouth of the Richelieu, but next morning, much to their horror, the two vessels were surrounded by British infantry and artillery on both sides of the river.

After a spirited resistance the *Growler* and *Eagle* were forced to strike their colours, and the captured vessels were taken back to Île aux Noix and repaired. They later entered British service as *Broke* and *Shannon* in honour of Captain Broke's victory over the American frigate *Chesapeake*, fought the month before.

Île aux Noix was never seriously threatened again, but the island continued as the only British naval base on Lake Champlain. The yard here produced the thirty-seven-gun ship rigged vessel *Confiance*, which became the flagship of Commodore George Downie at the Battle of Lake Champlain.

The War of 1812 pointed out the necessity of properly fortifying the island, and Fort Lennox was built during the period 1819 to 1829. Today the fort proudly stands on Île aux Noix, preserved in Fort Lennox National Historic Park. A good sense of the island's strategic position can be obtained from a visit to the site. A marker dedicated to the capture of the *Eagle* and *Growler* used to stand at the south end of the island but has long since been removed. A plaque placed by the Historic Sites and Monuments Board of Canada is at the entrance to the fort. The fort can only be reached by passenger ferry from the Visitor Centre, which is located 19 kilometres (12 miles) south of St. Jean sur Richelieu in the province of Quebec.

## BATTLE OF THE LACOLLE MILL — LACOLLE, QUEBEC

In the winter of 1778 a sawmill was built on the Lacolle River to provide planking for the new fortifications being built at Île aux Noix, St. Jean, and Fort Chambly. Later a blockhouse was added under the direction of Major William Twiss, the same officer who had created the defences at Coteau du Lac on the St. Lawrence.

In 1812 the blockhouse was reactivated, and on the early morning of November 20th, it was attacked by American regulars under Colonel Zebulon Pike. Pike had about six hundred men when he surrounded the blockhouse, but was unaware that the garrison had departed the evening before. In the early morning twilight another party of American militia, who had taken a different route, approached the blockhouse and began firing on Pike's men, believing them to be the enemy. What followed was a confused skirmish, with friend firing upon friend, but soon after the Canadian garrison under Lieutenant Colonel Charles de Salaberry, considerably reinforced, returned. After a short engagement, this time with a real enemy, the Americans retreated, leaving five dead and five wounded on the field.

Two years later the blockhouse was subject to a more ambitious attack. In March of 1814, Major General James Wilkinson, whose career had been so tarnished at the Battle of Crysler's Farm, moved once more against Montreal.

On March 30th his army of four thousand regulars marched north to the Lacolle Mill, though their progress was much impeded by the poor condition of the roads, and the barricades that had been placed by the Canadians. By three o'clock in the afternoon Wilkinson's troops were deploying in the fields south of the mill.

Lacolle Mill as Lossing sketched it in 1860

Lacolle Mill present day

The mill was on the south side of the Lacolle River near the bridge, and the blockhouse guarded the north. The mill was virtually a fortification, since it had walls eighteen inches thick buttressed with heavy timbers and windows that were loopholed for muskets. Defending the mill and the blockhouse were only two hundred soldiers of the 13th Regiment under Major Handcock, but reinforcements were expected soon

The ground over which Wilkinson's men moved was inundated by melting snow and difficult for manoeuvre. Heavy guns were out of the question, though the Americans did manage to bring up two twelve-pound cannons. Colonel Isaac Clark and Captain Forsyth commanded the advance and the reserves were under General Alexander Macomb.

Moving to the west, the advanced guard crossed the Lacolle River and surrounded the position from the rear, while the main force engaged the mill from the south. When the attack did come, the American musket firing was kept at long range, and the cannons could make no impression against the mill. Reinforcements from Île aux Noix and Burtonville later arrived for the British, and with these at hand, they now numbered about one thousand men. After several sorties by the British, Wilkinson realized that the mill could not be taken. With his men fatigued and running out of ammunition he decided to retreat back across the border. Disgusted with Wilkinson's performance, he was recalled back to Washington to face charges of misconduct. Although he was acquitted, his military career was over.

Presently the Lacolle Blockhouse is administered by the government of Quebec. Inside are fascinating displays on blockhouse construction and a history of the building. A plaque placed by the Historic Sites and Monuments Board of Canada is located south of the blockhouse on Route 221 at the intersection with 202 in the province of Quebec.

# SKIRMISH AT ODELTOWN — ODELTOWN, QUEBEC

During the spring of 1814 a party of U.S. riflemen under the ever-active Captain Benjamin Forsyth entered the hamlet of Odeltown. Their purpose was to capture a troublesome spy by the name of Perkins. Abducting him and bringing him over the border, he was later exchanged for another American citizen after the British retaliated with a raid of their own. That summer Captain Forsyth's riflemen returned once again to the Odeltown vicinity, where on June 28th they became engaged with a party of French-Canadian militia and Indians, under Captain Joseph St. Valer Mailloux. Mailloux's troops were known as the "Frontier Light Infantry" and they operated out of Odeltown.

It was Forsyth's plan to lure the column into an ambush, but in the early stages of the fight Forsyth was hit and mortally wounded. Even so, his skilled riflemen managed to drive off the French-Canadians. Captain Forsyth was taken to Judge Moore's house in Champlain, New York where he died the same day. On August 10th, sixteen men of the 1st Rifle Regiment, under Lieutenant Riley, crossed the border, determined to get Captain Mailloux and avenge their leader's death. They staged an ambush which severely wounded Mailloux, and ironically they took him to Judge Moore's house where British surgeons were allowed to treat him. The wounds were mortal however, and he died one week later. Although there is a marker at Odeltown indicating a skirmish during the Rebellion of 1837, there is presently no marker indicating the 1812 incident.

Judge Moore's house as Lossing sketched it in 1860

## JUDGE MOORE'S HOUSE — CHAMPLAIN, NEW YORK

A fine old house owned by Judge Pliny Moore during the war, was used numerous times as British headquarters during their various forays into New York State. Both American Captain Forsyth and Captain Mailloux died in the house in the summer of 1814. An exact replica of the original house still stands in the village of Champlain, although it is now a funeral home.

The replica of Judge Moore's house on the same site

# HUBBELL HOUSE — CHAZY, NEW YORK

During the War of 1812 this small stone structure was the law office of Julius C. Hubbell. On September 4, 1814, when the British army was advancing on Plattsburg, British officers used the building as their headquarters. Just over a week later the office was again appropriated by the British, only this time in their retreat after the Battle of Plattsburg. Local tradition states that fence rails that surrounded the property were burned in the fireplace by the British. Mrs. Hubbell returned to the office just in time to put out a fire that had started when the officers vacated the premises. Today the law office is the public library for the town of Chazy and is located on Route 9.

# PREVOST'S HEADQUARTERS — CHAZY, NEW YORK

The Commander in Chief and Governor of Canada, Sir George Prevost, utilized the home of Alexander Scott as his headquarters during the Plattsburg campaign. The home is a private dwelling and is not open to the public but still stands today at 9685 Main Street in the town of Chazy, New York.

Sampson's Tavern as the artist Lossing sketched it in 1860

# SAMPSON'S TAVERN — INGRAHAM, NEW YORK

On the evening of September 5, 1814 the British left wing under General Brisbane camped for the evening around a little tavern known as Sampson's.

The next morning the column marched directly south on their way to Plattsburg. The building still stands today although it is now a private residence and not open to the public. A New York State Marker is located near the house. The building is off of old Highway 9 at Ingraham Road and Stratton Hill Road in the community of Ingraham.

Sampson's Tavern as it looks today near Ingraham, New York

# FARNSWORTH TAVERN — BEEKMANTOWN, NEW YORK

According to local tradition, the British army in their march to Plattsburg fired on the Farnsworth Tavern, believing it to be a fort. A plaque describing the incident has been placed by the town of Beekmantown on Highway 9 at the junction with State Route 456.

# IRA HOWE HOUSE — BEEKMANTOWN, NEW YORK

On September 6, 1814, the right column of the British army, under the commands of General Manley Power and General Frederick Robinson, collided with a small party of about 250 regulars under Captain Wool that had been positioned around the home of Ira Howe the evening before. Falling back in an orderly manner, Wool's men made a brief stand on Culver Hill just to the south. The setting around the house has changed little since 1814, and the house still stands on route 22 at the Ashley Road in East Beekmantown. Though slightly altered since 1814 it is a private residence and not open to the public.

# SKIRMISH AT BEEKMANTOWN — BEEKMANTOWN, NEW YORK

Falling back before two British brigades numbering over 5000 men, Captain Wool's detachment of 250 regulars made a brief stand on Culver Hill. Joined by some other militia units that were also retreating, they opened fire as soon as the British troops appeared in column formation on the road. Lieutenant Colonel Wellington and Ensign John Chapman of the 3rd Regiment made a conspicuous target and were killed instantly. Faced with overwhelming numbers, Wool had little choice but to fall back to the main defences of Plattsburg, while losing only one man, Corporal Stephen Partridge of the Essex County Militia.

The wounded from the skirmish were cared for at the Daniel Culver house, which used to stand on the west side of the hill. A small monument erected by the "Plattsburg Institute" in 1895 marks the location of the skirmish and commemorates the three soldiers who were killed there. The monument is located on Route 22, Culver Hill just south of East Beekmantown.

## BATTERY PARK — BURLINGTON, VERMONT

Battery Park was the site of an encampment of over four thousand troops during the war, and in 1813 a battery of guns was mounted on the heights overlooking the harbour.

In July the British sloops *Broke* and *Shannon* and one gunboat made their way up to Burlington to seek out the American squadron. Arriving opposite the heights, they engaged in a long-range duel with the defences. Of the thirteen guns in the battery, only two could engage at long range, but soon the fire of these two guns became too accurate. Captain Thomas Everard broke off the action, and sailed his vessels away.

Today the site where the naval guns engaged the British, offers a good view of Lake Champlain. The battery and encampment are commemorated with a plaque placed by the Green Mountain Chapter, Daughters of the American Revolution. The plaque also describes a similar encounter with the British on June 13, 1813. The plaque is mounted on a boulder in Battery Park, off of Battery Street in the City of Burlington.

## MACDONOUGH SHIPYARD — VERGENNES, VERMONT

A lovely basin of water below the Otter Creek Falls was the site of Thomas MacDonough's shipyard. The location was well chosen, as it was easily defended and was far enough from Lake Champlain where the British had temporary naval superiority. Vergennes was also an ideal site because of the virgin timber nearby and the presence of an iron works, which meant MacDonough had all the materials for constructing a lake fleet immediately at hand.

The twenty-six-gun corvette *Saratoga*, which became MacDonough's flagship, was built at this site. No vestiges of the shipyard remain, but the Vermont Historic Sites Commission has placed a plaque, which is in a small park on MacDonough Drive at the foot of the falls in the town of Vergennes.

## MACDONOUGH BOULDER — VERGENNES, VERMONT

Thomas MacDonough was the American Naval Commander on Lake Champlain, and is remembered for the achievement of building a fleet at Vergennes, and wresting control of Lake Champlain from the British. His decisive victory at the Battle of Lake Champlain on September 11, 1814, greatly influenced the peace talks, which were at that time going on in Ghent, Belgium. The Daughters of the American Revolution have placed a memorial boulder to him near the spot where his flotilla was built. Simply inscribed "MACDONOUGH," it is at the intersection of MacDonough Drive and Comfort Hill in the town of Vergennes.

# LAKE CHAMPLAIN FLEET MONUMENT — VERGENNES, VERMONT

This monument erected by the United States Government and the State of Vermont commemorates the American vessels that fought and won the Battle of Lake Champlain, and pays tribute to the efforts of Thomas MacDonough in achieving that victory. The monument is located in a park on North Street in the town of Vergennes.

# SITE OF FORT CASSIN — OTTER CREEK, VERMONT

Anticipating that the British fleet would enter Lake Champlain before his fleet could be ready, Thomas MacDonough had Fort Cassin constructed in the spring of 1813. It was a hastily constructed earth work, mounting seven twelve-pound long guns, and named for MacDonough's second in command Lieutenant Stephen Cassin. Situated at the mouth of Otter Creek, it was well suited to command the entrance and protect the squadron which was being built at Vergennes.

The fort saw action on May 14, 1813, when the British squadron from Île aux Noix cautiously approached the position. The British vessels and the fort exchanged fire for about an hour and a half, but unable to make any impression on the fort, and noting that the shore was lined with militia, Captain Pring turned his vessels north to other potential targets. American casualties were light with only three wounded, while the British suffered one seaman dead and two wounded. The mouth of Otter Creek is accessible from a narrow road from Vergennes, but presently the site is unmarked and there are no above-ground remains of the fort.

# CHAPTER 17
## PLATTSBURG

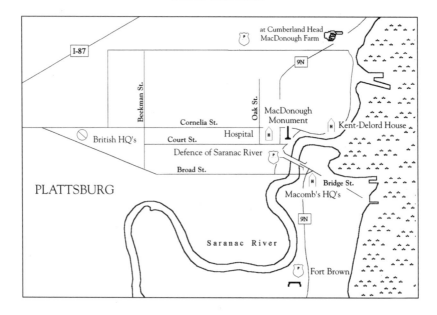

## BATTLE OF PLATTSBURG MONUMENT

On the morning of September 11, 1814, Sir George Prevost had seven thousand veteran troops deployed north of the Saranac River ready to assault the American lines. Facing him was General Alexander Macomb with 1,700 troops backed up with fortifications. Prevost's plan was to have Captain Downie's fleet round Cumberland Head in the early morning, and destroy the American fleet at anchor. While the two fleets engaged in the bay, he would then order an assault against the American lines. Theoretically the plan was sound, but when the land assault was delayed, the naval battle fought in the bay decided the issue. Although there was a small land skirmish in the battle, with his fleet destroyed Sir George had few options but to retreat.

The American fleet commander, Captain MacDonough, utilized an unusual tactic in the battle. He anchored his vessels on "springs," which was a procedure whereby the vessels could remain stationary but still turn, presenting a fresh broadside if required.

With this tactic the ships were robbed of their mobility, but gained greater accuracy in gunnery, since the vessel presented a more stable platform. The naval engagement began at 9:00 AM but unfortunately for the British, Captain Downie was killed in the first few minutes, and this left the command structure in a quandary during the critical opening stages. After a two-hour engagement at close range, the two fleets literally tore each other apart, but the Americans had the better of it, and at 11:00 AM the British struck their colours.

On land, Sir George Prevost had ordered his artillery to bombard the U.S. positions, and by the end of the naval engagement his troops should have been storming the American lines. But his orders to General Robinson, the commander of the flanking column, were given too late, and by the time these troops had started their march, the naval engagement was at its height.

As a further misfortune, the guide leading the flanking column lost his way, and another hour was lost in locating the ford on the Saranac river. By the time the troops finally reached the ford, the naval engagement was over, and just as they were about to cross the ford, they received an order from Prevost to retreat. At this point they had already come under fire from the Americans, and nothing could have been more galling to these veteran troops than to retreat in the face of militia! In frustration they obeyed the order and returned to camp. There was virtually no "land" battle of Plattsburg, only a spectacular bombardment and an ignominious retreat. MacDonough's naval victory in the bay was decisive.

Sir George Prevost's retreat from Plattsburg would hang like a shadow over his career, for people soon forgot his successful defence of Canada. Sadly, he was never able to clear his name, for he died one month before a court martial might have exonerated him of all charges. In retrospect, it is hard to imagine what more he could have done, with the British fleet destroyed and the Americans in command of the lake. The Battle of Plattsburg was truly decisive, because it influenced the peace talks which were then in progress at Ghent, Belgium.

An impressive monument to MacDonough's victory has been erected in the city of Plattsburg. It is made of Indiana Limestone, and has inscribed on the sides the names of his four main vessels,

*Saratoga, Ticonderoga, Eagle,* and *Preble.* The monument is 135 feet high and was dedicated in 1926. It is located in City Hall Place, Plattsburg.

## DEFENCE OF SARANAC RIVER

The main American defences in the Battle of Plattsburg were along the south side of the Saranac River, and they stretched from the river's mouth to a ford about two thousand yards west. Three earthwork forts were added between the river and the lake, and were named Fort Brown, Fort Moreau, and Fort Scott. In 1895, the faculty and students of the Normal school placed a plaque to commemorate the successful defence of the Saranac River Bridge. It is located on the lower bridge over the Saranac River on Bridge Street.

## KENT — DELORD HOUSE

The house was built by Nathan Averill Sr. in 1797 and owned by James Kent, who was a judge in the town of Plattsburg. In 1810 Kent sold the house to Henry Delord from Peru, New York who added to the house and later named the large front room his "winter parlor." Generals Scott, Brown, Totten, Pike, and Commodore MacDonough were all entertained in this front room at one time or another.

In July of 1813 Colonel Murray's raiders landed at the mouth of the river just opposite the Delord home. Mrs. Delord, seven months pregnant, fled the house and returned to the home of her family in Peru, but not before burying the family silver in the yard. Henry Delord operated a business at the southwest of his property which was called the "Red Store," and here trade goods were supplied to the U.S. Army. During Murray's raid the British carried off over one thousand dollars worth of Mr. Delord's supplies.

When the British Army returned to Plattsburg in September of 1814, Mrs. Delord had to vacate the house once more. During this sojourn the British stayed a little longer, camping in the woods to the north of the house, and establishing batteries to the east of the property near the river. Though the house was directly in the field of fire during the Battle of Plattsburg, it was miraculously spared.

After the battle Mrs. Delord returned to the house, to find the west or "Blue" room full of broken furniture and piled up clothing. In their haste, her British "guests" had left an officer's mess chest containing some silver, which can still be viewed in the house today. It appears to have been the property of Captain Graham of the Royal Army.

The War of 1812 ruined the Delord family financially, for they were never compensated for the supplies they gave to the American army. When the Delord family left Plattsburg permanently, they donated the "Red Building" to the Roman Catholic Church, and it was subsequently used as a place of worship for years.

Today the Kent–Delord house is open to the public and guided tours may be arranged. A New York State Historic Plaque is located in front of the building and indicates that the house was used as British officers headquarters during the Battle of Plattsburg. The house is located at 17 Cumberland Avenue in the city of Plattsburg.

## BRITISH HOSPITAL

This house was owned by Charles Dunham and was used by the British as a hospital during the battle. The British retreated quickly from the area and left their wounded in the house. The building has been modified since the war, but it still stands at the corner of Court and Oak Streets in the city of Plattsburg. It now houses the Clinton County Historical Museum, and a New York State Plaque is in front of the house.

# SIR GEORGE PREVOST'S HEADQUARTERS

The headquarters of the British Commander in Chief, Sir George Prevost, were located in the home of Edward Allen, which used to stand here in the tract of land formed by Broad and Cornelia Streets. The site is presently unmarked and a commercial office now occupies the ground.

# GENERAL MACOMB'S HEADQUARTERS

At the time of the War of 1812 this house was owned by Major General Benjamin Mooers of the New York State Militia. Although Mooers did not live in the house until after the war, it was used by Brigadier General Alexander Macomb as his headquarters during the Battle of Plattsburg. A stone placed by the Saranac Chapter, Daughters of the American Revolution, is imbedded into the brickwork at the front of the house. The home is a private residence and not open to the public, and is located at the corner of Bridge and Peru streets in the city of Plattsburg.

# FORT BROWN

Fort Brown is one of three forts that were commenced by Major General George Izard in the spring of 1814. The two other forts were named Fort Moreau and Fort Scott, but only the remains of Fort Brown exist today. They were part of a general defence plan to protect the line of the Saranac River against attack from the north. With the British invasion expected in the autumn of 1814, Fort Brown was completed by General Macomb when he was left in command by General Izard. Fort Brown is an earthwork structure, and is the last remaining vestige of the Battle of Plattsburg, and as such should be treated with respect. The fort is located on Route 9 at the south end of the city of Plattsburg. A New York State Plaque is located at the site.

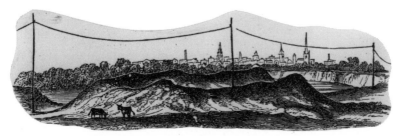

Fort Brown as Lossing sketched it in 1860

Fort Brown today

# MACDONOUGH FARM, CUMBERLAND HEAD, NEW YORK

Because of his great naval victory at the Battle of Plattsburg, the State of Vermont presented to Thomas MacDonough a farm located at this site. The farm was two hundred acres and overlooked the scene of his great victory in Plattsburg Bay. The State of New York was also grateful and presented him over two thousand additional acres of land. A New York State Plaque on Cumberland Head Road marks the farm's location.

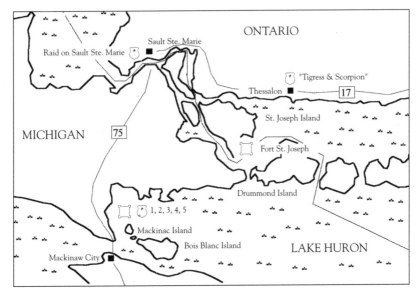

1. Fort Mackinac
2. British Landing
3. British Cannon
4. Battlefield of 1814
5. Fort Holmes

## RAID ON SAULT STE. MARIE — SAULT STE. MARIE, ONTARIO

In the summer of 1814 the Americans planned to recapture Fort Mackinac, but prior to their attack the fleet under Captain Arthur Sinclair, and an infantry force under Lieutenant Colonel George Croghan, moved against St. Joseph Island. Burning the abandoned fort, they respected individual private property and left the settlement and the North West Company stores intact, but with contrary winds they were forced to stay at the island. Here, while laying over they captured the North West Company schooner *Mink*, which was on its way to the falls of St. Marys, present day Sault Ste.

Marie. Utilizing their time to the maximum, they decided to destroy the North West Company's depot at the Sault by using the squadron's boats.

On July 21, 1814, a mixed force of 150 sailors and soldiers landed at the Sault under the command of Major Holmes and Lieutenant Daniel Turner. They proceeded to destroy the bateau locks, sawmill, and storehouses and burned the schooner *Perseverance*. They then left unmolested and returned to the fleet. With favourable winds, the squadron then proceeded to the abortive attack on Fort Mackinac. An Ontario Provincial Plaque describes the small raid, and is located at the east end of the Canadian locks in the city of Sault Ste. Marie.

## FORT ST. JOSEPH — ST. JOSEPH ISLAND, ONTARIO

By the terms of Jay's Treaty in 1794 the British were forced to give up Fort Mackinac at the junction of Lakes Huron and Michigan. The fort was in a strategic position to take advantage of the fur trade, the key to which was the loyalty of the western Indians. Economically, the British were forced to build a new fort in the vicinity or lose the goodwill of the Indians, for whom they were politically and morally allied.

Fort St. Joseph was constructed in the period 1798 to 1803 and was Upper Canada's most isolated outpost, but its importance far outweighed its physical size. When war was declared in June of 1812, a bizarre set of circumstances put the garrison of only thirty-nine men on the centre stage.

Due to the ineptness of the politicians in Washington, and communication being what they were at the time, Captain Charles Roberts knew of the declaration of war before the Americans at Fort Mackinac. With this intelligence, there was a splendid opportunity to capture Fort Mackinac before the Americans could react, and with Brock's approval, Roberts decided to make the attempt. Augmenting his meager garrison with Indians, fur traders, Canadians, and employees of the North West Company, Roberts eventually assembled a force of over six hundred men. Taking the schooner *Caledonia* and a number of canoes, they travelled the forty-five miles to Mackinac Island and landed in the early morning, catching the garrison totally by surprise. Not even knowing that war had been declared, Lieutenant Porter Hanks had little choice but to surrender.

The capture of Fort Mackinac won the loyalty of the western Indians, and had an impact hundreds of miles away. For the garrison of Fort St. Joseph, this was their shining hour. Captain Robert's men soon relocated to Fort Mackinac, which was in a superior position, and which they held until the end of the war. Their former site, Fort St. Joseph, was burned in 1813 when the Americans gained naval superiority on the Upper Lakes.

Fort St. Joseph was never rebuilt, though after the war the British maintained a small outpost on nearby Drummond Island. When the Montreal merchants finally lost their trading licence, they too abandoned the site and the community drifted into oblivion. The site of Fort St. Joseph today is maintained by Parks Canada. Numerous archeological excavations have taken place and some remains have been restored. A visitor centre is located at the site and tells the story of this historic landmark. The fort is accessible by a causeway from the mainland on Highway 17, west of Desbarats, Ontario. (see prior entry)

## CAPTURE OF *TIGRESS* AND *SCORPION* — THESSALON, ONTARIO

In the summer of 1814, after the successful defence from an American attack, the garrison of Fort Mackinac was still critically short of supplies. After the supply schooner *Nancy* was destroyed by the Americans on the Nottawasaga River, the situation became desperate. Fortunately for the British, the crew of the *Nancy* under Lieutenant Miller Worsley managed to escape their pursuers, and despite the loss of his vessel, Worsley was determined to relieve Fort Mackinac. He and his men proceeded up the Nottawasaga River to another cache of supplies, and loaded as much as possible into two bateaux and one large canoe. The party then made their way north to Georgian Bay to complete the dangerous mission — and dangerous it was, with the American squadron in full command of the Upper Lakes.

After a six-day journey, hugging the north shore of Lake Huron, they approached a narrow body of water called "the detour." Much to their dismay it was guarded by two American schooners, the *Tigress* and *Scorpion*. Worsley knew that the two bateaux would never make it through the detour without being spotted, so he hid them in a small bay and embarked his whole crew into the large canoe. They slipped by the two schooners on the evening of August 29th and by sunset of September 1st, the weary party had arrived at Fort Mackinac.

Worsley convinced Lieutenant Colonel Robert McDouall that the American schooners could be taken, and they proceeded to outfit an expedition for their capture. The force selected numbered about three hundred men, consisting of a large body of Indians, members of the Royal Navy, and a detachment from the Royal Newfoundland Regiment. Leaving the next evening, they approached the "detour" and found only one American schooner.

At about 9:00 PM the British party approached the anchored schooner, but with no reply given to their call sign, the sailors from the vessel fired on the approaching boats with musketry and a twenty-four-pound cannon. But the vessel was soon boarded from two sides by parties under Lieutenant Worsley and Lieutenant Bulger and soon surrendered to overpowering numbers. The vessel turned out to be the schooner *Tigress* under the command of sailing master Champlin. While making preparations to send the captured crew back to Mackinac, Worsley he sent out a canoe under Lieutenant Livingston to search for the other American vessel.

Livingston reported that the other schooner was slowly beating up towards them, and deciding on a ruse, Lieutenant Worsley kept the American flag flying from the captured vessel. The newly sighted vessel anchored some two miles away from the *Tigress*, completely unaware that she had now been taken by the British. The next day in the early morning hours, Worsley had the *Tigress* slip her cable and move down on the other vessel. Still flying the American flag, and now armed with the captured call signals, the *Tigress* lay alongside the enemy vessel, and took her within ten minutes.

The *Tigress* and the *Scorpion* had been captured, and Lieutenant Worsley had well avenged the loss of his schooner *Nancy* to these same two vessels. More important, the strategic naval picture had changed once more, for the Upper Lakes were once again in British hands, a power they held until the end of the war. An Ontario Provincial Plaque commemorating this amazing feat is located in the Municipal Park in the town of Thessalon. (see also The *Nancy* and Nancy Island Historic Site)

## FORT MACKINAC — MACKINAC ISLAND, MICHIGAN

Towards the end of the American Revolution, the British abandoned Fort Michilimackinac on the mainland, and erected Fort Mackinac on Mackinac Island. By the terms of Jay's Treaty signed in 1794 they were obliged to give up the fort to the Americans, but did not do so until two years later.

At the commencement of the War of 1812, it was garrisoned by sixty men under Lieutenant Porter Hanks of the U.S. artillery. On the early morning of July 17, 1812, Hanks was forced to surrender the fort to the British, completely unaware that the war had commenced.

The British held Fort Mackinac for the entire war, but in 1814 the American army and navy did make an attempt to recapture it, but were repulsed in the Battle of Mackinac just to the north. By the Treaty of Ghent, which ended the War of 1812, the fort was given back to the United States.

Fort Mackinac has been restored, and has seventeen original buildings, guides in period dress, and a museum. A plaque placed by the Michigan Historical Commission is located near the fort, and also describes Fort Holmes, formerly Fort George, which was constructed by the British in 1812. Fort Mackinac is accessible by ferry from Mackinaw City, Michigan. (see previous entry)

# BRITISH LANDING — MACKINAC ISLAND, MICHIGAN

The British under the command of Captain Roberts landed at this spot at about 3:00 AM on July 17, 1812. His force of over six hundred men, mainly Indians, but including men from the 10th Royal Veteran Battalion and members of the Northwest Company, proceeded south to attack Fort Mackinac from the rear. With the help of two oxen given to them by Michael Dousman, a local resident, they managed to drag two six-pound cannons to a height overlooking the fort. At 10:00 AM Lieutenant Porter Hanks, unaware that war had been declared on June 16th, surrendered the garrison. A plaque placed by the Michigan Historical Commission identifies the location, and is located on the northwest shore of Mackinac Island.

# BRITISH CANNONS — MACKINAC ISLAND, MICHIGAN

A plaque placed by the Michigan Historical Commission identifies the location where the British cannons were placed on July 17, 1812. The plaque is located on the high ground north of Fort Mackinac.

# BATTLEFIELD OF 1814 — MACKINAC ISLAND, MICHIGAN

After the Battle of Lake Erie in September of 1813, the United States had total control of Lake Erie and the Upper Lakes. With these advantages, Captain Richard Bullock, at Mackinac, surmised the Americans would now attempt the recapture of the fort. He wrote his superiors and asked for reinforcements, although he knew they could only arrive in spring. Fortunately for Bullock, the American army and navy were unable to begin their campaign against Mackinac before the end of the season.

Although the garrison suffered a terrible winter with short provisions, in early spring the reinforcements arrived, having left early in the season and taken the York-Nottawasaga Route. The men were from the redoubtable Royal Newfoundland Regiment, under Lieutenant Colonel Robert McDouall, the new commanding officer.

On July 26, 1814 the expected invasion finally came with the appearance of the American fleet, which included the brigs *Niagara*, *Lawrence*, *Caledonia*, and the schooners *Tigress* and *Scorpion*, all veterans from the Battle of Lake Erie. On board was a mixed force of regulars, militia, artillery, and marines numbering about 750 men.

The squadron commander, Captain Arthur Sinclair, used the next week to take soundings and reconnoitre the island, but much to his chagrin he discovered that the guns of the fleet could not reach the fort. With this development, the commander of the infantry force, Lieutenant Colonel George Croghan, decided to march overland to the rear of the fort. The plan duplicated the very tactics used by the British two years before.

After a heavy naval bombardment of the empty beach, the infantry force landed on August 4th. Pushing rapidly inland they reached the farm of Michael Dousman on the north end of the island. Meanwhile, the British under Lieutenant Colonel McDouall were not inactive themselves, and determined not to repeat the mistakes of the last siege, he marched his disposable force to meet the Americans. His field force consisted of 350 Indians, 100 men from the Royal Newfoundland Fencibles, 50 militia, and 2 cannons — in all about 500 men.

Reaching the area of the Dousman farm before Croghan's forces, he deployed them on the edge of the forest at the south end of the property. When the Americans finally entered the clearing they were met by musketry and cannon shot from the British, and after deploying their own cannons, Croghan's artillerists tried to drive the British from the position.

But neither side was having much success with cannons in the dense forest, and infantry charges against the British could not break their line. Finally the Americans tried to outflank the position, but the British managed to check two separate flanking manoeuvres against their right.

Major Andrew Hunter Holmes then tried a third flanking manoeuvre, only this time against the British left, but the column was met by a party of Menominee Indians who fired a volley that killed Major Holmes. In the resulting confusion, Croghan decided to call off the attack, and by nightfall they were back on board the fleet. The attack had been a costly failure, and the American fleet later bore off to try and find the schooner *Nancy*, which they knew was in the vicinity of the Nottawasaga River. A plaque has been placed by the Michigan Historical Commission to commemorate the battle and is located near the Wawashkamo Golf Club on Mackinac Island.

## FORT HOLMES — MACKINAC ISLAND, MICHIGAN

After the British capture of Mackinac Island in 1812, they built Fort George on the highest point of land on the island. It consisted of a blockhouse and stockade, and was part of a general defence plan against the recapture of the island. After the War of 1812 the Americans renamed it Fort Holmes, in honour of Major Holmes, who had been killed nearby in the Battle of Mackinac. A reconstruction of the fort, which dates from 1936, now occupies the site and a plaque placed by the Michigan Historical Commission is located on Fort Holmes Road north of town.

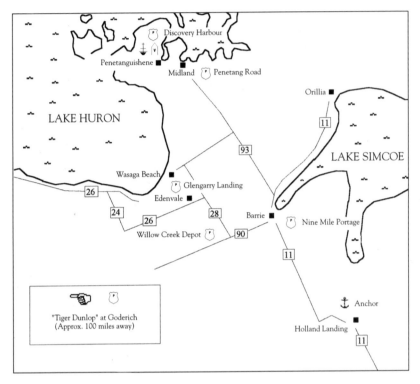

## PENETANG ROAD — MIDLAND, ONTARIO

During the winter of 1814–1815 a new road was commenced to connect the new naval base planned at Penetanguishene to the capital of York (Toronto). One company of Canadian Fencibles and some militia under Dr. William Dunlop were detailed to start the construction. Working under incredible hardships, with snow six feet deep, without horses and oxen, the men worked on the road throughout the winter. The snow was so deep that a pit had to be shovelled around each tree in order to give the men room to swing the axes.

The road was to play a key part in the strategic defence of the Upper Lakes for 1815, but fortunately the Treaty of Ghent, signed on Christmas Eve 1814, ended the War of 1812. Today an Ontario Provincial Plaque, located on Hugel Avenue off Highway 27 near Midland, marks a portion of the old road.

## NINE MILE PORTAGE — BARRIE, ONTARIO

The nine-mile portage was part of an important supply line for the British during the War of 1812. Supplies had to be carried from Kempenfeldt Bay on Lake Simcoe to the Willow Creek Depot, and from there travelled via Willow Creek to the Nottawasaga River, and thence to Georgian Bay. The portage became critically important after the American navy gained control of the Upper Lakes. During the winter of 1813–1814 a relief force under the command of Lieutenant Colonel Robert McDouall used the portage to come to the aid of beleaguered Fort Mackinac. An Ontario Provincial Plaque to the portage is located in the city of Barrie at Dunlop Street and Fred Grant Square. (see next entry and also Battlefield of 1814)

## WILLOW CREEK DEPOT — MINESING, ONTARIO

The Willow Creek Depot was the main staging area for supplies moving from Lower Canada and York to the Upper Lakes, and during the war it was surrounded by a wooden palisade and had eight buildings. Today no trace of the structures remain, but an Ontario Provincial Plaque is located in an obscure location near the Willow Creek in Vespra Township near Minesing, Ontario. This particular site is not easy to find and is recommended for only the most intrepid traveller. The exact location is on Lot 14, Concession IX on a side road in heavily forested terrain. (see prior entry)

# GLENGARRY LANDING — EDENVALE, ONTARIO

By the spring of 1814 the Americans had command of the Upper Lakes, and Fort Mackinac was the only British-held post left on Lake Huron. In the autumn of 1813, the commanding officer at Mackinac, Captain Richard Bullock, had written for reinforcements, but fortunately the high command had recognized the seriousness of the situation, and a relief expedition was already being planned.

Governor General Sir George Prevost, in a letter to the Earl of Bathurst, had said of Fort Mackinac "Its geographical position is admirable ... Its influence extends and is felt amongst the Indian Tribes at New Orleans and the Pacific Ocean; vast tracts of country look to it for protection and supplies, and it gives security to the great establishments of the Northwest and Hudson's Bay Companies by supporting the Indians on the Mississippi."

The relief expedition was organized in the winter of 1813–1814, and in February Lieutenant Colonel McDouall's party of twenty-one seamen, some shipwrights, eleven artillery men, and two companies of the Royal Newfoundland Regiment, crossed frozen Lake Simcoe and moved over the Nine Mile Portage. McDouall selected this site at the forks of the Nottawasaga, to build his fleet of bateaux for the relief of Fort Mackinac, and named it after his unit, the Glengarry Light Infantry. By April 19th McDouall's men had built thirty bateaux and loaded them with provisions and military stores.

Taking advantage of the mildness of the season, they descended the Nottawasaga and arrived at Fort Mackinac on May 18th, delivering all of the supplies, but having lost only one bateaux. This timely arrival saved Fort Mackinac from the amphibious attack that followed that summer. A cairn commemorating the Glengarry Landing has been placed by the National Historic Sites and Monuments Board of Canada and is located on Route 26 halfway between Barrie and Stayner, near Edenvale.

## ANCHOR AT HOLLAND LANDING — ANCHOR PARK, ONTARIO

In the closing days of the War of 1812 a large four-thousand-pound anchor was carried on sleighs from Kingston to Soldiers Bay, but when the news of peace was heard the anchor was promptly abandoned. In 1870 the anchor was brought here where it has remained ever since. The anchor can be seen in "Anchor Park" at Holland Landing, Ontario.

## *TIGRESS* AND *SCORPION* — PENETANGUISHENE, ONTARIO

The Historic Sites and Monuments Board of Canada has placed a cairn to commemorate the capture of the two American schooners, *Tigress* and *Scorpion* by a mixed force under the command of Lieutenant Worsley of the British Navy. The event is also commemorated by an Ontario Provincial marker at Thessalon, Ontario. The two vessels were captured in an area of water called "the detour," between the mainland of Michigan State and Drummond Island. (see capture of *Tigress* and *Scorpion*)

## THE *NANCY* — WASAGA BEACH, ONTARIO

After the failure of the attack on Fort Mackinac, Captain Sinclair of the American navy decided to institute a naval blockade of the island. From intelligence gained from the capture of the Northwest Company schooner *Mink*, he now knew the location of the supply schooner *Nancy*, and made plans for her destruction. The commander of the *Nancy*, Lieutenant Miller Worsley R.N., also gained intelligence of the American blockade, and made plans for her defence.

The *Nancy* was hauled up the narrow Nottawasaga River and her guns placed inside a hastily constructed blockhouse. Worsley utilized the natural cover of the sand dunes, which lay between the *Nancy* and the lake, and covered the vessel with branches. On August 13th the U.S. brig *Niagara* and the schooners *Tigress* and *Scorpion* arrived at the mouth of the Nottawasaga. On board the vessels was an artillery detachment and three companies of U.S regulars under the command of Lieutenant Colonel George Croghan, the same man who had successfully defended Fort Stephenson the year before, at Sandusky Ohio.

After landing his soldiers they began searching for a suitable campsite when they spotted the *Nancy*, her tall masts giving her away. The next morning Captain Sinclair anchored his three vessels opposite her location, and attempted to bombard the vessel from the lake, but the sand dunes screened the *Nancy's* too well. He then landed a couple of Howitzer's ashore, which were high trajectory cannons, and proceeded to bombard the helpless schooner. It was not too long before Worsley realized that the *Nancy* was doomed and determined to blow her up.

At that point however a lucky hit ignited some combustible material in the blockhouse, which soon reached the magazine and in a large explosion, the fire reached the *Nancy* and she went down sizzling into the waters of the Nottawasaga. With this action Captain Sinclair had destroyed British naval power on the Upper Lakes entirely.

Sailing the *Niagara* back to Lake Erie, he left Lieutenant Daniel Turner with the *Tigress* and *Scorpion* to maintain the blockade and intercept any fur canoes from Lake Superior. But he had not reckoned on the temerity of Lieutenant Worsley, who in a daring action less than three weeks later, would restore the naval balance to the British. A plaque has been placed by the Historic Sites and Monuments Board of Canada which commemorates the last gallant action of the schooner *Nancy*. The plaque is at the entrance to Nancy Island Historic Site, Wasaga Beach, Ontario. (see capture of *Tigress* and *Scorpion*)

# NANCY ISLAND HISTORIC SITE — WASAGA BEACH, ONTARIO

The schooner *Nancy* sank into the waters of the Nottawasaga River on August 14, 1814, and over the years her exact location was forgotten. It was in the summer of 1911 that an interested student of the lake vessels thought that he might be able to find her again. Browsing around a small island near the mouth of the Nottawasaga, an amazing discovery was made, moving aside some water lilies near the shore and staring into the clear water, a vessel could be seen! It was the *Nancy*, her one-hundred-year-old secret finally revealed. The man who found her was C.H.J Snider, who went on to write some of our earliest naval history of the War of 1812.

In 1814 there was no island at the mouth of the Nottawasaga, but after the *Nancy's* demise, she lay at the bottom of the shallow river with silt and debris forming all around her.

Decades went by, and an island was formed around the remains of the long lost schooner. Even though Mr. Snider had discovered her years before, it was not until the summer of 1924 that interest in the *Nancy* was revived. In August of that year an American twenty-four-pound round shot was found by Dr. F. J. Conboy, and it was this small find that provided the spark for the federal and provincial governments to take interest.

In 1927 the remains of the *Nancy* were raised and placed on the island, and the next summer on August 14, 1928, the first *Nancy* museum was opened to the public. In 1968 a completely new museum was built, and this is where the vessel lies today. The museum features audio visual displays, and a theatre which shows a film telling the *Nancy's* incredible story. The museum is run by the provincial government and is located on Nancy Island, Nottawasaga River, Wasaga Beach.

## UNKNOWN SOLDIER — NANCY ISLAND, ONTARIO

On July 23, 1949 the remains of a British soldier from the War of 1812 were found on the banks of the Nottawasaga River. On September 6, 1949 the soldier was re-interred on Nancy Island with full military honours. A stone dedicated to "service veterans past, present and future" marks the location. The stone is located on Nancy Island near the entrance to the museum.

## SCHOONER TOWN — WASAGA BEACH, ONTARIO

Schooner Town was the main naval base for the Royal Navy on Lake Huron and was located at the foot of navigation of the Nottawasaga River. It was also the terminus of a long supply line which stretched back to Kempenfeldt Bay on Lake Simcoe. With the establishment of a new naval base at Penetanguishene in 1815, Schooner Town was no longer needed. The site is now administered by Wasaga Beach Provincial Park. A small display and an Ontario Provincial Plaque is located on the River Road West, a few miles southwest from the mouth of the Nottawasaga River. (see Nine Mile Portage)

## DISCOVERY HARBOUR — PENETANGUISHENE, ONTARIO

For the first two years of the War of 1812, the British had control of the Upper Lakes, but after the disastrous Battle of Lake Erie in September 1813, their fleet had been eliminated. This meant that American vessels were now free to move into the Upper Lakes via the St. Clair River, and because of this the British had to consider an alternate location for a naval base.

At first Turkey Point on Lake Erie had been considered, but later Penetanguishene was chosen in Georgian Bay, and it was an ideal location. Utilizing the new road to Penetanguishene constructed during the winter of 1814, Colonel George Head arrived at Penetang in February, 1815 to commence construction of the new naval base. On March 9, 1815 Colonel Head received instructions to halt the work, as the peace treaty had been signed on December 24, 1814.

But the hard lessons learned during the war were not forgotten, for the campaigns had demonstrated that naval control was crucial to victory. During 1815 and 1816, during the years of uneasy peace, the work was recommenced at Penetang, and a small party completed the buildings and cleared the shore for docks. During the next five years the establishment reached its peak, with a complement of about seventy workmen, and by this time the site consisted of docks, workshops, barracks, and houses. A detachment of British regulars was stationed here, and ships called regularly, unloading naval supplies, tools, and cordage which were placed in a large storehouse.

In more recent times the base was administered by the Ministry of Tourism for the Government of Ontario, and was called the "Historic Naval and Military Establishments." The site is now called "Discovery Harbour" and consists of over fifteen restored buildings, dating from the period 1817–1834. Guides in period dress interpret the site and the visitor is given a glance at what life was like in those early days just after the War of 1812. There are also three working vessels established at the park. The schooners *Bee*, *Tecumseth*, and *Perseverance* are very much like their 1812 counterparts. The park offers afternoon and evening sails on the vessels, and visitors may participate as crew. Discovery Harbour is well worth a visit, and is located on the northeast side of Penetanguishene, Ontario.

# CAPTAIN JAMES KEATING —
# DISCOVERY HARBOUR, ONTARIO

During the War of 1812 James Keating, a sergeant in the Royal Artillery, was present at the surrender of Detroit in 1812, and was in the Battle of Crysler's Farm on November 11, 1813. In June of 1814 he accompanied the expedition led by Major William McKay for the recapture of Prairie du Chien on the Upper Mississippi River, and he was placed in command of the only field gun that was with the expedition.

On July 17th Major McKay's forces invested newly constructed Fort Shelby at Prairie du Chien. Aiding in the fort's defence was the gunboat *Governor Clarke* which was moored nearby in the river. Sergeant Keating's cannon opened up on the gunboat and after two hours forced it to drift down river. For the next two days the British and Indians maintained a close siege of the fort.

Sergeant Keating's cannon continued to bombard the fort, and when their only well went dry, the garrison was forced to surrender. A relief column for the fort had already been dispatched under Major Taylor, and Keating was also present when the British ambushed this column at the Rock Island Rapids on September 5, 1814.

His judicious handling of the three-pound gun and two swivel guns aided greatly to the success of that day. After the war, Keating was promoted to adjutant of Fort St. Joseph and also served on Drummond Island. When the establishment moved from Drummond in 1828, he accompanied the garrison to this site. Captain Keating died in 1849, and an Ontario Provincial Plaque dedicated to him is located in front of the Keating house on the grounds of Discovery Harbour at Penetanguishene.

# REMAINS OF *TECUMSETH* —
## DISCOVERY HARBOUR, ONTARIO

August 29, 1953 was a memorable one for the citizens of Penetanguishene. Citizens and families from miles around drove into town to see the historic occasion — the raising of a vessel from the War of 1812! and this was no ordinary vessel either. For this was the captured U.S. schooner *Scorpion*, renamed H.M.S. *Confiance* by the British, and an actual participant in the Battle of Lake Erie.

The raising operation began at 7:00 AM and after much trial and tribulation the remains of the vessel were on shore by late afternoon. When the sun went down the entertainment was over, and the crowds went home. But when the experts began examining the wreck days later, something was wrong, for the dimensions did not match the known dimensions of the American schooner. If this was not *Scorpion*, then what was she? A closer examination of the naval records and architects specifications, revealed that she must be the *Tecumseth* or *Newash*. These vessels had been built at Chippawa, Ontario in the closing days of the War of 1812.

Further research demonstrated that this was *Tecumseth*. *Newash* had been modified at some point in her career, and the skeleton of this vessel indicated no such modification. These twin schooners were designed to be more powerful than the American schooners that had fought at the Battle of Lake Erie and evidence showed that the British had learned from their mistakes. The armament of the vessels was two long twenty-four-pound guns and two thirty-two-pound carronades, which was formidable for vessels these size. They were twice as powerful as the American schooners of Perry's squadron.

The exact date of their launch is difficult to determine, because in some cases admiralty drafts were made only after the vessels were completed. Whether or not the schooners were launched during the war is immaterial. The fact that they were built showed that the British were determined to hold on to the Upper Lakes. *Tecumseth* and *Newash* were transferred to Penetang in the spring of 1815, where they did some work as supply vessels but were soon put "in ordinary" (covered up with wood to preserve them against the elements, or "moth balled"). The remains of *Tecumseth* are on display at Discovery Harbour, Penetanguishene, Ontario.

## SCHOONERS *BEE, AND TECUMSETH —* DISCOVERY HARBOUR, ONTARIO

The schooner *Bee* is a replica of the type of vessel that plied the Upper Lakes during the War of 1812. The vessel was launched in the spring of 1984 and is a faithful copy of the original, which was built at Penetanguishene in 1817. The vessel's main purpose was the carrying of supplies, and she bears a striking resemblance to other vessels of the war such as the schooner *Nancy*. Today the *Bee* and *Tecumseth* are moored at the wharf inside Discovery Harbour, and visitors may book passage for an afternoon sail. Discovery Harbour is located at Penetanguishene, Ontario. (see The *Nancy*)

## *TIGER DUNLOP —* GODERICH, ONTARIO

Doctor William Dunlop, a native of Scotland, served as an army surgeon in the 89th Regiment of foot during the War of 1812. He arrived at Quebec in November of 1813, but could not join his unit because the American army under General Wilkinson was between him and his regiment. Dr. Dunlop was put in charge of the wounded from the Battle of Crysler's Farm, where Wilkinson was defeated, and after that officer's retreat Dunlop rejoined his regiment then quartered at Fort Wellington, Prescott.

After the Battle of Lundy's Lane on July 25, 1814, Dr. Dunlop was once again placed in charge of the wounded at Fort George and later was present at the siege of Fort Erie in August of 1814. He was responsible for the cutting of the "Penetang Road" from Lake Simcoe to Penetang in December of 1814.

He later wrote of his experiences in Canada in a series of articles that appeared in The Literary Garland of Montreal in 1847, which he called "Recollections of the American War." This remarkable man had a fascinating history of travel, and his further adventures are described on an Ontario Provincial plaque, located at his tomb on Highway 21, north of Goderich, Ontario.

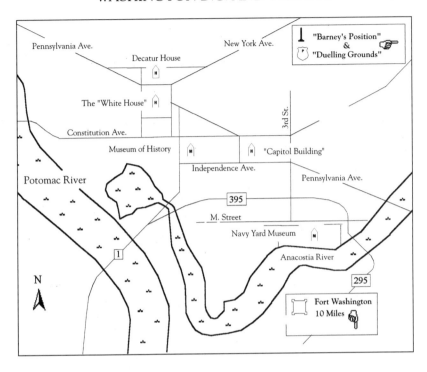

## BARNEY'S POSITION — BLADENSBURG, MARYLAND

In the summer of 1814 the British fleet commander, Rear Admiral George Cockburn, had convinced Major General Robert Ross that the city of Washington could be taken. On August 19, 1814 the army under Ross landed at Benedict, Maryland, and marching under the stifling heat of mid-summer, they marched rapidly through the Maryland countryside unopposed. At a place called the "Long Old Fields" they turned west and then counter-marched to the north. This manoeuvre caught the American commander Brigadier General Winder off guard, as he was desperately trying to gather enough forces together to oppose the British advance.

Ross's army numbered about 4,400 veteran soldiers, while Winder was able to assemble about 7000 men, but these were nearly all city and state militia. At the village of Bladensburg northeast of Washington, Winder's army made its stand. He deployed his men in three consecutive lines across the Bladensburg Road, but his arrangements were made in haste, and his deployment was faulty, for his three lines were not in supporting distance of each other. The main action of the battle occurred at the bridge over the east branch of the Potomac River, where the British, supported by Congreve rockets and artillery, stormed across and scattered the militia. When the militia retreated into the second line, causing even greater confusion, this line gave way, and was carried away in the general retreat. Only at the third line did the panic ebb a little, for it was here that Commodore Joshua Barney had his sailors and marines, supported with five heavy naval guns. Standing their ground, Barney and his men inflicted significant casualties on the British, but could not halt their advance. When the rest of the army retreated from the field, Barney was wounded and captured by soldiers of the 85th Regiment.

The victory for the British was amazing considering the numbers involved: Ross's engaged force of about 2,600 men had routed an army of over 6000! The battle laid open the door to the nations capital, which the British entered that evening. The Battle of Bladensburg has been called "America's Darkest Hour," and indeed at the time it must have looked so. The stand made by Commodore Barney's men is commemorated with a plaque and a small monument. They are located at the crest of the hill in Fort Lincoln Cemetery, on the Bladensburg Road, Bladensburg.

The bridge at Bladensburg as Lossing sketched it in 1860

The vicinity of the Bladensburg Bridge today, looking northeast

## THE DUELING GROUNDS — BLADENSBURG, MARYLAND

Although having little to do with the War of 1812 directly, this spot was well known as a dueling ground to settle affairs of "honour" in the nineteenth century. It has the dubious distinction of being the place where naval captain Stephen Decatur was fatally wounded on March 22, 1820. Decatur commanded the frigates *U.S.S. United States* and *U.S.S. President* during the War of 1812. His opponent in the duel was Captain James Barron who commanded the *U.S.S. Chesapeake* at the time of its encounter with the British frigate *Leopard*. A plaque indicating the site has been placed by the Maryland-National Capital Park Planning Commission and is located on the Bladensburg Road not too far from Fort Lincoln Cemetery.

## THE UNITED STATES CAPITOL — WASHINGTON, D.C.

On the evening of August 24, 1814, the third brigade of the British Army entered the city of Washington on the Bladensburg Road, via present-day Maryland Avenue. Accompanying the brigade were General Robert Ross and Admiral George Cockburn. Halting near

the Capitol Building, they paused to discuss their next move. Suddenly musket fire erupted, and General Ross had his horse shot from under him. Four of his men were also hit. The shots were thought to have come from a house owned by a Mr. Sewall, located on the north side of Maryland Avenue. British official policy was to burn all federal buildings, but private property was to be respected unless resistance was offered, therefore as an example, the Sewall house was quickly burned.

The Capitol Building was set aflame along with the treasury buildings, the arsenal, and barracks. The Capitol Building turned out to be very fire resistant, as its construction was nearly all marble and stone and at one point demolition was considered. The idea was abandoned when several citizens pleaded that such an action would destroy their homes also. After the War of 1812 the Capitol Building was rebuilt from the old.

The Capitol Building is one of Washington's most distinguishing features, and the first floor has historical displays: among these is a cross belt from the Royal North British Fusiliers. The Capitol Building is located at the intersection of Maryland Avenue and Pennsylvania Avenue in downtown Washington D.C.

## THE "WHITE HOUSE" — WASHINGTON, D.C.

Though there is nothing at the site to indicate that the president's mansion has any 1812 history, it was burned when the British occupied the city after the Battle of Bladensburg. When they entered Washington on August 24, 1814, British army official policy was to burn all public buildings. This was in retaliation for the burning of York by the Americans the previous summer.

After its destruction, only the walls of the president's mansion remained, and when the house was rebuilt after the war, the walls were "white washed" to conceal the marks of the fire. The name the "White House" has stuck ever since. The White House is still the residence of the president of the United States and is one of America's most historic buildings. The White House is located on Pennsylvania Avenue in downtown Washington. Tours at selected times are available.

# WASHINGTON NAVY YARD — WASHINGTON D.C.

The commander of the Washington Navy Yard, Commodore Thomas Tingey had orders to burn the facilities if the British entered the city. This he did at about 8:00 PM the evening of August 24, 1814, and about one-million-dollars worth of materials were lost. The modern Washington Navy Yard was resurrected from the old, and is on the same site as the 1812 yard. The Washington Navy Yard Museum interprets the entire naval history of the United States, featured in the collection are 1812 displays and a reproduction of the "fighting top" from the American frigate *Constitution*. The museum is on the grounds of the Navy Yard on "M" Street in Washington, D.C.

# NATIONAL MUSEUM OF HISTORY AND TECHNOLOGY

The Smithsonian Institution is a "must see" for any visitor to Washington D.C. The original building still stands, but the museum collection has grown so large that it is now housed in several different buildings. The National Museum of History and Technology has several displays and artifacts on the War of 1812. Of particular note is the original "Star Spangled Banner," which flew over Fort McHenry during the British attack on Baltimore in 1814. The shoulder wings of Captain Ben Burch who commanded a militia battery in the Battle of Bladensburg is also on display. The National Museum of History and Technology is located on Madison Drive in the city of Washington D.C.

# DECATUR HOUSE — WASHINGTON D.C

Captain Stephen Decatur is usually remembered for his daring action during the Tripolitan War, which prompted the famous Lord Nelson to say that it was "the most bold and daring act of the age." The U.S.S. frigate *Philadelphia* had been captured by the Tripolitans, and it was Decatur's mission to see that the vessel was never used again. With the vessel lying under the guns of a fortress, he managed to enter the harbour with seventy-five volunteers, and after overpowering the guards, the vessel was set on fire, while Decatur and his men made their escape. The *Philadelphia* soon exploded, and the amazing feat had cost Decatur only one injured sailor.

On October 25, 1812, Decatur commanded the frigate *United States* in her famous action with the British frigate *Macedonian*. Using superior gunnery and sailing skill, Decatur out-manoeuvred the British frigate and captured her. With the British blockade strangling American commerce for most of 1813 and 1814, Decatur proposed breaking out of New York with a small squadron.

On the evening of January 14, 1815, Decatur commanding the U.S.S. *President*, attempted to run the blockade in heavy seas, but the vessel struck a shoal off of Sandy Hook. Decatur eventually managed to work the vessel free, but her fast sailing speed was impaired. The next morning she was spotted by four British vessels, which immediately gave chase. It was not long before three frigates, *Endymion*, *Pomone*, and *Tenedos* over hauled her and got within firing range.

Numerous cannon shots began to pummel the *President*, and Decatur felt he had little choice but to surrender. It was an embarrassing end to a rather successful career, for unknown to both parties, the war had actually ended on Christmas Eve, 1814. A court martial exonerated him of all blame and he returned to the United States an untarnished hero.

Decatur also had a successful career in the war against Algiers, but it was in 1820 that tragedy struck. In an age where a man's "honour" could mean life or death, Decatur got involved in an old feud with a brother officer, Captain Barron.

When Captain Barron issued a challenge, Decatur could not refuse. At the "old dueling grounds" north of Washington, the two antagonists met. By the early evening of March 22, 1820, Decatur would be lying mortally wounded in this house. He and his wife Susan had lived in the house less than fourteen months. The Decatur house is open to the public and has been restored to the federalist period (1820), and the Victorian era (1880). The house is located at 748 Jackson Place in the city of Washington D.C. (see duelling grounds)

## OLD FORT WASHINGTON — FORT WASHINGTON, MARYLAND

The fort that existed at the time of the War of 1812 was called "Fort Warburton," and was a smaller work located closer to the river than the present fort. It mounted thirteen guns and was completed by 1809. Some of the fort's features were fourteen-foot-high earthen walls, a wide ditch facing the river, and an octagonal tower mounting six guns, which protected the fort's rear. There was also a barracks and a magazine.

By 1813 the fort was known as Fort Washington because of its close proximity to the city, and by the summer of 1814 the garrison consisted of eighty men under Captain Samuel T. Dyson. On August 17, 1814, Captain James Alexander Gordon, with a squadron of ships, began his ascent up the Potomac River acting under the orders of Vice Admiral Sir Alexander Cochrane. His instructions were to act against Fort Washington and mask the main effort, which would be directed against the city of Washington.

His squadron carried about one thousand men and consisted of the frigates *Sea Horse, Euryalus,* the bombships *Devastation, Aetna, Meteor,* and the rocket ship *Erubus.* Gordon was navigating the river based on an old chart dating back to the Revolution, and by "warping" or "towing" the vessels for five days, the fleet finally arrived opposite Maryland Point on August 24th. That night they witnessed the sky lit up from the burning of Washington.

Gordon guessed that his mission was now superfluous, but he decided to exercise his right of "initiative" and the squadron proceeded upriver past Mt. Vernon, where they saluted the home of their old adversary George Washington. At sunset the squadron anchored just out of range of Fort Washington's guns, but the bomb vessels commenced a bombardment in preparation for the main attack the next morning.

At 8:00 PM a tremendous explosion was heard: the defenders of Fort Washington had ignited the powder magazine and retreated! The next morning the surprised British landed an infantry force to complete the work of destruction, but they found the work thoroughly done as the departing Americans had spiked most of the guns.

To retire down river now would have accomplished every object of the mission and more, but this was not enough for the daring Captain Gordon. Re-embarking the land force they proceeded upriver to Alexandria, Virginia, where he accepted the surrender of the old city. Gordon did not harm the town, as it was completely un-defended, but he did lay it under tribute.

A prodigious amount of material was captured, among these were 21 merchant vessels, 18,000 barrels of flour, 18 hogsheads of tobacco, and 150 bales of cotton. Satisfied with the whole campaign, Gordon's fleet now retired down the Potomac River, but unknown to him was the fact that three of the United States' best naval officers were working on a plan to trap him.

Captain John Rodgers, Captain David Porter, and the hero of Lake Erie, Oliver Hazard Perry, were planning to destroy Gordon's flotilla as it passed down the Potomac. Their plan would utilize shore batteries and fire ships, but alerted by the brig H.M.S. Fairy sent by Admiral Cochrane, Gordon began making his way down the river to Chesapeake Bay.

In a daring escape, Gordon managed to defy all attempts to take his squadron, and at one point he even landed his own forces and wrecked a shore battery that had been firing on his vessels. Gordon's foray was one of the most daring episodes of the War of 1812, but has had little notice in formal histories of the war.

A new Fort Washington stands where Gordon's squadron caused the hasty retreat so long ago. The fort is interpreted to the period of the American Civil War and has a visitor centre with displays on the War of 1812, the American Civil War, and later periods. The fort is administered by the National Parks Service and is located in Fort Washington Park, Maryland. It is about twelve miles from Washington D.C. off Route 210 on the east side of the Potomac River.

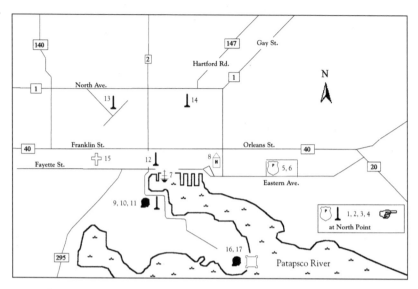

1. Methodist Meeting House
2. Battle Acre
3. Battlefield of North Point
4. General Ross Wounding Site
5. Rodgers Bastion
6. Star Spangled Banner Memorial
7. Frigate *Constellation*
8. Flag House
9. Federal Hill
10. George Armistead Monument
11. General Samuel Smith Monument
12. Battle of Baltimore Monument
13. Francis Scott Key Monument
14. Wells and McComas Monument
15. Old Western Burying Ground
16. General Armistead Statue
17. Fort McHenry National Historic Site

## METHODIST MEETING HOUSE — NORTH POINT, MARYLAND

On the evening of September 11, 1814, Brigadier General John Stricker's force of Baltimore militia marched out of the city on the North Point Road and encamped around the old Methodist Meeting House which stood at this spot.

Next morning Stricker deployed his forces in three separate lines, the first line was near here at the meeting house, the second line further west behind Bread and Cheese Creek and the third about one-half mile back on the main road. After the Battle of North Point, which ended in a success for the British, the meeting house was used as a hospital for the wounded of both sides. The original church was torn down around 1921, after the congregation moved to another location. A monument to the old church was placed by the "Patriotic Order Sons of America of Maryland" in 1914. The monument is located in a small clearing on the south side of Old North Point Road at German Hill Road, in North Point, Maryland.

## BATTLE ACRE — NORTH POINT, MARYLAND

Some of the heaviest fighting of the Battle of North Point occurred here, though intended only as a holding action, the casualties were heavy. The Americans lost 213 men, while the British had 341 men killed, wounded, and missing. The "Battle Acre" is located on the 3100 block of Old North Point Road in North Point. A plaque placed by the State Roads Commission of Maryland is located at the site.

## BATTLEFIELD OF NORTH POINT — NORTH POINT, MARYLAND

After the successful capture of Washington on August 24, 1814, the British selected Baltimore as their next target, and North Point was selected as the debarkation site, located about fourteen miles southeast of the city. Major General Robert Ross's five-thousand-man veteran army began debarking there at 3:00 AM on September 12th. Leaving North Point at about 8:00 AM, they made good time marching to the northwest.

At about the same time Brigadier General John Stricker of the Baltimore Militia was deploying his men in a defensive position, between Baltimore and Ross's marching columns. Stricker had with him about 2700 men, all militia, but he had chosen his ground well, and his line was deployed on a narrow peninsula with his right flank protected by Bear Creek and his left secured by the Back River. The only way the British could get to Baltimore was through Stricker's line.

Before the main battle was joined, General Ross was killed at the head of his advanced guard, and the command devolved on Colonel Arthur Brooke of the 44th Regiment. Brooke had the Royal Artillery and the Congreve Rockets bombard the American centre and left, while he ordered a flanking manoeuvre against the weakened side.

Against Brooke's regulars, the American militia were not disciplined enough to refuse their left flank, and began to give way. The British Light Infantry then pushed forward and soon the American force to the south was also outflanked. The "Union Artillery" and the 5th Maryland Regiment in the American centre inflicted heavy casualties on the British before being forced to retire.

General Stricker had done all that he was expected to do. He was merely to delay the British, and after pulling his brigade back to the city of Baltimore, he deployed them on Hampstead Hill. The plaque dedicated to the action was placed by the State Roads Commission of Maryland and is located beside the Aquilla Randall monument on Old North Point Road at 4000 Battle Grove Road.

## GENERAL ROSS WOUNDING SITE — NORTH POINT, MARYLAND

Before the Battle of North Point, General Stricker sent out a reconnaissance party of 250 men under Major Richard Heath from his main line. Meanwhile on the British side, General Ross, accompanied by Admiral Cockburn and a small advanced guard, had left the Gorsuch house to the east a little before noon. The two parties collided on the road and when firing began, General Ross turned back to order up the light infantry, and at a spot just west of the present monument, he was hit in the side from a rifle ball.

His men took him from his horse and carried him to a nearby

wagon, but on route back to the fleet, he died in the arms of his aide Duncan M'Dougall. The monument that marks the site of General Ross's wounding is actually dedicated to a young private soldier named Aquilla Randall. Randall was only twenty-four years old when he lost his life at the Battle of North Point. The monument was erected in 1817 and over the years has been vandalized and restored several times.

The mystery is that Randall is commemorated at all, for there were twenty-one other privates killed in the battle, but only he is mentioned. Over the years several misconceptions have arisen about the monument. One is that private Randall was responsible for the death of General Ross and this would appear to explain why both of their names are on the monument. But this is a misconception, as two other soldiers seem to be responsible for the death of Ross.

There is still debate today as to who killed the General. Two privates, "Wells and McComas" from Captain Aisquith's company, may have been responsible, but these two privates were also killed in the battle, and we will never know for sure. The monument also commemorates the "First Mechanical Volunteers" commanded by Captain Benjamin C. Howard, a militia unit that fought here. The old monument is located on the Old North Point Road at 4000 Battle Grove Road, and is very near the position where Ross was mortally wounded.

Monument where Ross fell as sketched by Lossing

The same site today

## RODGERS BASTION — PATTERSON PARK

Rodgers Bastion is so named because it was commanded by Commodore John Rodgers in the defence of Baltimore in September of 1814. Fortifications extended from the Patapsco River, to the site now occupied by John Hopkin's Hospital, and the entire line held some 1200 men and 100 guns. A plaque affixed to a small cannon was placed by the Star Spangled Banner Centennial Commission in 1914 and is located at the site of Rodgers Bastion in Patterson Park.

## STAR SPANGLED BANNER MEMORIAL, PATTERSON PARK

A memorial placed here by the pupils of the "Public Schools of Baltimore" honours the one-hundredth anniversary of the writing of the Star Spangled Banner, America's national anthem. The memorial is located in Patterson Park not far from the Rodgers Bastion monument. Patterson Park (in 1812 called Hampstead Hill)

is bounded by Eastern Avenue, Fayette Street, Patterson Park, and Ellwood Avenue in the city of Baltimore.

## FRIGATE *CONSTELLATION*, BALTIMORE

The frigate *Constellation* was launched on September 7, 1797, making her one of the oldest American vessels still afloat. She was rated as a thirty-eight-gun frigate, but as was the practice at the time actually carried forty-eight guns. Two other frigates built at about the same time were the *Constitution* and the *United States*, although these were larger and rated at forty-four guns.

The *Constellation*'s most famous voyages were in the quasi-war with France and her most famous action was against the French frigate *Insurgente* on February 9, 1799. In this seventy-five-minute encounter, she completely out-sailed her opponent and caused her to strike her colours.

Unlike her cousin *Constitution*, the *Constellation* had a very inglorious career during the War of 1812. For nearly the entire war she was blockaded in the Elizabeth River off Norfolk Virginia. On the morning of June 20, 1813, her crew did attempt one sortie to capture some British vessels that were becalmed in Hampton Roads, but the wind backed at the last moment and the enterprise was abandoned. The crew of *Constellation* did participate in the Battle of Craney Island on June 22, 1813.

The *Constellation* had the reputation of being one of the fastest American frigates, and earned the name the "Yankee Racehorse." In her long career, this historic vessel has been preserved and restored several times, and today she lies in Baltimore Harbor where a visit is well worth the time.

# FLAG HOUSE — BALTIMORE

"Flag House" was the home of Mary Pickersgill, a skilled seamstress who was locally known as "a maker of ships colours and Pennants etc." In the summer of 1813, Major Armistead, commander of Fort McHenry, requested that a large national flag be made to fly over the fort. Armistead insisted that the flag be large enough so the British fleet could see it from the water, and large it was, measuring thirty-two by forty-two feet!

The story has become a legend now, how Francis Scott Key could see the flag from miles away, and was inspired to write his epic poem, which in turn became America's national anthem. The "Star Spangled Banner" that flew over Fort McHenry can be seen in the Smithsonian Institution in Washington. The "Flag House" has been declared a National Historic Site, and is operated as a memorial and small War of 1812 museum. The house is located at Pratt and Albermarle streets in the city of Baltimore.

# FEDERAL HILL, BALTIMORE

Federal Hill, overlooking the Inner Harbour, has always been a popular spot for Baltimore citizens, and on the evening of August 24, 1814, they gathered here to see the sky lit up from the burning of Washington. Knowing that they were very likely to be attacked next, the citizens and military began preparing defences. The hill was fortified and Captain Daniel Schwartzaur of the Maryland Militia placed a six-pound signal gun here to give warning should the British fleet be sighted. Also from this spot citizens watched the bombardment of Fort McHenry on the evening of September 13, 1814. Federal Hill was an excellent observation point during the war and still offers good views of the inner harbour. The Maryland Historical Society has placed a plaque at the site which gives a brief history, it is located near the crest of the hill opposite Baltimore's Inner Harbor.

## GEORGE ARMISTEAD MONUMENT — FEDERAL HILL

This monument honours Major George Armistead, who was commanding officer of Fort McHenry during the Battle for Baltimore, and for his successful defence was brevetted Lieutenant Colonel. This is the second memorial to him, as an old monument used to stand at what is now Mercy Hospital. This monument was dedicated in 1882 but was originally located at Eutaw Place. Local citizens felt that the monument should be taller than their rooftops, so it was moved to Federal Hill where it still stands today. The monument is at the crest of Federal Hill opposite the Inner Harbour in the city of Baltimore.

## GENERAL SAMUEL SMITH MONUMENT — FEDERAL HILL

The city of Baltimore owes a great deal to the energy and ability of Major General Samuel Smith, who was in charge of the city's defences in September of 1814. The general was an experienced veteran and had fought at Brandywine, Fort Mifflen, and Monmouth during the American Revolution.

General Smith, exercising a great deal of foresight, began preparing the city's defences in the spring of 1813 and by the time of the British invasion, the city was well prepared, unlike Washington which was captured after a brief battle. The successful defence of Baltimore is largely due to the energy and capacity of this man, and a statue to him is located in Federal Hill Park.

# BATTLE OF BALTIMORE —
## CALVERT AND FAYETTE STREETS

This beautiful monument commemorates the Battle of North Point and the successful defence of Fort McHenry in September of 1814. The cornerstone of the monument was laid on September 12, 1815, exactly one year after the Battle of North Point. In 1827 the symbol of the monument became the official seal of the city of Baltimore. Depicted on the relief column are the Battle of North Point and the bombardment of Fort McHenry. At the top of the monument is a feminine figure holding a laurel leaf in her right hand, and her left guides a ships rudder and inscribed across the monument are the names of those who fell in the battle. This impressive monument is located at Calvert and Fayette streets in downtown Baltimore.

# FRANCIS SCOTT KEY —
## LANVALE STREET AND EUTAW PLACE

This very impressive monument was completed in 1911, and depicts the author of the "Star Spangled Banner," Francis Scott Key, in a small boat with a sailor. Above the two figures is a statue of "Columbia" holding the national flag above her. Francis Scott Key was a lawyer living in Georgetown at the time of the War of 1812, and witnessed the Battle of Bladensburg. Later he was a volunteer aide to General Walter Smith, commander of the First Brigade District Militia.

During the Washington Campaign, Dr. Beanes, a civilian from Marlborough, Maryland, was arrested by the British and taken aboard the flagship H.M.S. *Tonnant*, then lying in the Chesapeake. It seems that the British had good cause to arrest the doctor, as he had been dealing in some dubious matters concerning the capture of British soldiers. A friend of Dr. Beanes approached Francis Key and asked for his assistance in freeing the doctor.

Just before the attack on Baltimore, Key made his way to the flagship, which was now moored in the Patuxtent River, for the purpose of negotiating the doctor's release. Key had with him certificates signed by British officers, who could give good account of the doctor's behaviour after the Battle of Bladensburg. Francis Key dined with General Ross and Admiral Cockburn and after presenting the certificates secured the doctor's release. As the attack on Baltimore was in its advanced stages, Key was kept aboard the British vessel as a security precaution.

It was from the deck of this ship, while watching the bombardment of Fort McHenry, that Key was inspired to write his poem "The Star Spangled Banner." This poem of course, went on to become words for the American national anthem. This beautiful monument to Francis Scott Key and "The Star Spangled Banner" is located at Lanvale Street and Eutaw Place in the city of Baltimore.

## WELLS AND McCOMAS MONUMENT — GAY AND ASQUITH STREETS

This monument, dedicated to two heroes of the Battle of North Point, was placed here in 1871. Daniel Wells and Henry McComas were two young men enlisted in Captain Edward Aisquith's company of sharpshooters, 1st Rifle Battalion, Maryland Militia. At the Battle of North Point, Aisquith's company was part of the advanced guard sent forward by General Stricker to harass the British, and when the unit was ordered to fall back, the two boys determined to remain.

Tradition has it that Henry McComas had been at the humiliating defeat at the Battle of Bladensburg, where he observed General Ross and swore he would know him again on sight. At North Point, when Ross approached at the head of his troops, he was fired upon by Wells and McComas, who were under cover. The general was hit with ball and buckshot and died soon after.

The British skirmishers having come up they opened a volley fire, and both Wells and McComas were killed. The bodies were originally buried in Greenmount Cemetery, but were later moved here in 1858, before the erection of the monument, which stands at the corner of Gay and Asquith streets in a busy section of the city of Baltimore.

## WESTERN BURYING GROUND — FAYETTE AND GREENE STREETS

The old Western Burying Ground dates back to 1784, and a number of Revolutionary War soldiers are buried here, along with at least twelve general officers from the War of 1812. These include James McHenry, from whom the fort is named; David Stodder designer of the frigate *Constellation*; and Brigadier General John Stricker, who commanded the American forces at the Battle of North Point.

Major General Samuel Smith, the defender of Baltimore, is also buried here, and his tomb is quite prominent. One of Baltimore's most famous citizens — but having nothing to do with the War of 1812 — is also here: the poet Edgar Allan Poe was buried here in 1849. The Old Western Burying Ground is located at Fayette and Green streets in the city of Baltimore.

## GEORGE ARMISTEAD STATUE — FORT McHENRY

The city of Baltimore, in grateful remembrance of George Armistead, erected this second statue to him in September of 1914, one hundred years after his successful defence of Fort McHenry. The statue is located on the grounds of Fort McHenry National Historic Site.

# FORT McHENRY NATIONAL HISTORIC SITE — BALTIMORE

Fort McHenry had evolved from old Fort Whetstone that had stood here during the Revolutionary War, and later on was named after Secretary of War James McHenry, who was a Baltimore resident. Fort McHenry's shining hour was in the Battle of Baltimore in September of 1814. After their success at Washington on August 24th, the British Army and Navy began their movement against Baltimore. After the Battle of North Point was fought on September 12th, the British army encamped just two miles away from the city.

The army waited for the next moves which were now up to the navy, but in order for them to move into the inner harbour, Fort McHenry had to be reduced. At dawn on September 13, 1814 a squadron of sixteen vessels moved into position about two miles from the fort. Among these were five bomb vessels and a ship which could fire Congreve Rockets. The intense bombardment lasted all day and went past midnight.

Francis Scott Key, future writer of the "Star Spangled Banner" watched the "rockets red glare" from a British vessel where he was being detained until after the attack. After dawn though, "the flag was still there" and the British, failing to reduce the fort withdrew. For his successful defence of Fort McHenry, Major Armistead was brevetted Lieutenant Colonel.

Fort McHenry has been declared a National Historic Site, and the city of Baltimore is unique in the fact that two National Historic Sites are in her domain (the other is "Flag House" where the Star Spangled Banner was made). Fort McHenry is located on East Fort Avenue about three miles from downtown Baltimore.

# CHAPTER 22
## TIDEWATER

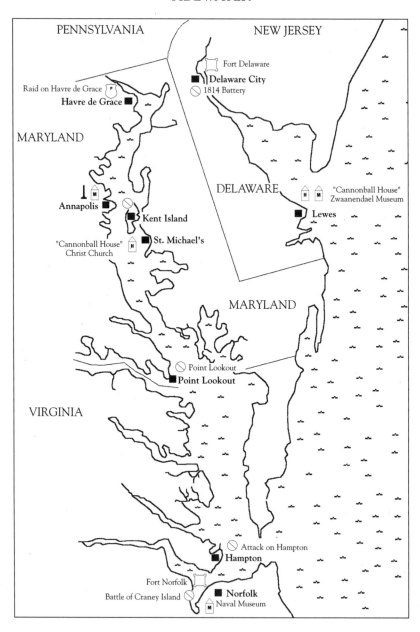

PENNSYLVANIA

NEW JERSEY

Fort Delaware

**Delaware City**

1814 Battery

Raid on Havre de Grace

**Havre de Grace**

MARYLAND

DELAWARE

"Cannonball House"
Zwaanendael Museum

**Lewes**

Annapolis

**Kent Island**

"Cannonball House"
Christ Church

**St. Michael's**

MARYLAND

Point Lookout

**Point Lookout**

VIRGINIA

Attack on Hampton

**Hampton**

Fort Norfolk

Battle of Craney Island

**Norfolk**

Naval Museum

## 1814 BATTERY — DELAWARE CITY, DELAWARE

In 1814 a battery and fortification was constructed here on Newbold's Point. There are no remains of the works today, but the name is commemorated in "Battery Park," which offers the same view of the river. Battery Park is located at the foot of Clinton Street in Delaware City.

## FORT DELAWARE — PEA PATCH ISLAND, DELAWARE CITY

In 1813 the State of Delaware ceded Pea Patch Island to the Federal Government, which at that time had only a small earthwork on it to command the river. In 1814 a party of thirty labourers and one hundred soldiers arrived there to build new wharves, dikes, and fortifications, and this work continued sporadically until 1824. In February of 1831 a good portion of the fort was destroyed in an accidental fire. Fort Delaware, a more substantial work, was completed in 1859 and was used as a federal prison during the Civil War. The site today has no 1812 interpretation, but the fort is preserved in Fort Delaware State Park, which is accessible by ferry from the foot of Clinton Street in Delaware City.

## RAID ON HAVRE DE GRACE, MARYLAND

Effective December 26, 1812, a British Order in Council declared Chesapeake Bay and the Delaware River under blockade. On April 1, 1813, the British fleet under the command of Admiral George Cockburn entered Chesapeake Bay for the purpose of enforcing the blockade and to engage in a series of raids on the coastal communities. Cockburn's policy, humane by any standards of warfare, was to respect private property and pay for any goods seized unless resistance was offered.

On April 28th, boats from Cockburn's squadron raided the small community of Frenchtown on the Elk River, seizing naval stores and merchandise but paying for some cattle. The squadron then made its way to Specucie Island. While passing Havre de Grace, the town defiantly raised the American colours and fired on the passing fleet. That evening Cockburn made plans to capture the town.

On the early morning of May 3rd, his naval brigade began rowing towards the town while the defenders manned two batteries and tried to drive the British off. Bombarding the defenders with cannons from their boats and utilizing rockets, the British soon took possession of the town. They also sent an expedition up the Susquehanna River about six miles, where at an ironworks they destroyed a number of cannons and stands of arms. By sunset the invaders had left Havre de Grace. The Maryland Historical Society has commemorated the raid with a state plaque located near the landing place of the British.

## U.S. NAVAL ACADEMY — ANNAPOLIS, MARYLAND

The United States Naval Academy features a fine museum dedicated to the United States Navy, and is located in Preble Hall. Featured in the collection are a number of artifacts and paintings from the War of 1812, such as the bullet that killed Stephen Decatur, a boatswain's pipe from the U.S. frigate *Chesapeake*, a cannonball taken from the corvette *Queen Charlotte* at the Battle of Lake Erie, a model of the British frigate *Shannon*, and other memorabilia. At the entrance to Preble Hall are flags taken from British vessels in the War of 1812, such as Commodore Barclay's flagship *Detroit* and the pennant from the British frigate *Guerriere*, which was captured by the U.S. frigate *Constitution*. On the grounds in front of Preble Hall is a monument to the capture of the British frigate *Macedonian* by the U.S. frigate *United States* on October 25, 1812. The United States Naval Academy is well worth a visit and is located in the beautiful city of Annapolis, Maryland, which has many buildings that date from pre-1812.

## KENT ISLAND — CHESAPEAKE BAY, MARYLAND

When Admiral Cockburn began his raids on the Chesapeake in the summer of 1813, a base was needed to intern captured vessels and supplies. Kent Island was ideally located for this task, and it became the British base for about three weeks in August. Admiral Cockburn has been harshly treated in the American press and throughout history. It was at Kent Island, however, that a demonstration of his humanity was shown.

At the north end of the island lived an American civilian, who found one evening that his house had been ransacked by the British and he applied to Cockburn for redress. The admiral asked him to state his loss, and when told that this amounted to some $350, the admiral immediately repaid him out of his own pocket. Presently there are no historical markers on Kent Island to commemorate the War of 1812.

## RAID ON ST. MICHAELS — CHESAPEAKE BAY, MARYLAND

St. Michaels had a long history of being a place where privateers were constructed and outfitted, and it became a natural target for Admiral Cockburn's raids when that officer returned to the Chesapeake in the summer of 1814. However, the local militia commander, General Derry Benson, had taken precautions for its defence, and two batteries had been constructed. One was located at the entrance to the harbour and the other on high ground in front of the town. When an expedition of eleven British gun boats attacked the town on the night of August 11th, they were met by the fire from these two batteries.

The British were still able to land and spike the first battery, but had to retire with some loss. Local tradition says that there was a previous attempt against the town on the night of August 9th. In this engagement the local people are accredited with extinguishing all of the town lights and hanging lanterns in the nearby trees. In the naval bombardment that followed, the British then overshot the town and missed many of the houses. Ever since, St. Michaels has been known as "the town that fooled the British" and indeed they did, as only one house was struck. St. Michaels is located on Route 33 off Route 50 on the eastern side of Chesapeake Bay. (see next entry)

## CANNONBALL HOUSE — ST. MICHAELS, MARYLAND

The house was constructed by shipwright William Merchant in 1805 and during the attack on St. Michaels, the house had the dubious distinction of being the only one struck during the bombardment. A British cannonball penetrated the roof, then rolled across the attic and down the staircase, frightening poor Mrs. Merchant half to death. The house is privately owned and not opened to the public and is located at St. Mary's Square in the town of St. Michaels. (see previous entry)

## CHRIST EPISCOPAL CHURCH — ST. MICHAELS, MARYLAND

This is the fourth Episcopalian church to stand on this location. The present church, although not dating from the War of 1812, does have an 1812 connection. During its construction, muskets from the War of 1812 were found under the floor boards. Research is unclear, but these may have been left behind by troops stationed near the church during the raid on St. Michaels. Christ Episcopalian Church is on Talbot Street in the town of St. Michaels.

# CANNONBALL HOUSE — LEWES, DELAWARE

In the spring of 1813, when Admiral George Cockburn was blockading Chesapeake Bay, he sent a small detachment of four vessels under Captain John P. Beresford to blockade the Delaware River. Beresford arrived off the port of Lewes and demanded supplies for which he offered to pay in hard cash, but when the mayor of Lewes refused, Beresford replied with a bombardment of the town on April 6th. Over one thousand rounds were fired into the town, but little damage was done and no lives were lost. Afterwards Beresford withdrew.

One of the cannonballs hurled by the British is still lodged in the basement of "Cannonball House" a part of the Lewes Historical Society Complex which is a collection of some of the town's oldest buildings. "Cannonball House" is home to the Marine Museum and is located at Bank and Front streets in the town of Lewes.

# ZWAANENDAEL MUSEUM — LEWES, DELAWARE

The Zwaanendael Museum interprets the history of southern Delaware and the town of Lewes. The collection emphasizes decorative arts of the 18th and 19th centuries, but includes artifacts dealing with military affairs at Lewes in the War of 1812, and a maritime collection. The building is a replica of the town hall in Hoorn, Holland, and is located at the intersection of the King's Highway and Savannah Road in the town of Lewes, Delaware.

# POINT LOOKOUT — SCOTLAND, MARYLAND

Point Lookout has always been a popular resort area situated as it is surrounded by the waters of Chesapeake Bay and the Potomac River. In the summer of 1813 it was a staging area for the local militia when Admiral Cockburn was conducting raids into Chesapeake Bay. Its main claim to fame was as a hospital and prisoner of war camp during the American Civil War. Author–historian Benson Lossing visited the site in the last century, and noted that a monument erected to the War of 1812 patriots had been much defaced. This monument is no longer at the site.

Point Lookout is now a State Park with nature trails, beaches and a picnic area. Ruins of a Civil War fortification are located here and a museum has local artifacts and displays with emphasis on the Civil War period. Point Lookout is located at the extreme tip of the State of Maryland on Chesapeake Bay.

# FORT NORFOLK — NORFOLK, VIRGINIA

In 1794, under the orders of President George Washington, Fort Norfolk and Fort Nelson were built to control the entrance to the Elizabeth River. They were mainly earthwork structures, and by the turn of the century had been neglected and were in poor shape, but after the "Chesapeake Affair" in 1807 the forts were restored and strengthened.

During the War of 1812 the fort was manned by Virginia militia, and when the frigate *Constellation* was trapped by the British blockade, her crew joined the garrison. After the war the fort was once again neglected, and presently is under restoration. The fort is open to the public, and has earthen remains and some buildings. The fort is located at Colley Avenue and Front Street in the city of Norfolk, Virginia.

# HAMPTON ROADS NAVAL MUSEUM —
## NORFOLK, VIRGINIA

This small museum has displays covering the entire history of the United States Navy. There is a display on the Battle of Craney Island fought near here on June 22, 1813. The museum is maintained by the United States Navy and is located at Pennsylvania House G-29 on the Norfolk Naval base. A pass is required which may be obtained at the visitors centre.

## BATTLE OF CRANEY ISLAND — NORFOLK, VIRGINIA

In the summer of 1813, Admiral George Cockburn had already scouted out the defences of Norfolk, and when his superior, Admiral Sir John Borlase Warren, arrived on June 19th, an attack on Norfolk was planned. The objectives were to destroy the shipyard and to capture the frigate *Constellation*, which was then blockaded in the river. The key to Norfolk's defence was Craney Island, situated close to shore and connected to the mainland by a bridge.

Cockburn had the channel carefully sounded out beforehand, and had recommended his Lieutenant Westphal to lead the attack. Warren, however, overruled Cockburn's wise decision and delegated Captain Pechell of his flagship to lead the attack. One of the regiments chosen for the assault was the Canadian Chasseurs, although they were "Canadian" in name only, as they were actually French prisoners of war recruited to fight for the British.

In the attack on June 22nd, the boats carrying the soldiers grounded on a shoal near the island, and were cut to pieces by American artillery. The attack was a complete disaster and the British had to withdraw to lick their wounds. Casualties are unknown but at least three of the lead boats were hit and sunk.

Craney Island is the site of the United States Navy's fuel depot and is now connected to the mainland. The property belongs to the U.S. Navy and is not open to the public.

## ATTACK ON HAMPTON — HAMPTON, VIRGINIA

After the failure of the attack on Craney's Island, the British under Admiral Warren decided to strike Hampton, Virginia, but this time the operational plan was under the command of Admiral Cockburn. While gunboats engaged the shore defences, the British landed to the west, and brushing aside the defenders took the town. They stayed in Hampton for ten days, but before departing they seized supplies and destroyed all batteries and ordnance. One of the units in the attack was the 102nd Regiment, which was composed of French prisoners of war who had elected to fight for the British.

This regiment brought everlasting disgrace to themselves for their conduct at Hampton. The looting, burning, and killing that took place there was largely the fault of this corps, and later on at a court martial the unit was publicly disgraced, and was never employed in North America again. Presently there is no marker to commemorate the events at Hampton during the War of 1812.

# CHAPTER 23

# EASTERN SEABOARD OF THE UNITED STATES

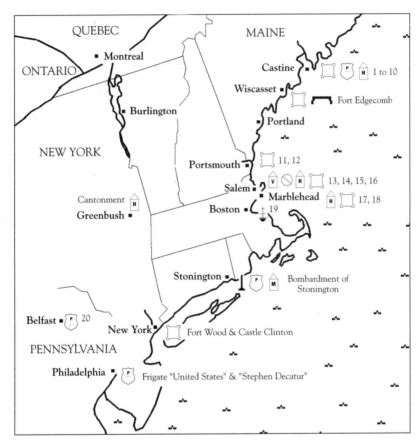

## Castine, Maine

1. Fort George
2. Fort Madison
3. Fort George Barrack
4. Paymasters Office
5. Hooke's Barn
6. Hawes Hall
7. Fort Furieuse
8. Customs House
9. Whitney House
10. British Headquarters
11. Fort Constitution
12. Fort McClary
13. Derby Wharf & Privateers
14. Funeral of Lawrence
15. Fort Lee
16. Fort Pickering
17. Old Powder House
18. Fort Sewall
19. *U.S.S. Constitution*
20. Henry's Gun Factory

## FORT GEORGE — CASTINE, MAINE

The town of Castine, at the mouth of the Penobscot River, was the centre of the lumber trade in the vicinity, and because of this the British built Fort George during the American Revolution. It was a large rectangular earthwork structure, and was successfully defended by the British in the colonists' abortive Penobscot Expedition of 1779. During the War of 1812 the British returned once more to the area, occupying most of the coast of Maine east of the Penobscot River. At that time Fort George was reactivated, and over sixty cannons were mounted. The British remained in possession of eastern Maine until well after peace was declared, finally evacuating Castine on April 25, 1815, but not before blowing up Fort George on their departure.

The town of Castine is quite charming, and the Chamber of Commerce has a very useful pamphlet walking tour that denotes many of the historic sites. The earthworks of Fort George have been restored in Fort George State Park on the corner of Wadsworth Cove Road and Battle Avenue at the north end of town.

## FORT MADISON — CASTINE, MAINE

With the likelihood that war was imminent, the United States built Fort Madison in 1811. It was an earthwork fortification, smaller than Fort George, but sited closer to the water. The armament of the fort consisted of four twenty-four-pound long guns, but when the British occupied eastern Maine in September of 1814, the guns were spiked and the garrison evacuated. The British renamed it Fort Castine and they remained in possession of the fort until the spring of 1815. The remains of Fort Madison are located on Perkins Street in the town of Castine.

# WALKING TOUR OF CASTINE

The next six sites are all found in the Walking Tour of Castine pamphlet, available at the local Chamber of Commerce

## FORT GEORGE BARRACK — CASTINE, MAINE

This house was used by occupying British troops as a barracks during the War of 1812. A local wooden marker is located in front of the house. On the "Walking Tour of Castine."

## PAYMASTERS OFFICE — CASTINE, MAINE

The title says it all. The house was used as the British paymasters office during their occupation of the town of Castine. On the "Walking Tour of Castine."

## HOOKE'S BARN — CASTINE, MAINE

During their long occupation of eastern Maine, the British had time for a few amusements, and Hooke's Barn was used as a theatre on the evening of January 2, 1815. It was here that the play *The Comedy of the Poor Gentleman* was enacted by officers of the 29th and 62nd regiments. Unknown at the time to either side was the fact that the war had ended on Christmas Eve with the signing of the peace treaty at Ghent, Belgium. Hooke's Barn was primarily used as a hospital during the British occupation, and a local marker is in front of the building, which is located on the "Walking Tour of Castine."

## HAWES HALL — CASTINE, MAINE

Hawes Hall was used by British officers as a mess hall during their occupation. The building is on the "Walking Tour of Castine."

## FORT FURIEUSE — CASTINE, MAINE

Fort Furieuse was built under the direction of General Girard Gosselin in 1813, and was evacuated by the British when they left Castine in 1815. There are no remains of the fortification today, but there is a marker which is on the "Walking Tour of Castine."

## CUSTOMS HOUSE — CASTINE, MAINE

The first customs house was built on this site in 1789, and when Lieutenant General Sir John C. Sherbrooke took the town in 1814, one of his first actions was to occupy the building. Josiah Hooke, who was the American collector of customs, fled into the woods after burying documents to prevent them from falling into British hands. The building is no longer standing, but a local sign marks the site, which is on the "Walking Tour of Castine."

## WHITNEY HOUSE — CASTINE, MAINE

A British officer who stayed in the house left a "graffiti" that was scratched on one of the window panes. It depicted an upside down American flag and the slogan "Yankee Doodle Upset." The house is currently unmarked and is privately owned, but is on the right hand side of the loop, off Court Street.

## BRITISH HEADQUARTERS — CASTINE, MAINE

General Girard Gosselin, the British commander, used the Dyer house as his headquarters during the British occupation. The house, constructed in 1796, is unmarked, but is located on the east side of Dyer Street at the intersection of Water Street.

## FORT EDGECOMB — WISCASSET, MAINE

Fort Edgecomb was a simple structure, consisting of a blockhouse and earthworks and was completed just in time for President James Madison's inauguration on March 4, 1809. By 1814, with much of the New England coast under close blockade, the garrison was constantly on the alert answering numerous false alarms and causing much anxiety to the local populace. News of the end of the war reached Wiscassett on February 14, 1815, and with much rejoicing the fort's garrison fired a final salute. The troops remained until the summer of 1816, at which time the fort's guns were moved to Fort Independence in Boston.

The fort still stands today and features an unusual octagonal blockhouse, a reconstructed palisade, and remains of earthworks.

The fort is administered by the Bureau of Parks and Recreation, State of Maine and is located south of U.S. Route 1 on the east side of the Sheepscott River, Wiscasset.

## FORT CONSTITUTION — NEW CASTLE, NEW HAMPSHIRE

The history of Fort Constitution dates back to 1631, but its most famous incident was when it was raided by the colonists during the American Revolution. At that time the fort was know as "William and Mary" and the patriots seized the fort months before the skirmishes at "Lexington and Concord." After the Revolution it was known as "Fort Castle" and in 1791 it was ceded to the federal government by the state of New Hampshire. Under federal ownership, the fort was garrisoned by an artillery company and renamed "Fort Constitution."

After the "Leopard — Chesapeake Affair" in 1807 the fort was upgraded, and by the next year the walls were considerably higher and new brick buildings had been added. At the commencement of the War of 1812 it was a fully serviceable, up-to-date fortification. With New England under blockade a Martello tower was added, and on October 2, 1814 the tower was named "Castle Walbach" in honour of the German commanding officer. "Fort Constitution," as with many other New England forts, was not seriously threatened by the British during the War of 1812. The fort is open to the public and is located on State Route 1B east of New Castle (Portsmouth), New Hampshire.

## FORT McCLARY — KITTERY, MAINE

Fort McClary, though small, has been utilized in five of Americas wars, the American Revolution, the War of 1812, the Civil War, the Spanish American War and World War I. The fort was constructed in 1809 when relations with England were strained. The salient feature of the fort today is the blockhouse, which dates from 1844, ,and strewn around the grounds are numerous granite blocks from various periods of construction. There are remains of a granite wall, a caponier, powder magazine, and earthworks. The site is administered by the Bureau of Parks and Recreation–Maine Department of Conservation. This charming site is located on the coast two miles east of Kittery on SR 103 not far from Portsmouth, New Hampshire.

## DERBY WHARF AND SALEM PRIVATEERS — SALEM, MASSACHUSETTS

Once America's sixth largest harbour, Salem was an important naval and commercial centre and during the American Revolution and the War of 1812 numerous privateers operated from its many wharves. Derby Wharf was constructed in 1762, and is an excellent example of the type of wharf that used to dominate the harbour. Today Derby Wharf, Central Wharf, and Hatch's Wharf are all preserved in Salem Maritime National Park. Buildings such as the Central Wharf Warehouse (1805), Hawkes Warehouse (1780) and other buildings from Salem's long maritime history have been restored. The park is administered by the National Park Service and a visitor centre is located on Derby Street on the Salem waterfront.

## FUNERAL OF JAMES LAWRENCE — SALEM, MASSACHUSETTS

In the decisive naval battle fought on June 1, 1813, the American frigate *Chesapeake* commanded by Captain James Lawrence was taken by *H.M.S. Shannon* under Captain Philip Broke. Captain Lawrence was killed in the action and Captain Broke was severely wounded.

The *Chesapeake* was towed to Halifax, Nova Scotia and in an impressive ceremony, the body of Captain James Lawrence was interred. Captain George Crowinshield Jr. of Salem had witnessed the battle, and he determined that the Americans killed in the action should be returned to American soil. With President Madison's approval he secured a pass to the British lines.

On August 18, 1813, Captain Crowinshield returned from Halifax in his brig *Henry*, with the bodies of Captain Lawrence and his first lieutenant, Augustus Ludlow. On Monday, August 23rd the harbour was full of vessels with flags at half mast, while the funeral procession left the "India Wharf" and passed through town, witnessed by thousands of people who had come from miles around. The ceremony ended at the Reverend Mr. Spalding's meeting house.

At the request of the Lawrence family, his body, along with Ludlow's, was ultimately buried in New York City and in a third funeral service, the two heroes were buried in a common vault in Trinity Church burying ground. There are no remains of the India wharf today, the site now being occupied by the Salem Harbor Power Company. The wharves preserved in Salem National Historic Park, however, can give the visitor a sense of what the events at India Wharf must have been like. Presently the funeral of Lawrence is uncommemorated.

## FORT LEE — SALEM, MASSACHUSETTS

The earliest fort to occupy this site was built in 1742, but in the summer of 1775 General Henry Lee selected the site for a stronger work, which later bore his name. It was an earthwork structure and mounted four guns which effectively commanded the outer harbour. At the commencement of the War of 1812 the fort seems to have been in fairly good repair, but by 1814 it was in a state of deterioration, which hints that it was not garrisoned. That summer, under the direction of major generals Amos Hovey and David Putnam, the fort was strengthened utilizing local militia. Reports indicate that there was even a small barracks. But the port of Salem was never seriously threatened during the war and with the Treaty of Ghent, the fort once again fell into oblivion. Fort Lee is owned by the city, and is one of Salem's "hidden secrets" tucked away on Salem Neck between Fort Avenue and Memorial Drive. (see next entry)

## FORT PICKERING — SALEM, MASSACHUSETTS

Fort Pickering is a more substantial structure than Fort Lee, and has evolved from several forts that have occupied Winter Island. The site dates back from the old Dutch Wars and has variously been called Fort Ann or Fort William. During the quasi-war with France in 1796, the fort had major repairs and a second restoration was done in 1799.

At that time the fort was renamed "Pickering" in honour of Timothy Pickering, a local Salemite, and quartermaster in Washington's army. The fort had a third restoration in August of 1814, but like its sister Fort Lee it was never seriously threatened. Incidentally, the American warship *Essex*, which fought in the War of 1812, was built at Winter Island, which was the ship-building centre of old Salem. Fort Pickering is maintained by the city of Salem, and can be reached by a causeway to Winter Island. (see prior entry)

## OLD POWDER HOUSE — MARBLEHEAD, MASSACHUSETTS

The old powder house, a circular brick structure with a shingled roof, dates back to the Seven Years' War, and was used to store muskets and powder during the War of 1812. The powder house is located at 37 Green Street in the town of Marblehead.

Fort Sewall as Lossing sketched it in November of 1860

## FORT SEWALL — MARBLEHEAD, MASSACHUSETTS

The British constructed Fort Sewall in 1742 to protect Marblehead against French privateers, and named it after Samuel Sewall, a member of the House of Representatives, who once lived in Marblehead.

It is mainly an earthwork structure but effectively commands the harbour, and in 1812 a garrison was stationed here. On April 3, 1814 the guns of the fort aided the frigate *Constitution* in her escape from two British frigates, *Tenedos* and *Junon*, which had chased her into the bay. The fort is now a public park maintained by the Marblehead Recreation and Parks Department. A plaque placed by the Massachusetts Bay Colony Tercentenary Commission is near the entrance to the fort, which is located at the northeast end of Front Street in the town of Marblehead.

Fort Sewall today

# U.S.S. CONSTITUTION — BOSTON, MASSACHUSETTS

The frigate *Constitution* is one of America's most famous fighting ships and her record in the War of 1812 is particularly distinguishable. Laid down in 1794 she was superbly built and was designed to fight any vessel of her class, and outrun anything she couldn't fight. Her main battery consisted of twenty-four-pound guns, and although rated as a forty-four-gun frigate, she in fact carried over fifty-four guns. She was a formidable opponent, as British vessels found out during the war. Her first "action" of the War of 1812 was actually a magnificent "flight," when on the morning of July 18, 1812 under Captain Isaac Hull, she found herself practically surrounded by a British squadron under Captain Broke.

Broke had with him his own *Shannon* and four other vessels: *Africa*, *Belvidera*, *Aeolus*, and *Guerriere*. What followed was one of the most famous sea chases in history. Captain Hull utilized every naval manoeuvre known to him to outdistance the pursuing British, and in the light winds that prevailed, some amazing tactics were resorted to.

"Kedging" was used, whereby the ship's boats were rowed ahead of the ship, an anchor dropped, and then hauled in to propel the ship forward. Seamen were sent aloft to throw water on the sails, as a wet sail holds more wind than a dry one. Stern guns were fired at the British and with each firing, the ship gained precious inches more. The chase lasted into the night, with over twenty-fours hours of back-breaking toil. At dawn a breeze finally arrived and *Constitution*, a superb sailor, finally left the astonished British.

After a hasty refit in Boston, Hull took *Constitution* to sea once more as he feared being blockaded in the harbour. On August 19th he fell in with His Majesty's frigate *Guerriere*, one of the same vessels that had pursued him just weeks before.

Though the two vessels manoeuvred for several hours, the actual combat lasted for less than thirty minutes, when the *Constitution*'s well-aimed broadsides reduced the *Guerriere* to matchwood. His vessel completely dismasted, brave Captain Dacres had little choice but to surrender. It was in this famous engagement that *Constitution* earned her nickname "Old Ironside." At one point in the action an American sailor observed one of the British cannonballs bounce off her side, and a nickname was born.

For her second cruise *Constitution* was under the command of William Bainbridge and on December 29th off the Brazilian coast, she fell in with the British frigate *Java*. Captain Lambert of *Java* utilized different tactics than Captain Dacres by remaining at long range, but the end result was the same: *Constitution* had defeated and captured a second British frigate.

On April 3, 1814, now under the command of Charles Stewart, *Constitution* had another close call. Making easy sail in a light breeze, she was headed toward Boston when she spied two British frigates bearing down on her. Taking advantage of a brisk breeze that had not reached *Constitution*, the frigates *Tenedos* and *Junon* closed the distance quickly. With the escape to the sea cut off, Captain Stewart was forced to run into Salem Harbor, where the ship could be protected by the guns of Fort Sewall.

By 1814 the British blockade of the American coast was quite effective, and when *Constitution* finally did enter Boston Harbor, she remained blockaded there for over eight months. On December 18, 1814, taking advantage of a winter gale, Captain Stewart managed to slip *Constitution* out of the harbour, but unknown to anyone at the time the war was to end just six days later. In a postscript to a glorious career she managed to defeat two smaller British vessels *Cyanne* and *Levant* on February 20, 1815.

*Constitution* has had a long and glorious career: a famous poem has been written about her, and she was the subject of a famous silent film. The *U.S.S. Constitution* Museum is located just yards away from the famous vessel. Today she is preserved in the city of Boston at the Charlestown Navy Yard, and is under the jurisdiction of the National Park Service.

## BOMBARDMENT OF STONINGTON — CONNECTICUT

On August 9 and 10, 1814, one of the most remarkable sidelights of the War of 1812 occurred. Lying offshore was a British squadron under the command of Sir Thomas Hardy ("Nelson's Hardy" of Trafalgar fame). Hardy sent a deputation ashore informing the townspeople they had one hour to evacuate the women and children, as his intention was to destroy the town by naval bombardment. The townspeople adamantly refused to give up without fighting, and despatch riders were sent into the countryside to rouse the militia. Hardy commenced the bombardment three hours later, with the vessels *Ramilies*, *Pactolus*, *Dispatch*, *Nimrod*, and *Terror*. The bombardment was halted after four hours, but not a single building was consumed. The next morning the action recommenced with local defenders manning a three-gun battery.

Despite hundreds of shells thrown into the town, little damage was done and remarkably no one was killed. By one o'clock a deputation under a flag of truce was sent to Captain Hardy, and appealing to his humanity, they informed him that the "unoffending habitants" had departed, and that they were anxious about the fate of their town. Hardy replied in writing, stating that since the town was not responsible for the creation of local "torpedoes" (floating mines in those days) it would be spared, and the next morning the squadron bore away.

This seemingly pointless action originated when Sir George Prevost wrote to Admiral Cochrane in Bermuda, suggesting a retaliatory raid in response for the burning of Dover in Upper Canada. Taking into account the tardy communications of the period, the raid on Stonington occurred nearly two months after the order was suggested. A light-hearted song was later written about the battle wherein two verses say:

> The Shells were thrown, the Rockets flew,
> But not a shell of all they threw,
> Though every house was in full view,
> Could burn a house in Stonington,
>
> Now some assert on certain grounds,
> Beside their damage and their wounds,
> It cost the King Ten Thousand Pounds,
> To have a fling at Stonington

Today Stonington is a picturesque little village located on the southern coast of Connecticut. The town has not forgotten the famous bombardment and there are many local reminders of this fact. A monument at Cannon Square, with two of the eighteen-pound cannons used in the action, commemorates the heroic defenders and a plaque affixed to a building on Water Street indicates the position of the land battery.

On Main Street on top of a period hitching post is one of the cannonballs lobbed by the British. Inside the Bank on Water Street is the flag which flew in the battle, and the Old Lighthouse Museum on the point displays artifacts from the War of 1812. A small stone marker denoting the action is in front of the museum. The Stonington Historical Society has published a pamphlet walking tour of the town and this indicates many of the historic sites. Stonington is East of Mystic Seaport, Connecticut and west of Westerly, Rhode Island.

## CASTLE CLINTON — NEW YORK CITY

Castle Clinton was constructed in 1811 when war with Great Britain seemed imminent. It was also known as "the West Battery" and its primary purpose was to protect the harbour. In 1812 it was the headquarters for the United States Army. The fort has been reconstructed and can be visited today in Battery Park at the tip of Manhattan Island.

## FORT WOOD — BEDLOE'S ISLAND, NEW YORK CITY

Fort Wood is scarcely remembered today, because it is far outshadowed by the more famous structure that lies on top of it. The fort is actually the base for the Statue of Liberty, which is visited by millions of people each year. The fort was constructed in the latter part of 1814 and is unusual because it features eleven pointed bastions, which form a star. The main armament of the fort consisted of twenty-four mortar guns, and was named after Lieutenant Colonel Eleazer D. Wood, who was killed during the War of 1812. The fort is located on Bedloe's Island and is accessible by ferry.

## FRIGATE *UNITED STATES* — PHILADELPHIA, PENNSYLVANIA

A plaque placed by the city of Philadelphia commemorates the launching of the frigate *United States* on May 10, 1797. The *United States* was commanded by Captain Stephen Decatur in her famous fight with His Majesty's frigate *Macedonian* on October 25, 1812. In this action Decatur managed to outmanoeuvre the enemy frigate and rake her several times. The *Macedonian* was captured and later did many years of service in the American navy. The *United States* remained on the navy list until 1866 when she was scrapped at Norfolk, Virginia. The plaque dedicated to this historic vessel is at the south end of Penns Landing in the city of Philadelphia.

# STEPHEN DECATUR, PHILADELPHIA, PENNSYLVANIA

Stephen Decatur was born in Maryland in 1779, but soon after his family moved to Philadelphia and young Stephen grew up in a house that once stood at this site. As a young man he enjoyed making models of sailing vessels, and he was actually on board the frigate *United States* when she was launched in 1797. Little did he know that he would one day command this vessel in one of her most famous actions. On October 25, 1812 the *United States*, under his command, defeated and captured the British frigate *Macedonian*. In the closing days of the War of 1812, with the United States coast almost completely blockaded, he tried running the frigate *President* out to sea. Unfortunately for him he was cornered by three British frigates and forced to surrender. In 1820 Decatur was tragically killed by naval officer James Barron in a duel and a historic plaque to him is located in the 600 Block of South Front Street in the city of Philadelphia. (see Decatur House)

# CANTONMENT GREENBUSH — GREENBUSH, NEW YORK

The headquarters and training centre for the Northern Division of the United States Army was located three miles east of Greenbush during the War of 1812. The site occupied four hundred acres and contained four barracks which could house approximately four thousand men. Of the vast complex only one building remains today, completely remodeled into modern apartments and privately owned. The site is presently unmarked. Greenbush is on the east side of the Hudson River opposite Albany, New York.

# HENRY'S GUN FACTORY — BELFAST, PENNSYLVANIA

A State of Pennsylvania Historical Marker denotes the site of a rifle factory built by William Henry around 1800. Rifles and other firearms were produced here during the War of 1812. The marker is located on State Route 1005, Belfast in Northampton County, Pennsylvania.

# CHAPTER 24
## EAST COAST OF CANADA

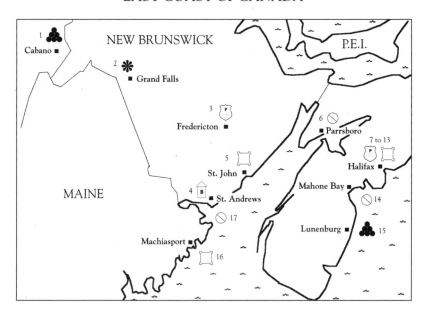

1. Temiscouata Portage
2. The Grand Falls
3. March of the 104th Regiment
4. St. Andrews Blockhouse
5. Carleton Martello Tower
6. Blockhouse
7. Grave of General Robert Ross
8. St. Paul's Church — Memorials
9. Prince of Wales Martello Tower
10. York Redoubt
11. *Shannon* and *Chesapeake*
12. Cannon from *H.M.S. Shannon*
13. *Shannon* memorial
14. Blowing up of the *Teazer*
15. Liverpool Privateers
16. Fort O'Brian
17. Campobello Island

## TEMISCOUATA PORTAGE — CABANO, QUEBEC

The Temiscouata Portage was the longest and most grueling portage on the old postal route from New Brunswick to Quebec. The route had been in use for over thirty years, instituted under the governor ship of Frederick Haldimand. It followed the St. John River to the Madawaska, then to Lake Temiscouata, across the lake and over the Grand Portage to the St. Lawrence. The 104th Regiment used the portage during its epic march from New Brunswick to Upper Canada during the winter of 1812–1813. A cairn placed by the Historic Sites and Monuments Board of Canada recalls the historic portage and the march of the 104th Regiment. The cairn is located in front of Fort Ingall in Cabano, Quebec.

## THE GRAND FALLS — GRAND FALLS, NEW BRUNSWICK

The "Grand Falls" were mentioned by Lieutenant John Le Couteur in his journal when his regiment, the 104th, marched passed them on the first of March 1813, on their way to Upper Canada. Le Couteur was much impressed by the falls and mentions that they were eighty-four feet high and nine hundred feet in width. The Grand Falls are still an impressive site today, and they are on the St. John River in the town of Grand Falls, New Brunswick. Markers are at the foot of the falls, but none relate to the War of 1812.

## MARCH OF THE 104TH REGIMENT — FREDERICTON, NEW BRUNSWICK

The 104th Regiment of Foot, also know as the New Brunswick Regiment, was composed mainly of veterans from New Brunswick and Nova Scotia. Having held off the American invasions in 1812, Sir George Prevost, Governor of Canada, expected a renewed offensive directed against Upper Canada. He ordered the regiment to reinforce the Upper Province before the spring thaws.

In the dead of winter, the regiment made a heroic march from Fredericton, New Brunswick to Kingston, Upper Canada. As fate would have it, that particular winter had heavy snowfall and was particularly cold. The Grenadier Company, leading the van, left Fredericton on February 16, 1813 and on each succeeding day, one company of the line followed. The light company, which was the last to leave Fredericton, departed on February 21st. The fatiguing ordeal is described by Lieutenant John Le Couteur, who participated in the march, and illuminates many of the events in his military journal. The company he travelled with crossed the Temiscouata Portage on March 6th, and they arrived at Quebec City nine days later. The entire march had taken twenty-four days.

When the Commander in Chief, Sir George Prevost, inspected the regiment it numbered 550 men. After a ten day rest he ordered the regiment to push on to Fort Chambly on the Richelieu River, arriving there on April 1st, but the next day they were ordered to march to Kingston and they arrived there on April 12th. It was indeed an incredible feat, for some companies of the regiment had marched over eight hundred miles in just six weeks.

The arrival of the 104th Regiment in Upper Canada materially aided the defence of the province. A plaque placed by the Historic Sites and Monuments Board of Canada commemorates this great march, and is located in the military compound where the march began, at Fredericton, New Brunswick.

## ST. ANDREWS BLOCKHOUSE —
## ST. ANDREWS, NEW BRUNSWICK

Of the twelve blockhouses that were built to defend New Brunswick during the War of 1812, only the St. Andrews Blockhouse remains. Although the province of New Brunswick was still doing business with its neighbours at Eastport, Maine, it was still vulnerable to American Privateers based further south. This was why senior militia officer Lieutenant Colonel Gibbons recommended that fortifications be built at St. Andrews.

Work commenced in 1813, with funds supplied by local businessmen, and by the summer were largely complete. There were other batteries placed around the town, but in the opinion of one Royal Engineer, these were poorly located and he noted that at high tide, the water actually reached one of the embrasures. A garrison remained at the blockhouse for the entire war, and after was reactivated periodically during the Fenian troubles and the Maine Border Dispute. The St. Andrews Blockhouse is administered by Parks Canada and is located on the waterfront in the town of St. Andrews, New Brunswick.

## CARLETON MARTELLO TOWER — SAINT JOHN, NEW BRUNSWICK

Saint John was an important commercial centre during the War of 1812, but with the Royal Navy in complete control of the waters around New Brunswick, there was little danger of attack from the sea. However, in a report by Captain Gustavus Nichols of the Royal Engineers, it was noted that the city was vulnerable to a land attack from the west. Nichols recommended four redoubts and a Martello tower be built to defend the city. The redoubts were never constructed, but the Martello tower was, and this is the tower that may be visited today. Construction commenced in 1813 and was only completed after the war. Carleton Martello Tower has never witnessed a shot fired in anger, but she has served her country during the Maine Border Dispute, the Fenian scare, and during World War II, as a fire control tower and observation point. The tower is administered by Parks Canada and is located above the harbour in West Saint John.

## BLOWING UP OF THE *TEAZER* — MAHONE BAY, NOVA SCOTIA

During the War of 1812 the *Young Teazer* was an American privateer schooner operating out of New York. She was seventy-five feet long, and was about 124 burthen tons. Her figurehead was a carved alligator with jaws agape, she was very fast, and in light winds was particularly adept at combining sail power with "sweeps" or oars.

The *Teazer* had many British captures to her credit and she was a thorn in the side of the Royal Navy. On the morning of June 27, 1813, the *Teazer* was spotted off of Halifax harbour by Captain Joseph Freeman of the *Sir John Sherbrooke*. Captain Freeman immediately gave chase, but lost the vessel in the forenoon fog. Not long after she was sited again by Captain Hugh Pigot of the *Orpheus* off of Lunenburg.

As the *Teazer* tried to make her escape to sea another British vessel joined the chase, H.M.S. *La Hogue*, with seventy-four guns, under Captain Thomas Bladen Capel. With her escape to sea now cut off, the *Teazer* had few options, but her captain put the helm over and made for the shallow waters of Mahone Bay, where the larger vessels could not follow.

By now signal guns were firing and the local militia gathered to prevent the crew escaping by land. The *Teazer* made it into Mahone Bay, but the British were not to give up so easily, manning several ships' boats they pulled for the trapped ship. At this point the *Teazer's* lieutenant, a man named Johnson, fled below with a crazed look in his eyes. Before anyone could react, he had put a firebrand to the powder magazine, and a terrific explosion occurred, which was heard twelve miles away. Of the crew of thirty-eight men only eight survived and two of these were horribly mangled.

The story of the *Teazer* is barely remembered today, and is not commemorated in any tangible way. But a chancel cross, which was made from the Keelson of the *Teazer*, is in the Anglican Church of St. Stephen in Chester, Nova Scotia. Two of the victims of the explosion are buried in the Chester Cemetery.

## GRAVE OF GENERAL ROBERT ROSS — HALIFAX, NOVA SCOTIA

Major General Robert Ross, commander of the British army in the campaigns against Washington and Baltimore, is buried in St. Paul's cemetery. Ross and Admiral Cockburn engineered the attack which allowed them to capture the city of Washington on August 24, 1814. Ross was killed several weeks later near North Point, Maryland while riding ahead of his troops. St. Paul's Cemetery is on Barrington Street near Spring Garden Road in the city of Halifax. Ross's burial site is located on a key which is at the entrance to the cemetery. (see also General Ross Wounding Site)

## ST. PAUL'S CHURCH MEMORIALS — HALIFAX, NOVA SCOTIA

St. Paul's Church contains several memorials to the War of 1812. At the front of the church to the right of the altar, is a memorial stone to Lieutenant General Sir John Harvey who fought in the battles of Stoney Creek and Crysler's Farm and was later a lieutenant-governor. He died at Halifax on March 22, 1852 at the age of seventy-four.

A very old sandstone grave marker is located at the back of the church and this tombstone originally stood in the naval hospital burying ground on Barrington Street. It commemorates two young men of *H.M.S. Shannon*, who lost their lives in the engagement with the *U.S.S. Chesapeake* on June 1, 1813. The engagement resulted in the capture of the U.S. vessel after a string of British naval defeats at sea. St. Paul's Church is located on Barrington Street in downtown Halifax.

## PRINCE OF WALES MARTELLO TOWER — HALIFAX, NOVA SCOTIA

With the arrival of Edward, Duke of Kent to Halifax in 1794, a new more durable series of fortifications was commenced to defend the harbour. One of these was the Martello Tower located on Point Pleasant, which started construction in 1796 and continued with interruptions until 1798. The tower's main purpose was to cover the batteries placed on the peninsula, and to defend against a landing in the Northwest Arm. The tower mounted four sixty-eight-pound carronades and two long twenty-four-pound guns. Various modifications were made over the years, and in 1812 a bomb-proof arch was added, the upper staircase was removed, and a door at ground level was cut into it. The Prince of Wales Tower is Canada's oldest example of a Martello tower still standing. The site is administered by Parks Canada and is located in Point Pleasant Park in the city of Halifax.

## YORK REDOUBT — HALIFAX, NOVA SCOTIA

The fortifications commenced at Sandwich Point in 1794 were all part of the Duke of Kent's general defence plan for Halifax Harbour. The fortifications here have been in a constant state of evolution, and were used during both World Wars before finally being abandoned in 1956. Collectively they were called York Redoubt.

The redoubt named for the Duke of York was built in 1798 as a sea battery, and had walls four feet thick. Only a portion of the original redoubt remains, which consists of a section of wall bulging out from the main walls of a later structure. The site is under the care of Parks Canada and is located off of Purcell's Cove Road eight miles south of Halifax.

The stamp issued by Canada Post to commemorate York Redoubt

# SHANNON AND CHESAPEAKE —
## HALIFAX, NOVA SCOTIA

In the opening months of the War of 1812, the American frigates gained a number of amazing victories at sea in single ship actions with British frigates. This shook the confidence of the British people, who were beginning to believe that the American frigates were invincible. But this illusion was shattered on June 1, 1813 when His Majesty's frigate *Shannon* under Captain Broke, defeated and captured the United States frigate *Chesapeake* under Captain Lawrence, in the ferocious action off Boston Harbor. Captain Broke's victory restored the confidence in the British navy at a time when it had been badly shaken.

In this hard fought battle fought on the decks of the *Chesapeake*, Lawrence was killed, and his last words "Don't Give Up the Ship," passed into U.S. naval history. Captain Broke was incapacitated with a cutlass wound to his skull and the victorious *Shannon*, under Halifax's own Lieutenant Provo Wallis, towed the *Chesapeake* back to Halifax Harbour. It was on a Sunday morning when the signal station at the citadel deciphered the news that *Shannon* was approaching towing a prize, which appeared to be a thirty-eight-gun American frigate! When told of the news it was said that the congregation of St. Paul's Church emptied in minutes, clergy, choir, men, women, and children all rushing to the harbour to see the historic event.

Captain Broke eventually recovered from his wound, though he suffered from it for the rest of his life, and never served at sea again. He was made a Baronet of the United Kingdom, and a Knight Commander of the Bath, and was given the Naval Gold Medal, which was only given to post captains who distinguished themselves in action.

Broke retired to Broke Hall in Suffolk, where he spent the rest of his days. As for the *Shannon* herself, not much is known about her after 1886, where she was serving as a training ship on the river Shannon in Ireland. The encounter between the *Shannon* and the *Chesapeake* was quite well known to Haligonians of the last century, but is little remembered today. A plaque commemorating the action from the Historic Sites and Monuments Board of Canada is located in Point Pleasant Park in the city of Halifax.

*H.M.S. Shannon* towing the *U.S.S. Chesapeake* into Halifax Harbour. From an old print derived from the painting by J.C. Schetky.

## LONG GUN FROM *H.M.S. SHANNON* — HALIFAX, NOVA SCOTIA

The Nova Scotia Historical Society has placed a plaque, which identifies a twenty-four-pound long gun, as having been used on the frigate *Shannon* in her historic engagement with the *U.S.S. Chesapeake*. The gun was fired at noon and evening in the city of Halifax from 1882 to 1905. The long gun and the plaque are on the grounds of Government House on Hollis Street on the right side of the building.

## NAVAL HOSPITAL — HALIFAX, NOVA SCOTIA

Sailors who were wounded on board the *Shannon* and *Chesapeake* during that famous engagement in 1813, were brought here to the old naval hospital. A monument and a plaque is dedicated to the sailors who died at the hospital, and is on the grounds of the Canadian Forces Base Halifax. The monument may be viewed only with special permission. The naval cemetery may be viewed from Barrington Street, but caution must be exercised as it is a busy thoroughfare.

## LIVERPOOL PRIVATEERS — LIVERPOOL, NOVA SCOTIA

During the War of 1812 hundreds of privateer vessels operated out of Liverpool, Nova Scotia, and one of the most successful was the *Liverpool Packet*, commanded by Captain Joseph Barss. This incredible vessel managed to capture and bring into port fifty American vessels. Proceeds from privateering helped establish the Bank of Nova Scotia and a cairn commemorating these bold adventurers has been placed by the Historic Sites and Monuments Board of Canada. It is located in a small park by the sea, in the town of Liverpool, Nova Scotia. Perkins house on East Main Street, has a model of the *Liverpool Packet* on display.

## BLOCKHOUSE SITE — PARRSBORO, NOVA SCOTIA

The origins of the blockhouse that stood at Parrsboro are obscure, but it appears to have been constructed prior to 1814. A local tradition has it that during the War of 1812, an American privateer anchored close to the town of Parrsboro, and sent a boat ashore for plunder. The sailors met with resistance from the local populace, and after losing two of their men, withdrew back to the ship.

There are no above-ground remains of the blockhouse today, and the site remains unmarked. A sketch dated from 1836 does show the blockhouse and the small community of Parrsboro in front. The blockhouse was located on the hill behind the "Ottawa House," which is still standing today, just outside of Parrsboro, Nova Scotia. The "Ottawa House" is from a later time period but does have on display a painting depicting the blockhouse.

## FORT O'BRIAN — MACHIASPORT, MAINE

At the commencement of the American Revolution the townspeople constructed an earthwork here under the direction of Jeremiah O'Brian. It was designed to protect the mouth of the Machias River, and the town of Machias, which was a major lumbering centre. Consisting of only a breastwork, containing two nine-pound guns and one six-pound gun, it was later strengthened in 1777, and a barracks added.

During the War of 1812 the fort was reactivated once more, and in 1814 during a general offensive to occupy eastern Maine, the British landed about nine hundred troops here, forcing the defenders to abandon the fort. The British remained two days, burning the barracks and making off with the cannons. During the Civil War the fort was reactivated once more to defend against confederate raiders, and new earthworks were added and the fort expanded. Largely what remains today is from this period.

The fort is maintained by the state of Maine and has earthworks, a cannon, and a plaque marking the site of the ammunitions magazine. The fort is located just outside the town of Machiasport on Route 92.

# CAMPOBELLO ISLAND — MAINE

The Maine–New Brunswick border was relatively quiet during the War of 1812, since the British navy commanded the waters around Maine, and the local citizens were not in favour of the war. But in 1813 a small party of U.S. regulars was sent to Fort Sullivan at Eastport, Maine and this triggered a response from the British.

On July 11, 1814 a British force of five hundred troops disembarked from barges at Eastport, supported by a frigate and a Ship of the Line. The defending officer, Major Putnam was forced to surrender, and thus Eastport was captured without firing a shot, and remained in British hands until the Treaty of Ghent. During their lengthy stay, British troops also occupied Campobello Island. Today there is little memory of this sidelight of the War of 1812, and the events are unmarked.

## THE NATCHEZ TRACE — COLBERT'S FERRY, ALABAMA

The Natchez Trace is a historic roadway that stretches over four hundred miles and passes through three states. General Andrew Jackson's army utilized the trace when they left Nashville on January 7, 1813 on their march to New Orleans. At Colbert's Ferry, George Colbert is reported to have charged Jackson $75,000 to cross his army. Numerous sites along the roadway have been marked by the National Park Service and portions of the old road can be seen at many places. The visitor centre is at Tupelo, Mississippi, and features exhibits and a film presentation on the history of the trace.

# OLD PENTAGON BARRACKS — BATON ROUGE, LOUISIANA

The Old Pentagon Barracks was the staging area for troops engaged in the Creek Indian Campaign of 1813 and a museum at the site tells the story of this old building.

The old powder magazine is located at the corner of River Road and State Capital Avenue in the city of Baton Rouge.

# FORT CONDE — MOBILE, ALABAMA

Fort Conde has had a long history under the control of four different nations: France, Great Britain, Spain, and the United States. Its 1812 history began when General Wilkinson seized it from the Spanish in 1813, and left a garrison there which remained for the entire war. It was also a staging area for two of General Jackson's operations: his army left here for the Pensacola and New Orleans campaigns.

The fort declined after the war, and by 1820 the expanding city of Mobile had no use for the old structure and the fort was demolished. In the early 1970s archaeological digs were conducted, and portions of the wall and bastions restored. For the American Revolution Bicentennial in July of 1976, the fort was reopened to the public.

Today two tunnels, which are part of Interstate 10, go below the foundations of the old structure. The fort is administered by the city of Mobile and is the official welcome centre for the city. It is located at 150 South Royal Street at the corner of Church Street in the city of Mobile.

During the War of 1812, Mobile was part of Spanish Florida, but acting under the orders of President Madison, General James Wilkinson seized it in 1813. When Major William Lawrence, of the 2nd U.S. Infantry arrived with 161 soldiers, the Spanish garrison departed peacefully. The regiment proceeded to construct a small sand and wood fort which they named after their Colonel Bowyer.

The fort eventually consisted of three buildings, a powder magazine, and mounted seventeen guns. On September 12, 1814 a small British force under Lieutenant Colonel Nichols, consisting of 130 marines and six-hundred Indians landed in the rear of the fort. That evening, four supporting British vessels, the *Hermes*, *Sophia*, *Caron*, and *Anaconda* arrived and anchored near the fort.

The next day the British dragged a howitzer to within seven hundred yards of the fort, and began throwing shells into it, but with little effect. While the single cannon engaged the fort's batteries, the fleet took soundings of the harbour. On September 15th at about two o'clock in the afternoon, the British vessels bore down on the fort and engaged it at close range. Meanwhile on land, Lieutenant Colonel Nichols managed to deploy another twelve-pound cannon, and soon this gun added its fire to the bombardment. By late afternoon the *Hermes* had her cable shot away and she drifted out of control. The British then withdrew, but not before evacuating the crew of *Hermes* and setting her aflame.

This victory by the Americans, though small, resulted in a loss of prestige for the British, and it hurt them considerably when the local Indians began to desert them in droves. On the other hand, the victory boosted American morale and stimulated recruiting for the defence of New Orleans.

After their defeat at New Orleans, the British returned in force to Fort Bowyer, and on February 9, 1815 it was forced to surrender. Unknown to both sides, the war was actually over, and with the Treaty of Ghent, Fort Bowyer was returned to the Americans. A tropical storm destroyed old Fort Bowyer in the 1820s and Fort Morgan was constructed nearby. Fort Morgan State Park is administered by the Alabama Historical Commission and is located at the Gulf Shores.

## FORT MIMS MASSACRE — STOCKTON, ALABAMA

In the summer of 1813 a small stockade was built around the home of Samuel Mims, a local settler and operator of the ferry. The stockade was about one acre and had no blockhouses, but in July of 1813, General Ferdinand L. Claiborne sent Major Daniel Beasley to garrison the small community. On August 7th, General Claiborne inspected the fort, and recommended that it be strengthened, but Major Beasley declined to do so.

Several weeks later the fort was overwhelmed by one thousand warriors from the Red Stick band of the Creek nation, led by Red Eagle. A general massacre ensued with only thirty-six survivors, among the fallen was Major Beasley. The departing Red Sticks burned the fort and it was not until September 9th that a detachment arrived to bury the dead.

The site was long abandoned, but in 1955 it was donated to the State of Alabama. The site is undeveloped, but a monument erected by the Daughters of the Confederacy, is located near the approximate location of the stockade. The site of Fort Mims is twelve miles north of Stockton, in Baldwin County.

## FORT JACKSON — WETUMPKA, ALABAMA

In his campaign against the Creek Indians, General Andrew Jackson's army established a supply depot at this site. After the battle of Horseshoe Bend, the army returned here and commenced construction of a new fort, under the direction of General Joseph Graham. Built near the ruins of old Fort Toulouse, it was completed by the time of the Treaty of Fort Jackson in June of 1814, which put an end to the Creek Indian War.

In 1817 the residents of the community moved to Montgomery and the site was used as farmland. The Alabama Historical Commission has excavated the site, and Fort Toulouse has been restored to its original appearance. There are little remains of Fort Jackson, but there is a small monument on the site. Fort Toulouse–Jackson Park is on Route 6, twelve miles northeast of Montgomery, and three miles south of Wetumpka, Alabama.

## HORSESHOE BEND NATIONAL
## MILITARY PARK — ALABAMA

On March 27, 1814 General Jackson, with his Tennessee Militia and the 39th U.S. Infantry, dealt a decisive blow against the Creek Indian Confederacy, by defeating the Red Stick faction under Menawa. Horseshoe Bend is distinguished because it was one of the few battles where Indians utilized entrenchments.

The main force under Jackson approached the Red Stick fortifications about mid-morning, and utilizing two cannons, a six-pound and a three-pound, they began to fire at the fortifications, but the cannons could make no impression. Meanwhile, General Coffee and his troops had worked around the rear of the Indians' main position, but they were isolated by the Tallapoosa River which intersected the position. A number of friendly Cherokee Indians, and some infantry under Colonel Gideon Morgan, bravely crossed the Tallapoosa and engaged the Red Sticks from the rear. But the Red Sticks were fighting tenaciously and Morgan's men also could make no impression.

At around noon the turning point of the battle occurred, when Jackson saw that the cannons were useless against the position, and when he could hear firing from the direction of the Tallapoosa, he decided on a frontal assault. The 39th Regiment bore the brunt of the attack, but they gained the entrenchments after ferocious hand to hand fighting at the barricades. The remaining Red Sticks broke and ran to the river, but with their retreat cut off by Coffee's men, they fought in complete desperation. No quarter was asked for or given, and at this stage of the battle, it was little less than a massacre.

Nightfall ended the killing, with scattered remnants of the

Creeks making their own way off of the battlefield. Remarkably, Menawa, though wounded seven times, escaped on his own. As expected, the casualties suffered by the regulars was high, since they had to charge over open ground, and then engage a desperate enemy at close quarters.

The Battle of Horseshoe Bend is remembered mainly because of Jackson's participation, and the public's awareness of him grew because of it. The battle occurred at a time of national misfortune, and his victory there was in stark contrast to the failed campaigns on the Canadian frontier. His later victory at New Orleans eventually paved his way to the presidency in 1828. After the Battle of Horseshoe Bend, the Creeks were forced to sign the Treaty of Fort Jackson, which ceded millions of acres of land to the United States.

Horseshoe Bend National Military Park preserves the site of Jackson's victory. The park has a visitor centre and museum and there is an auto-tour with historical markers that interpret the action. The park is located twelve miles north of Dadeville, Alabama on U.S. Route 49.

## FORT GADSEN — SUMATRA, FLORIDA

Fort Gadsen was constructed by British Marines under the command of Lieutenant Colonel Edward Nichols in the fall of 1814. It was constructed on the east bank of the Apalachicola River, at that time part of Spanish Florida. Its purpose was to attract local Seminole Indians as allies, but this was unsuccessful, and the British abandoned the fort in 1814. After that it became a haven for local runaway slaves and Seminoles.

In 1815 the fort was seized by local fugitive slaves, and they renamed it Fort Apalachicola. Southern slave holders now felt threatened, and an expedition was mounted against what was called the "negro" fort. Under the direction of General Edward Gaines the fort was destroyed, and 270 negro men, women, and children were killed.

In 1818 a new fort was built over the ruins of the first, and was renamed Gadsen. The fort remained in U.S. hands when Florida was annexed from the Spanish. The fort is preserved in Fort Gadsen State Park, and is located six miles southwest of Sumatra, Florida, in Franklin County.

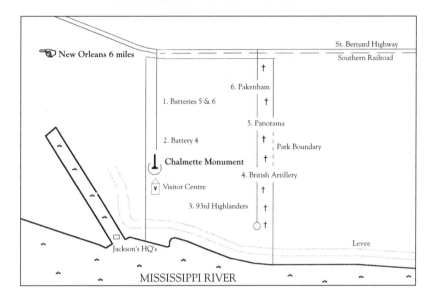

1. Site of batteries 5 and 6
2. Battery number 4 — 32-pound
   Naval gun
3. 93rd Highlanders attacked here
4. British artillery position
5. Panoramic view of battlefield
6. General Pakenham wounding site

## CHALMETTE NATIONAL
## HISTORICAL PARK — NEW ORLEANS, LOUISIANA

The plans to capture New Orleans were formulated by the Earl of Bathurst in September of 1814 and instructions were sent to Admiral Sir Alexander Cochrane and Major General Robert Ross, who were then engaged in the Chesapeake Bay Campaign. After their successful capture of the city of Washington, Ross and Cochrane then moved on to Baltimore, but Ross was killed in a small skirmish just outside the city, and never saw the orders which would direct him to capture New Orleans. His replacement was Sir Edward Michael Pakenham, brother-in-law to the Duke of Wellington.

Arriving from England on a fast frigate, Sir Edward took command of the army while the campaign was already in its advanced stages, in fact he joined the army after the Battle of Lake Borgne, and the night battle of December 23rd. His arrival on Christmas Day with reinforcements brought his total force to about 14,000 men, and was a great morale booster to the army. However, he was largely committed to a plan that he had no part in formulating.

General Andrew Jackson on the other hand, had a smaller less disciplined force of about four thousand men, but his army was in a superb position, with the Mississippi River guarding his right flank, and an impassable swamp guarding his left. The only way to New Orleans was to come across the open fields of the Chalmette Plantation.

On the evening of December 31st, with immense effort, the British managed to haul some heavy guns from the fleet and erect them before the American lines. On New Years Day the British guns opened up on the Americans, but the bombardment was a complete failure as more British guns were knocked out than American, and the Royal Artillery, with morale severely damaged, withdrew. Pakenham now waited for reinforcements and when General Lambert's brigade joined the army, he set the main attack for January 8th.

The original plan called for another column to turn the American flank across the river, but when the water level fell in the feeder canals, the British were unable to bring up sufficient boats to carry them across. There were supposed to be 1200 men on the other side of the river, but only about 350 could cross at any one time.

On the morning of January 8th there was a heavy fog over the battlefield. Pakenham waited impatiently for the sound of guns from the other side of the river, which would indicate that the American batteries were being assaulted, and then he could launch his main attack. Finally, Pakenham ordered the assault before the fog lifted, but the attack was poorly executed, and units that were supposed to carry ladders to scale the American works were found not to have any at all.

Much time was lost, and when the fog suddenly cleared many British columns found themselves within rifle and artillery range. The columns moved forward in a charge but were decimated at long range. It was the Battle of Bunker Hill all over again, but this time much worse. Dense British columns were mowed down by the deadly fire from the heavily entrenched American line, and Pakenham, leading one of the columns, fell mortally wounded. The column on the other side of the river captured the American works, but all to no avail. The army retreated from the Mississippi completely demoralized and utterly defeated.

The Battle of New Orleans was one of the worst defeats ever suffered by a British army. The losses alone are quite astounding and demonstrate the importance that field fortifications were to have in the years to come. British casualties were over two thousand killed, wounded and missing, but incredibly American losses were only seven killed and six wounded!

Ironically though, this amazing battle did not affect the outcome of the war in any way, for the war had ended two weeks before at Ghent, Belgium, where a treaty of peace had been signed between the United States and Great Britain. Communications being what they were, Pakenham and Jackson were completely unaware of this fact. Though the battle did not effect the war itself, it did have two effects on American history.

For one thing it shaped American mythology on the War of 1812, for in time they came to believe that they had actually won the war. Such a great victory at the end of the conflict assuaged feelings of disappointment with the failed campaigns on the Canadian front. The battle would also make Andrew Jackson a national figure, and his reputation because of New Orleans would help launch him into the White House in 1829.

Today most of the battlefield is preserved in Chalmette National Historical Park. Due to the change of shoreline of the Mississippi River since 1815, part of the battlefield has been inundated. Jackson's right flank is now under the Mississippi. But what remains is well interpreted and there is a visitor centre, a large monument dedicated to the battle, and a well-marked tour route. The battlefield is located about six miles south from the city of New Orleans on State Route 39.

The remains of the Rodriguez Canal, Jackson's main position, with the Battle Monument in the distance, as sketched by Lossing in 1861

The remains of the Rodriguez Canal today, preserved in Chalmette National Historical Park

# CHAPTER 27

# OTHER 1812 SITES

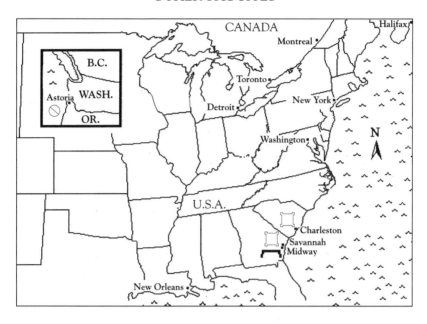

## FORT MORRIS (FORT DEFIANCE) — MIDWAY, GEORGIA

Fort Morris was constructed in 1776 during the American Revolution and its primary purpose was to protect the valuable seaport of Sunbury. It was the object of two separate British attacks, one in November of 1778, and the other in January of 1779. In the second attack the British destroyed the town of Sunbury and departed. At the commencement of the War of 1812 "Fort Defiance" was constructed over the ruins of old Fort Morris — like its predecessor an earthwork fortification — mounting eight cannons.

In January of 1813, Sunbury was again threatened by the British under Admiral Cockburn who had captured St. Marys, Georgia to the south. The fort was reactivated and manned by students, but Admiral Cockburn never came this way.

The town of Sunbury gradually declined in population and

eventually disappeared, but the site has been preserved in Fort Morris Historic Site. The visitor centre features displays on the history of the fort and the town of Sunbury. A pamphlet may be obtained to take a walking tour of the grounds. Fort Morris is located eleven miles east of Midway, Georgia on U.S. 17.

## FORT JACKSON — SAVANNAH, GEORGIA

Fort Jackson was named after James Jackson, a former governor of Georgia and hero of the American Revolution. Construction began in 1808 but by 1812 there was only a brick battery and barracks. The small garrison consisted of both local militia and federal troops. The fort was never seriously threatened during the war and after the Treaty of Ghent two different periods of construction began.

A moat and drawbridge were added and another brick barracks and powder magazine erected. After these enhancements the fort bore little resemblance to its 1812 appearance. The fort is maintained by the "Coastal Heritage Society of Georgia." There are displays on the fort's history and a self-guided tour. Fort Jackson is located on the banks of the Savannah River three miles south of the city of Savannah.

## FORT MOULTRIE — CHARLESTON, SOUTH CAROLINA

Fort Moultrie's most famous action was during the American Revolution when the fort withstood a combined naval and land attack by the British. There were no battles fought in the state of South Carolina during the War of 1812. But in the summer of 1813 British Admiral Sir George Cockburn launched a series of raids along the eastern seaboard of the United States. On July 12, 1813 Cockburn anchored his vessels off of Ocracoke Inlet, North Carolina. After cutting out a few coastal vessels he proceeded south, hugging the coast. Threatened with possible attack, Fort Moultrie was reactivated and garrisoned.

The present fort dates from the period 1807–1811. The site has been interpreted to various periods during the fort's history. Fort Moultrie is administered by the National Park Service and is located on Sullivan's Island opposite the city of Charleston. Battery Park in the city of Charleston has a monument commemorating Fort Moultrie's roll during the American Revolution.

## FORT ASTORIA — ASTORIA, OREGON

To fully appreciate the events at Fort Astoria one must take into account its great isolation from the East. When the United States declared war on Great Britain in June of 1812, the inhabitants of Astoria did not hear the news until January of 1813, nearly six months later.

In 1811 American entrepreneur John Jacob Astor had established a post here for his Pacific Fur Company. Located on the south side of the Columbia River at Point George, the post was named after its founder. At that time it consisted of merely a log residence, a storehouse, and a powder magazine.

In September of 1813 the employees learned that their company vessel, the *Isaac Todd*, had left England bound for Astoria. At the same time the British had dispatched the Sloop of War *Phoebe* with orders to capture the post. Fearing that they could not resist the warship's guns, and making the best of a bad situation, the owners promptly sold the post to the British-owned North West Company.

In October the new owners took possession of the fort, adding picketed bulwarks and four light cannons. On December 13, 1813 the British sloop of war *Racoon* arrived with orders to take the post. Captain Black's feelings must have been mixed ones of surprise and disappointment, for with the post now in British hands he and his crew would be denied valuable prize money. But all was taken in good stead. After a formal dinner and flag raising ceremony the post was renamed "Fort George" in honour of the king.

In March of 1814 the *Isaac Todd* finally arrived, bringing a strange passenger. The local Indians were quite curious at the arrival of Miss Jane Barnes, the first white woman they had ever seen. Today the site of Fort Astoria has been obliterated by the modern city of Astoria. The site is presently unmarked.

# CHAPTER 28
## BELGIUM

## TREATY OF GHENT — GHENT, BELGIUM

With the signing of the Treaty of Ghent on December 24, 1814, the War of 1812 came to a close, and the end to this embarrassing conflict was welcomed by both sides. A plaque commemorating this historic event was unveiled 150 years after the signing of the treaty. The text is quoted in full.

TREATY OF GHENT
1814–1964
HERE RESIDED FROM JULY TO
DECEMBER 1814 THE U.S.A
DELEGATION, HEADED BY
JOHN QUINCY ADAMS
LATER VIth PRESIDENT OF THE U.S.A
DURING THE NEGOTIATIONS WITH
THE BRITISH PLENIPOTENTIARIES
LEADING TO THE SIGNATURE OF THE
PEACE TREATY OF GHENT
ON DECEMBER 24th, 1814

The plaque is fixed to the old Lovendeghem Mansion in the rue des Champs, Ghent, Belgium.

# APPENDICES

## APPENDIX A
## CHRONOLOGY OF THE WAR OF 1812
### (Major Events in Boldface)

### 1811

November 7 - Battle of Tippecanoe

### 1812

June 18 - **United States declares war on Great Britain**
June 29 - Schooners *Sophia* and *Island Packet* taken by the British in the St. Lawrence
July 12 - Hull's army invades Upper Canada at Sandwich
July 16 - Skirmishes at the Canard River
July 17 - **British capture of Fort Mackinac**
July 19 - Provincial Marine attacks Sackets Harbor
August 5 - Skirmish at Brownstown
August 8 - Brock embarks at Port Dover for the relief of Amherstburg
August 8 - Skirmish at Maguaga
August 15 - Garrison massacred at Fort Dearborn (Chicago)
August 16 - Brock crosses over to Detroit
August 16- **Surrender of Detroit**
August 19 - Frigate *Constitution* defeats the Frigate *Guerriere*
September 3 - Massacre at Pigeon Roost (Indiana Territory)
September 6 - Fort Wayne attacked by Indians under Tecumseh
September 12 - Harrison arrives at Fort Wayne with reinforcements
September 14 - Major Muir commences his expedition to Fort Wayne
September 21 - Forsyth's raid on Gananoque
October 7 - General Winchester's army arrives near Fort Defiance
October 13 - **Battle of Queenston Heights**
October 25 - Frigate *United States* defeats frigate *Macedonian*
November 9 - Escape of the corvette *Royal George*
November 10 - Commodore Chauncey's attack on Kingston Harbour
November 28 - Skirmish at Frenchman's Creek
December 9 - Lieutenant Jesse Elliot captures *Caledonia* and *Detroit*
December 18 - Battle of Mississinewa

### 1813

January 22 - **Battle of the River Raisin**
February 6 - Forsyth's raid on Elizabethtown (Brockville)
February 16 - 104th Regiment commences its march from Fredericton to Upper Canada
February 22 - Macdonell's raid on Ogdensburg
March 3 - Admiral Cockburn's squadron arrives in Lynnhaven Bay
March 19 - Sir James Lucas Yeo appointed Commander in Chief of the Lake squadrons
April 1 - Commerce raids begin in Chesapeake Bay
April 6 - Lewes, Delaware bombarded by British
April 13 - General Wilkinson takes Mobile, Alabama
April 27 - **General Dearborn and Commodore Chauncey capture York (Toronto)**
May 1 - **Siege of Fort Meigs commences**
May 3 - British raid on Havre de Grace, Maryland

May 5 - Sir James Lucas Yeo arrives at Quebec
May 27 - **General Dearborn and Commodore Chauncey capture Fort George**
May 27 - British abandon Fort Erie
May 27 - Colonel Harvey retreats to Burlington Heights
May 29 - Sir George Prevost and Commodore Yeo attack Sackets Harbor
June 1 - Frigate *Shannon* captures frigate *Chesapeake*
June 6 - **Battle of Stoney Creek**
June 8 - Skirmish at the Forty Mile Creek
June 9 - Americans abandon Fort Erie
June 13 - British vessels repulsed at Burlington, Vermont
June 19 - Commodore Barclay's squadron appears off of Cleveland, Ohio
June 20 - Crew of frigate *Constellation* attempt capture of blockading vessels off Hampton, Virginia
June 22 - Battle of Craneys Island, Virginia
June 25 - Attack on Hampton, Virginia
June 24 - **Battle of Beaver Dams**
June 27 - Privateer *Teazer* blown up in Mahone Bay, Nova Scotia
July 3 - Capture of Sloops *Growler* and *Eagle* near Île aux Noix
July 5 - Raid on Fort Schlosser
July 8 - Action at Butler's Farm
July 26 - General Proctor quits the siege of Fort Meigs
July 31 - "Murray's Raid" on Plattsburg
July 31 - Second occupation of York
August 2 - General Proctor's assault fails at Fort Stephenson
August 7 - Schooners *Hamilton* and *Scourge* founder on Lake Ontario
August 10 - Naval engagement between Chauncey and Yeo, *Julia* and *Pert* captured
September 10 - **Battle of Lake Erie**
September 28 - "Burlington Races"
October 5 - **Battle of Thamesville**
October 26 - **Battle of Chateauguay**
November 6 - General Wilkinson's flotilla runs past the batteries at Fort Wellington
November 10 - Skirmish at Hoople's Creek
November 11 - **Battle of Crysler's Farm**
November 13 - Skirmish at Nanticoke
November 15 - Funeral of General Covington at French Mills
November 15 - Wilkinson's army goes into winter quarters
December 10 - **Burning of Newark (Niagara-on-the-Lake)**
December 15 - Skirmish at Thomas McCrae's house
December 19 - **Fort Niagara taken by British in a night assault**

1814

March 4 - Battle of the Longwoods (Battle Hill)
March 27 - **Battle of Horseshoe Bend**
March 30 - General Wilkinson's army turned back at Lacolle Mill
May 1 - General William Clark leaves St. Louis, Mo. to establish a post at Prairie du Chien
May 6 - **Commodore Yeo's raid on Oswego, New York**
May 14 - British attack on Otter Creek, Vermont
May 14 - Campbell's raid into Upper Canada
May 18 - Relief expedition to Fort Mackinac arrives under Lt. Col. Robert McDouall
May 29 - Skirmish at Sandy Creek
June 2 - Post at Prairie du Chien established under General William Clark
June 28 - Maj. William McKay's expedition leaves Fort Mackinac to capture Prairie du Chien
July 5 - **Battle of Chippawa**
July 18 - Burning of St. Davids
July 20 - Fort St. Joseph burned and schooner *Mink* captured by Sinclair's squadron

July 20 - Trials at the Ancaster Assizes
July 21 - Raid on Sault Ste. Marie
July 20 - Fort Shelby, Prairie du Chien surrenders to British
July 25 - **Battle of Lundy's Lane**
July 26 - Sinclair's squadron arrives off Mackinac Island
August 1 - Schooner *Nancy* warned of blockade of Fort Mackinac by Sinclair's squadron
August 2 - **Siege of Fort Erie commences under General Drummond**
August 4 - Americans repulsed at Battle of Mackinac Island
August 10 - Raid on Stonington, Connecticut
August 12 - Capture of *Somers* and *Ohio* on Lake Erie
August 13 - Part of Sinclair's squadron arrives at the mouth of the Nottawasaga River
August 14 - The schooner *Nancy* destroyed
August 15 - **Drummond's failed night assault on Fort Erie**
August 24 - **Battle of Bladensburg and entry into Washington**
August 27 - Point Lookout, Maryland occupied by the British
August 27 - Fort Washington, Maryland blown up by retreating garrison
September - Construction of Penetang Road commences
September 1 - British occupy Castine, Maine
September 3 - Capture of *Tigress* and *Scorpion*
September 4 - Commencement of Plattsburg Campaign
September 5 - Skirmish at Rock Island Rapids
September 6 - Skirmish at Beekmantown, New York
September 9 - Fort O'Brian, Maine capture by British
September 11 **Battle of Plattsburg**
September 12 - **Battle of North Point**
September 13 - **Bombardment of Fort McHenry**
September 14 - First assault on Fort Bowyer, Alabama repulsed
September 17 - General Brown's counter-attack at Siege of Fort Erie
October 19 - Battle of Cook's Mills (Lyons Creek)
October 26-November 17 - Macarthur's Raid through the Thames Valley
November 6 - Skirmish at Malcolm's Mills
December 24 - **Treaty of Peace signed in Ghent, Belgium**

1815

January 8 - **Battle of New Orleans**
February - Work commences on new naval base at Penetanguishene
February 12 - Fort Bowyer surrenders to British

# APPENDIX B

## NAVAL ACTIONS AT SEA DURING THE WAR OF 1812
{Rate of vessel in brackets - Victor in italics}

August 19, 1812 *Constitution* (44) vs Guerriere (38)
October 18, 1812 *Wasp* (18) vs Frolic (18)
October 25, 1812 *United States* (44) vs Macedonian (38)
December 29, 1812 *Constitution* (44) vs Java (38)
February 24, 1813 *Hornet* (18) vs Peacock (18)
June 1, 1813 *Shannon* (38) vs Chesapeake (38)
August 5, 1813 *Dominica* (15) vs Decatur (Privateer) (7)
August 12, 1813 Argus (20) vs *Pelican* (20)
September 25, 1813 *Enterprise* (16) vs Boxer (14)
March 28, 1814 Essex (32) vs *Phoebe* (36) and *Cherub* (18)
April 29, 1814 *Peacock* (20) vs Epervier (18)
June 28, 1814 *Wasp* (18) vs Reindeer (20)
September 1, 1814 *Wasp* (18) vs Avon (16)
January 16, 1815 President (44) vs *Endymion* (40) *Pomone* (44)
    *Tenedos* (38)
February 20, 1815 *Constitution* (44) vs Cyanne (32) and Levant (20)
March 23, 1815 Penguin (16) vs *Hornet* (18)

# APPENDIX C

## THE NAVAL WAR

Naval battles by their very nature are difficult of commemoration, unless the action was fought close to a body of land, they are not often commemorated by any monument or marker. In the case of the War of 1812, there have been some notable exceptions. For instance, the battles of Lake Champlain and Lake Erie have both been commemorated with impressive monuments to the victors. Even some of the obscure "cutting out expeditions" and naval manoeuvres have earned an historic plaque, like the "Burlington Races" and the "Capture of the *Tigress* and *Scorpion*."

Of the many actions that took place at sea, this author found only two that were commemorated with markers on land. At Halifax, Nova Scotia, the famous action between the *Shannon* and the *Chesapeake* has been commemorated with a plaque mounted on a granite base. And at Annapolis, Maryland, on the grounds of the Naval Academy, there is a monument to the action between the *Macedonian* and the *United States*.

Naval actions throughout history have usually been commemorated in art. Fortunately for the War of 1812, there are an abundance of paintings and prints still in existence. Listed below is a partial list of paintings of particular note. Edgar Newbold Smith's book, *American Naval Broadsides*, is a particularly useful work, and lists many 1812 prints and illustrations.

### SUBJECT and AUTHOR

| | |
|---|---|
| "*Constitution* and *Guerriere*" | by W.A.K Martin |
| "The Capture of H.B.M Sloop of War Frolic" | by F. Kearny |
| "*United States* Capturing *Macedonian*" | by T. Birch |
| "*Constitution* and the *Java*" | by N. Pocock |
| "The Boarding and Capture of *Chesapeake*" | by G. Webster |
| "Capture of the *Argus*" | by T. Whitcombe |
| "The Battle of Lake Erie" | by Sully and Kearny |
| "Sloop of War Gen. Pike and Sloop of War *Wolfe*" | by R. Rawdon sc. |
| "Attack on Fort Oswego" | by I. Hewett, Lt. Royal Marines |
| "The *Wasp* and the *Reindeer*" | by A Bowen sc. |
| "The *Wasp* and the *Avon*" | by A Bowen sc. |
| "MacDonough's Victory on Lake Champlain" | by H. Reinagle |
| "The *President* and *Endymion*" | by Hill Aquat (officer R.N) |
| "Capture of H.M. ships *Cyanne* and *Levant*" | by T. Birch |
| "The *Hornet* and the *Penguin*" | by A Bowen sc. |

## PHOTOGRAPH AND ILLUSTRATION CREDITS

Cover Watercolour *The Death of Isaac Brock* by C.W. Jefferys courtesy of the Arts Associates — Toronto

Photographs courtesy of the author

Benson Lossing sketches taken from *The Pictorial Fieldbook of the War of 1812*. New York: Harper and Brothers, 1868

Stamp reproductions courtesy of Canada Post Corporation

Portrait of Lt. Col. Joseph Wanton Morrison courtesy of the McCord Museum, Montreal

*H.M.S. Shannon* towing *U.S.S. Chesapeake* adapted from the sketch by Captain R.H. King

# BIBLIOGRAPHY

## BOOKS

Allen, Robert S. *The British Indian Department and the Frontier in North America*. Occasional Papers in Archaeology and History #14 Canadian Historic Sites, Parks Canada, 1975.

Allen, Robert S. *A History of Fort George*. Occasional Papers in Archaeology and History #11 Canadian Historic Sites, Parks Canada, 1974.

Auchinleck, G.A. *History of the War between Great Britain and the United States of America during the Years 1812, 1813 and 1814*. Arms and Armour Press, 1972 Orig. Pub. 1855.

Ashlee, Laura R. *Travelling Through Time-A Guide to Michigan's Historical Markers*. Bureau of History Michigan Historical Commission, 1991.

Barnes, James. *Naval Actions of the War of 1812*. London: Cornmarket Press, 1969.

Barry, James. *Georgian Bay: the Sixth Great Lake*. Toronto Clarke, Irwin & Co., 1968.

Battle of New Orleans Sesquicentennial Commission. *Battle of New Orleans Sesquicentennial Celebration*. Washington D.C., 1965.

Berton, Pierre. *The Invasion of Canada 1812-1813*. McClelland & Stewart, Toronto, 1980.

Berton, Pierre. *Flames Across the Border 1813-1814*. McClelland & Stewart, Toronto, 1981.

Bilow, John A. *Chateauguay, N.Y. and The War of 1812*. Printed in Canada, 1984

Benn, Carl. *Historic Fort York*. Natural Heritage, Toronto, 1993.

Bird, Harrison. *Navies in the Mountains —The Battles on the Waters of Lake Champlain and Lake George*. Oxford University Press, 1962.

Bowler, Arthur R. Ed. *War Along the Niagara*. Old Fort Niagara Association, 1991.

Bradford, James C. Ed. *Command Under Sail-Makers of the American Naval Tradition*. Naval Institute Press, 1985.

Cain, Emily. *Ghost Ships*. Musson, Toronto, 1983.

Charbonneau, Andre. *The Fortifications of Ile Aux Noix*. National Historic Sites-Parks Canada, 1994.

Cooper, James Fenimore ed. *Ned Myers or A Life Before the Mast*. Naval Institute, 1989, orig. pub. 1843.

Crisman, Kevin J. *The Eagle:An American Brig On Lake Champlain During the War of 1812*. Shelburne: The New England Press, 1987.

Cruikshank, Ernest Alexander. *Documentary History of the Campaigns on the Niagara Frontier*. Welland Tribune, 1907.

Cruikshank, Ernest Alexander *Documents Relating to the Invasion of Canada and the Surrender of Detroit* Government Printing Bureau Ottawa, 1912 Reprint Arno Press 1971.

Currie, Emma A. *The Story of Laura Secord and Canadian Reminiscences* St. Catharines, 1913.

De Kay, James Tertius. *The Battle of Stonington* Annapolis: Naval Institute Press, 1990.

Department of Mines and Resources, *Guide to Fort Wellington and Vicinity Prescott - Ontario* 1937

Dunnigan, Brian Leigh *The British Army at Mackinac* Mackinac Island State Park Commission, Reports in Mackinac History and Archaeology #7 1980.

Everest, Allan S. *The War of 1812 in the Champlain Valley* Syracuse University Press 1981

Flemming, David *Navy Hall, Niagara on the Lake* National Historic Sites - Parks Canada 1976

Gellner, John Ed. *Recollections of the War of 1812-Three Eyewitness Accounts* Baxter, Toronto 1964

Graves, Donald E. *The Battle of Lundy's Lane*, The Nautical and Aviation

Publishing, Baltimore 1993

Graves, Donald E. *Red Coats & Grey Jackets : The Battle of Chippawa* Dundurn Press, 1994

Graves, Donald E. Ed. *Soldiers of 1814* Old Fort Niagara Association, 1995

Graves, Donald E. Ed. *Merry Hearts Make Light Days — The War of 1812 Journal of Lt. John Le Couteur of the 104th Foot* Carleton University Press 1993

Gunckel, John E. *The Early History of the Maumee Valley* Toledo: The Schmit Press,1913

Hamil, Fred Coyne *The Valley of the Lower Thames 1640 to 1850* University of Toronto Press, 1951

Hannay, James *A History of The War of 1812* Morang & Co. Toronto, 1905

Heine, William C *96 Years in the Royal Navy* Lancelot Press Hantsport, Nova Scotia 1987

Hickey, Donald R. *The War of 1812: A Forgotten Conflict* Urbana & Chicago: University of Illinois Press,1989

Hitsman, Mackay J. *The Incredible War of 1812* Toronto: University of Toronto Press,1965

Holden, James A *The Centenary of the Battle of Plattsburg* New York State University 1914

Horgan, Thomas B. *Old Ironsides* Yankee Books, Camden Maine 1990

Jenkins, John S. *The Generals of the Last War with Great Britain* Derby Miller & Co. Buffalo, 1849

Lossing, Benson J. *The Pictorial Field Book of the War of 1812* New York: Harper & Brothers, 1869

Litt, Williamson, Whitehorne *Death at Snake Hill — Secrets from a War of 1812 Cemetery* Dundurn Press 1993

Lord, Walter *The Dawn's Early Light* Norton & Co. New York 1972

Lundy's Lane Historical Society, *Centenary of the Battle of Lundy's Lane* Niagara Falls 1919

Mahan, Capt. A. T *Sea Power in its Relations to the War of 1812* 2 vols. Greenwood Press, New York repr. 1968 orig. pub. 1903

Malcomson, Thomas *H.M.S Detroit: The Battle for Lake Erie* Vanwell Publishing, St. Catharines 1990

Morden, James C. *Historical Monuments and Observatories of Lundy's Lane and Queenston Heights* Lundy's Lane Historical Society Niagara Falls 1927

Nelson, Larry L. *Men of Patriotism, Courage and Enterprise-Fort Meigs in the War of 1812* Daring Books Canton, Ohio 1985

Nowlan, Alden *Campobello The Outer Island* Clarke Irwin & Co., Toronto — Vancouver, 1975

Nursey, Walter R. *The Story of Isaac Brock* McClelland & Stewart, Toronto, 1923

Pack, Jame *The Man Who Burned the White House* Naval Institute Press 1987

Pickles, Tim *New Orleans 1815* Osprey, Great Britain 1993

Pullen, H.F *The Shannon and the Chesapeake* McClelland & Stewart, Toronto, 1970

Quaife, Milo Milton *War on the Detroit — The Chronicles of Thomas Vercheres de Boucherville and the Capitulation by an Ohio Volunteer* Lakeside Press, Chicago 1940

Raymond, Ethel T. *Tecumseh: Chronicles of Canada Series* Glasgow Brook & Co. Toronto 1920

Richardson, John *Richardson's War of 1812* Coles Canadiana Collection orig. pub. Toronto 1902

Roberts, Robert B. *Encyclopedia of Historic Forts* Macmillan, 1988

Roosevelt, Theodore *The Naval War of 1812* 2 vols. Charles Scribner's Sons New York 1906

Saunders, Ivan J. A *History of Martello Towers in the Defence of British North*

America, 1796-1871 Occasional Papers in Archaeology and History #15 Canadian Historic Sites, Parks Canada 1972

Sheppard, George *Plunder, Profit, and Paroles: A Social History of the War of 1812 in Upper Canada* McGill-Queen's University Press, Montreal & Kingston, 1994

Sheads, Scott S. *The Rockets' Red Glare — The Maritime Defence of Baltimore in 1814* Tidewater Pub. Centreville, Maryland 1986

Smith, Edgar Newbold *American Naval Broadsides: A Collection of Early Naval Prints (1745-1815)* Philadelphia Maritime Museum & Clarkson Potter Inc, New York, 1994

Snider, C.H.J *The Glorious Shannon's Old Blue Duster* McClelland & Stewart, Toronto, 1923

Snider, C.H.J *Under the Red Jack* Musson Book Co. Toronto, No Year

Snider, C.H.J *The Story of the Nancy and other Eighteen Twelvers* McClelland & Stewart, Toronto, 1926

Squires, Austin W. *The 104th Regiment of Foot 1803-1817* Brunswick Press, Fredericton 1962

Stanley, Gerge F.G. *The War of 1812 Land Operations* Canadian War Museum, Macmillan 1983

Temperley, Howard ed. *Gubbins' New Brunswick Journals 1811 and 1813* New Brunswick Heritage Publications Fredericton, 1980

Suthren, Victor *The Battle of Chateauguay* Occasional Papers in Archaeology and History #11 Canadian Historic Sites, Parks Canada 1974

Whitehorne, Joseph *While Washington Burned: The Battle for Fort Erie 1814* Nautical and Aviation Publishing, Baltimore 1992

Whitfield, Carol *The Battle of Queenston Heights* Occasional Papers in Archaeology and History #11 Canadian Historic Sites, Parks Canada 1974

Wilder, Patrick A. *The Battle of Sackets Harbor* Nautical & Aviation Publishing Baltimore 1994

Wilder, Patrick A. *Seaway Guide Trail to the War of 1812* Seaway Trail Inc. Oswego 1987

Wohler, Patrick J. *Charles de Salaberry* Dundurn Press Toronto & Charlottetown 1984

Young, Richard J. *Blockhouses in Canada, 1749-1841 A Comparitive Report and Catalogue* Occasional Papers in Archeology and History #23 Canadian Historic Sites, Parks Canada 1980

Zaslow, Morris ed. *The Defended Border* Toronto: The Macmillan Company, 1964

## ARTICLES

Antal, S *Myths and Facts Concerning General Proctor* Ontario History Vol. 79 # 3 Sept. 1987

Bingham, R.W *The Cradle of the Queen City* Buffalo Historical Society

Cruikshank, Ernest Alexander *General Hull's Invasion of Canada in 1812* Transactions of the Royal Society of Canada, Section II 1907

Cruikshank, Ernest Alexander *The Contest for Command of Lake Ontario in 1812 and 1813* Transactions of the Royal Society of Canada, Series III Sept. 1916

Cruikshank, Ernest Alexander *From Isle aux Noix to Chateauguay: A Study of the Military Operations on the Frontier of Lower Canada in 1812 and 1813 Part 1* Transactions of the Royal Society of Canada, Section II 1913

Cruikshank, Ernest Alexander *From Isle aux Noix to Chateauguay: A Study of the Military Operations on the Frontier of Lower Canada in 1812 and 1813 Part 2* Transactions of the Royal Society of Canada, Section III June 1914

Cruikshank, Ernest Alexander *Harrison and Proctor — The River Raisin* Transactions of the Royal Society of Canada, Section II 1910

Cruikshank, Ernest Alexander *The Battle of Stoney Creek and the Blockade of Fort George* Niagara Historical Society Publications # 3

Cruikshank, Ernest Alexander *The Contest for Command of Lake Ontario in 1814* Ontario Historical Society Publications Vol. 21 1924

Curry, Frederick C. *Little Gibraltar (Bridge Island Blockhouse)* Ontario Historical Society Vol. 33 1939

Curry, Frederick C *A Letter from Ogdensburg in 1814* Ontario History Vol. 41 # 4 1949

Eaton, H. B *Bladensburg* Journal of the Society for Army Historical Research Vol. 55 # 221 1977

Fredriksen, John C *The War of 1812 in Northern New York: General George Izard's Journal of the Chateauguay Campaign* New York History April, 1995

Grant, John *The Extraordinary March from St. John to Kingston* Atlantic Advocate, March 1973

Harris, Commander R.F. *The Ghost Ship of Mahone Bay* Atlantic Advocate November, 1966

Kimball, Jeffery *The Battle of Chippawa: Infantry Tactics in the War of 1812* Military Affairs, Vol. 31, 1967-68 Washington D.C.

Malcomson, Bob HMS *St. Lawrence: Commodore Yeo's Unique First-Rate Fresh Water* Vol. 6 # 2, 1991 Pub. Marine Museum of the Great Lakes at Kingston

Patterson, William J. *The Battle of Crysler's Farm* St. Lawrence Parks Commission (unpublished)

Stacey, C.P ed. *Upper Canada at War, 1814: Captain Armstrong Reports* Ontario History Vol. 17 1956

Stickney, Kenneth *The Taco Bell in Lundy's Lane* Idler Magazine, May-June 1987

Taylor, Blaine *Gordon's Daring Strike at Fort Washington* Sea Classics October 1990

## DISCOGRAPHY

House, Wallace *War of 1812 Songs* Folkways Records & Service Corporation FP 5002 1954